MANAGEMENT BY EXCEPTION

MANAGEMENT

McGRAW-HILL BOOK COMPANY

BY EXCEPTION

Systematizing and Simplifying
the Managerial Job

LESTER R. BITTEL

Editor-in-Chief, FACTORY Magazine

with a Foreword by H. B. MAYNARD

New York   San Francisco   Toronto   London

MANAGEMENT BY EXCEPTION

05484

4567 VB 987

To Edythe

FOREWORD

Managing a business enterprise has become an increasingly complex task in modern times. Growing competition has forced the manager to become more and more concerned with costs and profit contribution in all areas of the business, and has multiplied the number of activities which he would like to bring under close control. Without an organized, systematic plan of managing, the manager can easily become swamped with a mass of detail which will grow beyond his capacity to handle, no matter how many hours he works each day.

The problem of simplifying the task of managing is by no means new, and a logical approach to its solution was proposed many years ago. Back near the turn of the century, Frederick Winslow Taylor, the father of scientific management, wrote, "Under (the exception principle) the manager should receive only condensed, summarized, and invariably comparative reports covering, however, all of the elements entering into management, and even these should all be carefully gone over by an assistant before they reach the manager, and have all of the exceptions to the past averages and standards pointed out, both the especially good and the especially bad exceptions, thus giving him in a few minutes a full view of the progress which is being made, or the reverse, and leaving him free to consider the broader lines of policy and to study the character and fitness of the important men under him."

This statement describes all of the elements which are necessary for management by exception. First, there must be standards, preferably based on measurement. It has been said that if you don't measure, you don't know. Measurement, even the measurement provided by past performance, is essential for control.

Then actual performance must be compared with the standard. This step, Taylor pointed out, can be performed by an assistant who then brings to the attention of the manager the very good and very bad exceptions to normal or acceptable performance in brief reports. The manager is thus spared the task of reviewing performance where things are going well and can devote his attention only to those areas which really require his managerial attention.

Taylor pointed out that the exception principle applies to all areas of the business. The managers of his day, however, were concerned chiefly with manufacturing management, and they tended to limit measurement and control largely to this area. Taylor's pioneering work with time study gave them a tool of measurement which was easy to understand and apply. They used it to develop labor standards and thus were able to know which people in the work force were performing satisfactorily and which were not.

As time passed, methods of controlling factory costs were refined and perfected while not losing sight of the exception principle. Standard cost systems, for example, were designed to bring variances in standard labor and material costs to the manager's attention without burdening him with a mass of detail. Eventually measurement and control through management by exception was seen to be applicable to other areas of business as well, but it was not until comparatively recently that the more progressive managers made Taylor's early vision a reality by practicing management by exception on "all of the elements entering into management." The idea is so sound and so practical that one can only wonder why its full realization took so long.

Perhaps it is because up until now there has been no really complete written discussion of the exception principle. There have been articles and fragmentary statements dealing with the subject, but this is the first full-length book to be written about management by exception. As such, it will be a welcome addition to the management literature.

In the pages that follow, the author gives a full explanation of management by exception as a systematic way to better results. He first develops the concept, then explains the system on which the concept is based, and finally shows how management by exception can be applied to the major activity areas of a business.

The text is enriched throughout by numerous case illustrations of the various points which are made, describing actual applications of the exception principle. Managers reading the book will find that this treatment will generate many ideas which they can put to work to good advantage in their own businesses. Thus the book will make its contribution to the search for better methods of managing in which all serious managers are forever engaged.

H. B. MAYNARD
Maynard Research Council, Inc.
Pittsburgh, Pennsylvania

PREFACE

Mark Twain is supposed to have said, "Everybody talks about the weather but nobody does anything about it." I have come to much the same conclusion about management by exception. Nearly every management authority acknowledges its virtue, but virtually nothing substantial about management by exception exists in the literature. Almost every successful executive practices it, at least informally, but more often he does not recognize it as such. And more serious, no one until now has taken the concept of management by exception apart to find out what makes it tick. So that is what I've tried to do in this book. I've arbitrarily broken the concept up into its several parts. Then I've put them back together again in systematic order. My hope is that by following a step-by-step procedure, any executive might put the principle to work to his advantage in a variety of business situations.

Management by exception, I've concluded after long study, is truly the foundation upon which most modern management practices are based. Without a clear-cut understanding of its principles, most executives will have difficulty in planning wisely or in acting or controlling effectively.

Management by exception, while not a pure science, has evolved many reliable laws of its own. A vast wealth of empirical data has been accumulated in many management areas. These data and rules of thumb have been collected here—especially in the third part of the book.

Management by exception also seems to hold the key needed to

xi

release the benefits promised by high speed, computerized handling of business information. One of its key values is that it enables management to cull from a monumental mass of trivia the essential and vital data needed in order to manage well.

Management by exception, however, is not a magic bullet that will solve all management problems. It has its limitations as well as its values. And it is especially limited by the vagaries and intractability of human beings at work. So I've tried to provide perspective on these matters, too.

In developing this text, I readily acknowledge the great contributions made by the early management pioneers like Frederick W. Taylor, Henry Laurence Gantt, and Frank Bunker Gilbreth. I owe a great debt to them and to many, many more whose perceptive thoughts have found their way into my own. I'm indebted, too, to M. Joseph Dooher, who saw the need for a full-scale book on management by exception and who suggested the idea to me. Phil Carroll has been a welcome counsellor in the preparation of this book, and Roger W. Christian furnished much of what appears here about computers.

Finally, I should concede that this has been a difficult book to write. Its weaknesses will be evident to some. But its strength lies in the conviction that management by exception can make management life simpler and more effective.

Lester R. Bittel

CONTENTS

PART 4 *The Variables in Management by Exception*

PART 1

THE CONCEPT
of Management by Exception

What it is and what it can do for you.
What it needs from you to make it work.

Chapter 1

MANAGEMENT BY EXCEPTION

The time is the present. Four managers have just taken action in order to solve a pressing business problem:

Charles Ryerson, purchasing agent for East Coast Electronics, rejects a shipment of cathode tubes because a systematic sampling of the lot showed that the percentage of off-specification tubes exceeded a predetermined allowable number.

Avery Prentice, chairman of Amalgamated Alloys, calls a meeting of the board when a monthly statement shows that the brass division has failed to meet its sales target for the third successive time.

Elmer Bond, plant superintendent of the Seattle Stamping Works, authorizes overtime in the plating department when his weekly "late report" pinpoints plating delays as the cause for late shipment of six orders.

Joseph Schaeffer, office manager for Lifetime Insurance Mutuals, has a heart-to-heart talk with his chief clerk after an attitude survey reveals growing employee unrest in the clerical section.

Charles Ryerson, Avery Prentice, Elmer Bond, and Joseph Schaeffer have been solving problems that differ in nature and degree. But all four executives have one thing in common. They are all practicing management by exception. Every day thousands of other business managers practice management by exception, too. Most of them do so, not so much by conscious intent as by instinct. Fortunately this instinct is soundly based upon their own experience.

3

Experience has taught most seasoned managers that much of what happens in business life is a repetition of what has occurred in the past. Consequently, an alert manager can project yesterday's occurrences into today and tomorrow. This way he can know ahead of time what is likely to happen. Knowing this, he can preplan what to take for granted and what to get excited about. Those *routine,* expectable occurrences permit him to set up a plan of action for dealing with them. Only the *exceptional* occurrences—and not even all of these—need bring on new and difficult problems.

For example, let's take another look at the case of Charles Ryerson, the purchasing agent. Ryerson was employing a statistical technique based upon a "normal," or typical, distribution of product characteristics throughout a "lot" of any size. Ryerson was able to predetermine, to a high degree of accuracy, how many tubes would be off-quality. When his sampling showed that the actual number had exceeded the expected—that it was, in fact, "exceptional"— Ryerson's decision was easy. He followed an established buying policy of rejecting an entire shipment when sampling showed an exceptional amount of off-quality goods.

How did Avery Prentice practice management by exception? His method was technically simpler than Ryerson's. With the aid of the division manager, he had previously set up monthly profit goals for brass products. Experience, however, had taught him that if the division failed to meet profit goals for more than two months running, something unpredictable was happening to the brass market. As company chairman, he knew it was his responsibility to deal with the unpredictable. While his action technique was simple, even unscientific, his problem to be solved was difficult. This is so because no amount of accumulated data has taken market prediction out of the realm of art and into science.

Elmer Bond, too, was using a simple, time-saving management method. Instead of examining the progress of each of the thousands of orders as they moved through the shop, he studied only those items that were not on schedule. A reporting system that flagged these exceptional items helped him to make sense out of what would otherwise be an unintelligible mountain of data. The action he took was also relatively simple. It was dictated by existing company policy. In the face of a tough competitive situation, late deliveries could not be tolerated. Bond knew he was expected to correct the delivery problem before he could take long-term measures to produce on-time deliveries without the extra cost of overtime.

Finally, Joseph Schaeffer was managing by exception, too, because he was comparing measurements of attitudes in his department with average measurements in his company and in his industry. The survey earmarked the chief clerk's employees as having a lower than average—or exceptional—attitude. In this instance, the measurement method isolated the exception, and existing knowledge of human behavior indicated an approach Schaeffer might follow.

Management by Exception Defined

Management by exception, in its simplest form, is a system of identification and communication that signals the manager when his attention is needed; conversely, it remains silent when his attention is not required. The primary purpose of such a system is, of course, to simplify the management process itself—to permit a manager to find the problems that need his action and to avoid dealing with those that are better handled by his subordinates.

It is easier to tell you what the *ingredients* are in management by exception than to provide a simple definition. For instance, one might say that management by exception has six key elements. They are measurement, projection, selection, observation (or remeasurement), comparison, and decision making.

Measurement assigns values—often numerical—to past and present performances. Without measurement of some sort, it would be impossible to identify an exception.

Projection analyzes those measurements that are meaningful to business objectives and extends them into future expectations.

Selection pinpoints the criteria management will use to follow progress toward its objectives.

Observation is that phase of measurement that informs management of the current state of performance.

Comparison of actual performance with expected performance identifies the exceptions that require attention and reports the variances to management.

Decision making prescribes the action that must be taken in order to (1) bring performance back into control or to (2) adjust expectations to reflect changing conditions or to (3) exploit opportunity.

In many ways the concept of management by exception is inseparable from other management essentials. All planning, for instance, is based upon this concept. The philosophy of management by exception is also deeply rooted in the principles of the division of labor, delegation of responsibility and authority, and span of control. But it has as its taproot the concept of measurement, to which a later chapter will be devoted.

Its Historical Background

You have only to look around you in business today to find dozens of modern management practices that directly utilize, support, or reflect the management by exception principle. To name just a few, there are:

Statistical control of product quality

Economic order quantities and order points for control of inventories and supplies

The Gantt chart for production control

Break-even points for determining operating levels

Trends in ratios of indirect to direct labor used in apportioning overhead

Attitude surveys for gaging employee morale

Dozens of financial ratios (such as net sales to net working capital) to measure the economic health of a business

There is no managerial function that cannot practice management by exception in some form or other. In fact, management by exception has become such an obvious—often unconscious—way of life that it is hard to realize that it is relatively new as a crystallized concept. There is little doubt that its application could be documented by a historical search of early cultures—such as the Roman's. The world's military organizations and many religious organizations have used it for centuries. But it was not until the end of the nineteenth century that management by exception was identified as a principle that could be applied to business situations in general.

In order to enlarge your own foundation in applying this principle, it is helpful to see it as some of management's more notable pioneers have seen it. Here is a sampling of their views.

Frederick W. Taylor

Under [the exception principle] the manager should receive only condensed, summarized, and invariably comparative reports covering, however, all of the elements entering into the management, and even these summaries should all be carefully gone over by an assistant before they reach the manager, and have all of the exceptions to the past averages or standards pointed out, both the especially good and the especially bad exceptions, thus giving him in a few minutes a full view of progress which is being made, or the reverse, and leaving him free to consider the broader lines of policy and to study the character and fitness of the important men under him.[1]

Henry Robinson Towne

The primary object [of records and paperwork] is the systematic recording of the operations of the different departments of the works, and the computation therefrom of such statistical information as is essential to the efficient management of the business, and especially to increased economy of production.[2]

Henry Laurence Gantt

In order to be sure that they all got the assistance possible from the foreman he, too, received a definite premium for each machine under his charge that made its bonus, and in order that the poorer men might receive sufficient instruction from the foreman, it was made to his interest to give them special attention. That was accomplished in this way: While the foreman was given a definite amount for each machine that earned its bonus, he was given an additional fifty per cent if all the machines under his charge earned their bonus, thus making it to his interest to give special attention to the men most likely to fall behind.[3]

Leon Pratt Alford

Experience is the knowledge of past attainment. It includes a knowledge of *what* has been done, and also *how* it has been done. It is inseparably associated with standards of performance, that is with the ideas of quantity and quality in relation to any particular method of doing something. . . . The great instrument of experience, which makes progress possible, is comparison. By systematic use of experience is meant the careful analysis of what is about to be attempted, and its reference to existing records and standards of performance.[4]

Frank Bunker Gilbreth

The personal work of the executive should consist as much as possible of making decisions and as little as possible of making motions. General recognition of this fact has resulted in the common practice of assigning to the executive one or more secretaries, or clerks, to relieve him of certain parts of his work which involve mere motions and less important decisions than that part of the work retained by the executive. This procedure varies in degree according to the kind of work done by the executive and how well he realizes the possibilities of eliminating waste through the use of the "exception principle" in management.[5]

Peter Drucker

Any serious attempt to make management scientific or professional is bound to lead to the attempt to eliminate those disturbing influences, the unpredictabilities of business life—its risks, its ups and downs, its wasteful competition, the irrational choices of the consumer—and, in the process, the economy's freedom and its ability to grow. It is not entirely accident that some of the early pioneers of Scientific Management ended up by demanding complete cartelization of the economy (Henry Gantt was the prime example); that the one direct outgrowth of American Scientific Management abroad, the German Rationalization movement of the twenties, attempted to make the world safe for professional management by cartelizing it; and that in our own country men who were steeped in scientific management played a big part in Technocracy and in the attempted nation-wide super-cartel of the National Recovery Act in the first year of Roosevelt's New Deal.[6]

This was management by exception as the pioneers of scientific management saw it. Its big advantage lay in making management more effective and in preventing management from "overmanaging." Today, however, management by exception has taken on a new dimension. In an era of phenomenal technical growth and harassing economic change, a management by exception system stimulates a manager to actively search for exceptions that allow him to apply his creative ability. Consequently, management by exception is not only a technique of control but also a method for seeking out opportunities.

The early pioneers—and critics—of scientific management and the exception principle have had their say. Because of them, or in spite of them, the principle has stood the test of time well. Today it is applied in broad scope to every conceivable management function in every kind of organization—in America or abroad. This is so because its rewards to management are so generous.

What Management by Exception Can Do for Management

Taylor's analysis of the exception principle highlights its obvious advantages—executive timesaving and an objective view of progress made toward established goals. A more penetrating examination justifies another dozen more. For instance, the practice of management by exception:

• Saves personal time. You apply yourself to fewer problems—the ones that really count. It minimizes time-consuming work on trivia and details that others on your staff can handle.

• Concentrates executive effort. Instead of spreading managerial talent thinly across all sorts of problems, you place your effort selectively only where and when it is needed.

• Reduces distractions. The management by exception system only flags attention to critical areas. It remains silent on matters that are under control or that are delegated automatically to your subordinates.

• Facilitates broader managerial coverage. Concentrated, more effective management effort enables you to increase the scope of your activities and your span of control. This frees you to tackle promising projects that otherwise might be left undone.

• Lessens frequency of decision making. The system makes most of the minor decisions for you. You don't have to check every item under your supervision every day to see if it is okay or not. The system passes along to you only the few important problems for you to rule on or act on. But these decisions are, of course, the more difficult ones.

• Makes fuller use of knowledge of trends, history, and available business data. Management by exception, when applied systematically, forces an executive to review past history and to study related business data, because these are the foundations upon which standards are derived and from which exceptions are noted.

• More fully utilizes highly paid people on high-return work. Because delegation is planned, it more carefully relates and assigns the more complex problems to the more talented and highly paid people.

• Identifies crises and critical problems. As much as anything, management by exception helps you to avoid uninformed, impulsive pushing of the panic button. Yet a crisis is almost always recognized because seemingly unusual variations can be reliably and quickly compared with anticipated conditions.

• Provides qualitative and quantitative yardsticks for judging situations and people. Management by exception takes much of the prejudice out of performance appraisals by making individual and organizational goals and measurements tangible and specific.

• Enables inexperienced managers to handle new assignments with a minimum of related experience and training. A new man benefits from measurements and projections that have been established as standard for his function in the past. He can depend upon the system to alert him to problems rather than having to rely solely upon his own experience.

• Alerts management to opportunities as well as difficulties. Managing by exception helps to counterbalance purely negative, control-minded management. Attention is directed to "breakthrough" variations as well as to omissions or shortcomings.

• Encourages more comprehensive knowledge of all phases of business operations. You cannot practice management by exception systematically without continually gathering and updating real facts about your organization and its operation.

• Stimulates communications between different segments of an organization. With its focus on results, management by exception seeks to relate causes, regardless of their place in the organization, with overall organizational results. As such, it encourages exchange of measurements between functions as well as between a function and the cost or profit center to which it reports.

How Companies Are Using Management by Exception

Hardly a successful company exists today that does not practice management by exception. As indicated earlier, this conclusion is more often inferred by observation than confirmed by positive evidence of an active system. Nevertheless, the evidence is considerable. For example, see how these topflight companies are making management by exception work for them:

In Decision Making. Bell & Howell Co. uses the practice of management by exception to make its policy of delegation work. Its policy is threefold: (1) Delegate to the lowest possible level. (2)

Step in only when problems warrant. (3) Tap optimum capabilities of everyone. Charles H. Percy, company chairman, says that under this system, executives have been able to remove up to 90 per cent of the routine work from their desks. Furthermore, he points out that it has additional value because it serves to "get management people *out* of the act" and to let others have an opportunity to participate to the extent of their capabilities.[7]

In Marketing. Smith-Corona Marchant, Inc., directs executive attention to exceptional marketing problems by classifying products annually according to their sales potential. In the first group are those products that are expected to hold their own in the ensuing year. These get only superficial attention from top management. In the second group are those products with the greatest immediate potential. Top management examines these intensively from many corporate viewpoints, including engineering, finance, and production. The intention here is to exploit an opportunity. The third group of products are those adversely affected by a dwindling market. These also come up for sharp executive consideration. The problem here is one of improvement and/or control.[8]

In Corporate Finance. Westinghouse Electric Corporation greatly reduces the time required by top management to review capital expenditure requests by establishing a table of amounts that may be approved by lesser management without higher approval. For instance, individual projects up to $50,000 go to the division manager, projects from $50,000 to $100,000 go to headquarters management, and those over $100,000 go to the board of directors. In one year, as an example, about 500 projects, representing in dollars 15 per cent of the total program, went to the division managers, while only about 150 projects, which represented 85 per cent of the dollars, required headquarters or board approval.[9]

In Production. St. Regis Paper Company expects its managers of production to delegate most day-to-day matters to subordinates. To quote William R. Adams, president, "Most of the prime duties of the production manager will necessitate his being freed of routine functions (but) there are routine matters . . . of which he will need to inform me. Usually they are the result of decisions arrived at long before. Reports of this kind serve to acquaint me with the progress made in his area. Sometimes they give me the option to exercise control, sometimes to inform managers in other areas." [10]

In Organization Staffing. International Business Machines Corporation after World War II expanded its engineering force by over 400 per cent. Most of the new people held M.A.'s and Ph.D.'s. However, an appraisal of executive resources brought to the attention of president Thomas J. Watson, Jr., the fact that practically none of the engineering and research management positions were staffed by people of similar educational background. In order to bring IBM management into phase with a rapidly changing technology, a policy was instituted to promote to top administrative posts those people who best understood the technology with which they were dealing. Consequently, IBM promoted large numbers of the advanced-degree men into positions of executive responsibility.[11]

In Upgrading Performance. Otis Elevator Company operates throughout the United States in ten districts. In setting standards of performance for each zone, the company holds up for example the best performance set by any of its components. It then makes comparisons on the basis of a composite picture made up of the selected best features to be found in the entire ten districts.[12]

In Reducing Costs. Rockwell Manufacturing Company recently performed a conclusive experiment documenting the value of measurement, standards, and management by exception. Two plants were tooled up at the same time to make the same product. At one plant methods were studied and controls prescribed by the industrial engineering department. In the second plant the industrial engineering department did not see the job until it was in operation. *The result:* the first plant's production averaged 50 per cent more as a result of this preplanning for management by exception for the executive group who took over the plant.[13]

Where Its Limitations Lie

Peter Drucker's criticism of management by exception expressed a fear that management might interpret the exception as only a nuisance to be reduced through refinements in measurement, more careful planning, and stricter controls. Management by exception has other pitfalls, of course. Here are some that come to mind:

- It breeds "organization-man" thinking.
- It is often dependent upon unreliable data.
- It requires a comprehensive observing and reporting system.
- It tends to proliferate paperwork.
- It often assumes an unnatural stability in business affairs.

• In the absence of exceptions it can give management a false sense of security.

• It is silent about conditions predetermined not to be critical.

• Standards of comparison tend to become obsolete (such as the ratio of indirect to direct labor).

• Some critical business factors (such as human behavior) are difficult, if not impossible, to measure.

Finally, the process of management by exception cannot be a substitute for thinking—nor for decision making. Its big advantage lies in the fact that much of the time-consuming process of thinking and decision making can be done in *advance*. A progressive system of action can be prescribed beforehand, much as a troubleshooter's manual can give an instrument repairman step-by-step directions to isolate a fault. As a result, only radical exceptions, either good or bad, need be interpreted and acted upon under pressure of time.

The executive's problem, therefore, is threefold. First, he must convert his instinctive, unconscious approach to management by exception to a positive, systematic way of handling every kind of management problem—men, money, machines, and materials. Secondly, he must guard against the conformity and false sense of security that systems of any kind tend to nourish. Thirdly, freed from the demands of routine work, he must fill his time with creative effort directed toward improving his plans, organization, staff, and decisions.

References

1. Frederick W. Taylor, "Shop Management," 1911, reprinted in *Scientific Management*, Harper & Row, Publishers, Incorporated, New York, 1947, p. 126.
2. Henry R. Towne, "The Engineer as an Economist," *Transactions of the American Society of Mechanical Engineers*, vol. 7, p. 428, 1886.
3. Henry L. Gantt, "A Bonus System of Rewarding Labor," *Transactions of the American Society of Mechanical Engineers*, vol. 23, p. 341, 1901.
4. L. P. Alford with Alexander H. Church, "The Principles of Management," *American Machinist*, May 30, 1912.
5. Frank B. Gilbreth, "Graphical Control on the Exception Principle for Executives," Paper 1573a, American Society of Mechanical Engineers, New York, December, 1916.
6. Peter F. Drucker, *The Practice of Management*. Harper & Row, Publishers, Incorporated, New York, 1954, p. 10.

7. R. R. Conarroe, *The Decision Makers,* The Bureau of Business Practice, New London, Conn., 1958, p. 16.
8. Gordon H. Smith, "Direction and Control of Expansion," in H. B. Maynard (ed.), *Top Management Handbook,* McGraw-Hill Book Company, New York, 1960, pp. 1026–1029.
9. Ross G. Walker and Russell B. Read, "Capital Investment Control," in Edward C. Bursk and Dan H. Fenn, Jr. (eds.), *Planning the Future Strategy of Your Business,* McGraw-Hill Book Company, New York, 1956, pp. 85–102.
10. William R. Adams, "Top Management and Production," in Maynard (ed.), *op. cit.,* pp. 559–567.
11. Thomas J. Watson, Jr., "Promotion Innovation," in *ibid.,* pp. 514–515.
12. LeRoy A. Petersen, "Establishing Objectives," in *ibid.,* p. 186.
13. Willard F. Rockwell, Jr., "Managing a Highly Decentralized Organization," in *ibid.,* p. 930.

Chapter 2

HOW TO MANAGE BY EXCEPTION

Listen to the words of these two giants of industry:

Giant No. 1: "I believe in changing the policies every time the door opens."

Giant No. 2: "There are two ways of running any kind of business. They are the 'hunch' method and the scientific way. I have always followed the latter. It has paid me big returns and it will for others."

Of these two men, both multimillionaires, can you guess which one ended up broke? You're right. Giant No. 1, the fabulous William C. Durant, founder of the General Motors empire, wound up his career financing a string of bowling alleys that went bust. Giant No. 2, his successor as president of General Motors, was the administrative genius Alfred P. Sloan, Jr. He helped pull GM out of near bankruptcy by setting up a system of delegated authority, systematic planning, and executive control by exception. His administrative techniques, instituted in 1930, still exist today at GM in much the same form as they were originally.

Why did Will Durant finish on his back? Not because he wasn't one of the world's greatest financial wizards. Not because he didn't have extraordinary vision. (Bowling alleys, so successful now, were a fiasco in 1929. Durant's venture was roughly twenty years ahead of schedule.) Nor was he a poor leader of men. And he didn't lack courage. Durant's problem was that he just couldn't get the hang of that vital ingredient of twentieth-century management—manage-

15

ment by exception. Walter P. Chrysler, Durant's operations chief for a short period, recalls urging Durant this way: "Billy, please now, say what your policies are for General Motors. I'll work on them. Whatever they are, I'll work to make them effective. Leave the operations alone; the building, the buying, the selling and the men—leave them alone, but say what your policies are." As the words of Giant No. 1 indicate, Durant would never say. Neither would Durant leave his subordinates alone. He couldn't resist over-managing. He lived by hunch. And he couldn't learn to manage by exception.[1]

Practice Self-Control

Unlike Will Durant, today's successful executive *must* learn to manage his business affairs by applying the principles of management by exception. And one of the prime principles is that of self-control. It often *is* easier to rush ahead on impulse. It often *does* give you a feeling of relief just to be able to do something—especially when it pertains to something that you have delegated to a subordinate. And especially when the necessary action seems obvious to you. It is also less demanding personally to be able to make plans based upon intuition. Playing your hunches can give you a feeling of excitement similar to that many people get from playing cards. Such taking off into the wide blue yonder gives a person a sense of freedom. And then it's not abnormal to satisfy some deeply hidden urge by clobbering a subordinate who appears to be getting out of line. This is even more true when you don't have to judge his off-standard performance by more than a single factor—in other words, if you don't have to spend time sifting through a mass of evidence. The trouble is that acting on these kinds of impulses is rarely effective.

We're all prone to interpret any administrative system as something that is set up to control others. Or, conversely, we're sure that controls are needed to punish people—even ourselves—who stray too far from the path laid out by corporate plans. However, if you adopt this attitude toward a methodological approach to management by exception, you're likely to be missing an essential, but subtle, point. Yes, there *are* systematic ways for applying management by exception. In fact, the next section of this book will be devoted to describing how to develop such a system. But no amount of paperwork and punitively oriented controls will make even a good system work. What is needed first is a belief in the underlying purpose of the system. And then it's up to you to exercise self-control in making it work for *you*.

In the San Francisco office of a life insurance company where the management practiced a policy of delegation, salesmen for some months failed to meet underwriting quotas. Company officials in the New York headquarters pressed the Western states vice-president for improvement. He assured New York that the situation was well in hand. Results in the next few months did not bear him out. Finally, the company auditor, who was making his annual tour of the regions, had an opportunity to talk with the manager of the San Francisco office. The manager complained that he was having an unusual morale problem with his staff. His story was that another East Coast firm had moved into the Bay area several months ago and was furnishing intense competition. He felt that his sales force had begun to make headway after its initial difficulty in handling this competition. But a couple of months ago the regional vice-president had started to call all the shots—even going so far as to issue ultimatums to individual salesmen who were below quotas. In simple terms, the regional vice-president, when faced with an off-standard condition, had panicked. And he had resorted to a kind of overmanaging that, far from helping the situation, had speeded its deterioration.

Take another example. Ron Burke is plant superintendent for an Ohio Valley gray-iron foundry. The controller has set up a simple schedule of reports for determining unit costs of various products. The reports take into account direct and indirect labor, wage incentive payments, materials, supplies, etc. Ron Burke's operations sheets show that he has kept costs regularly within the prescribed limits. What the sheets *don't* show is that in order to meet these cost standards, Burke has gradually been sacrificing product quality. Now, he *can* get away with this, perhaps for a long while if the market is good. Or he can suggest to the controller that another factor must be plugged into the cost schedules—the cost of maintaining quality against specified standards. This would impose, at Burke's expense, another management control. It would take self-discipline on Burke's part to invite it. But, in the long run, it would work to his advantage to provide management with a fairer measure of his performance.

Discard Preconceived Notions

One of the hardest management qualities to find, says one executive research organization, is true objectivity. As a matter of fact, true objectivity is hard to find in anybody. This is so because we spend most of our lives learning how to be prejudiced. Although this may sound a little peculiar, it really isn't if you stop to think about it for a moment. From the day we are born, we get most of our knowledge from experience. A baby touches a hot stove and is burned. Stoves burn, says the baby to himself. A week later he touches the same stove and he isn't burned. That's strange, he says. Next time he touches the stove when his mother is preparing dinner, and he's burned again. Oh, he observes, stoves burn at mealtimes. And so on. What the baby has acquired is a bias toward stoves. The bias doesn't mean that he doesn't like them. It means that his bias has given him a knowledge of stoves that isn't exactly accurate or complete. In the same manner, almost all people, including too many executives, have acquired bias about just the things they should be objective about.

How many times, for instance, have you heard someone in your organization say, "We've tried it before and it didn't work." Or, "Smith isn't the kind of man who can handle this assignment." Or, "Our experience has proved that the way we are doing the job now is the best." Or, "It's smart to buy commodities now when prices are falling."

Any of these statements *may* be true. Chances are, however, that they represent someone's preconceived notion rather than an objective assessment of the facts.

Take the man who says we've tried it before and it didn't work. Has he asked himself these questions: Were the circumstances then identical with those today? Were the people involved as flexible, or competent, as those we now employ? What was the competitive situation then? Has it changed since? Did the method get a fair trial, or was it given only short shrift? Was this the idea actually tried, or has the speaker's memory confused it with another that had failed?

Now take the man who says that Smith isn't the man to handle the assignment. Has anyone asked these questions: Has Smith ever been given a chance to demonstrate competency in that area? What sort of training has Smith been given for such work? Exactly which of the job demands can Smith handle, and on which is he weak?

Or look at the fellow who says that our experience shows us that the way we are doing things now is best. How does he know? Can he back up this judgment with facts and figures documenting results? Is he judging present performance by obsolete standards? Is he aware of what potential there is in completely new methods as compared with those tried in the past?

Finally, how about the manager who says it's smart to buy now? Financial experts tell us that more firms fail because of poor inventory management than for any other technical reason. Apparently most managers can't resist a bargain. While the adage of buying cheap and selling dear makes sense, unfortunately it's only a fragment of *average* knowledge that may or may not fit a specific situation.

Management by exception is based upon a respect for documented facts that have shown a relationship to desired results. Few things will negate the exception principle like the adherence to preconceived notions and the failure to strive for objectivity.

Be Guided by Policy

So much has already been said about the value of policy in guiding executive decisions that there is a danger in being redundant. Nevertheless, there seems always to be those who resent policy. They see it as an intrusion into their prerogatives or a slur on their ability to think for themselves. Such was the attitude of the early, barnstorming pilots when navigational aids to flying were introduced. These intrepid birdmen wanted to keep on flying by the seat of their pants. Some of them did, but a whole new generation of pilots have come along who fly better, higher, faster, and more safely by using instruments.

According to one expert, Capt. Harold Blackburn, the oldest jet pilot flying international routes for Trans World Airlines, the problem was equally difficult in transferring from propeller-driven aircraft to jets. It involves a new concept known as "attitude" flying. Captain Blackburn says,

Getting used to the idea of attitude flying is the essential point in making the transition to jets. Basically, the idea is that for every maneuver there is a specific attitude—a specific thing to do. If you do that, the certified performance will be delivered. The most important rule about jet flying is that *you must fly by the book.*

On takeoff, for example, we know exactly how many feet of runway this airplane needs in relation to its weight, the barometric pressure, and so on. If the temperature increases one degree, we need another 50 feet of runway. If the barometric pressure decreases one-tenth of an inch, we need another hundred feet of runway. And we need to know how much fuel it will use during takeoff, climb, cruise, descent, and every other phase of flying. All this has been worked out very very accurately with electronic computers, and all the information is in our manual—charts, tables and graphs. So you consult the book, and you fly by the book. What it amounts to is that you fly this airplane by an I.B.M. machine. If you play it exactly by the book, it's going to perform exactly on the money. If you try to fly by the seat of your pants, you can be in a lot of trouble in a hurry.[2]

Like today's jet pilot, modern executives must also be guided by the book. Their policy book is rarely so rigid, but if it's a good book, and electronic data processing will make policy increasingly dependable, then it's wise to follow it. Not that policy will ever do away with decision making. Even the jet pilot continually makes decisions—whether to follow through at takeoff or to "abort," whether to climb at the prescribed rate or to seek a new flight level, whether to land at Brussels or continue on nonstop to Paris, etc. With the same attitude toward your book, you too can learn to know when to lean on policy and when to use it as a springboard to a better decision.

Learn to Live with Accountants

There's a possibility that your own sad experience has caused you to downgrade accountants, industrial engineers, statisticians, operations research people, and electronic-data-processing specialists as pencil pushers, paper shufflers, and "Figure Filberts." If that's your inclination, the time has come for you to abandon it. It won't serve you well in an organization bent upon managing by exception. Measurement, fact finding, data collection, and reporting and analysis form the foundation upon which the exception principle is built. And no habitually successful organization lives without it.

Henry Ford II, chairman of the Ford Motor Company, was asked by *The Saturday Evening Post* to advise young men entering business on this point. He said,

Every company is different from any other. But no matter what company he may be in, a young man is always faced with the job of bringing a tremendous number of variables under his control. Hunches won't do. Simples rules of thumb won't do. These things may help, but what it takes to achieve order and steady progress is system, and the young man must learn to master that system.

Lightning-fast communications, for example, regularly put information from around the world at his fingertips. Highly trained specialists tell him what is happening in the world and something of what will happen. And if the experts bog down, they can run alternative courses of action through computers and get quick, accurate answers that used to be available only after weeks or months or even years of strenuous work.[3]

Contrary to the wishes of many of the old guard in management and of many of the young reactionaries who seem to proliferate its ranks, this army of statistical specialists is going to keep on growing. The race to get to market ahead of your competitor, and in better shape, is intensifying, not slackening. And your competitors are turning to every available kind of statistical help in collecting and assessing business information. So don't fight it. Instead, try to describe for the Figure Filberts in your organization the kind of information you need to know in order to manage your operation better. Above all, don't make the mistake of assuming a hands-off attitude that gives the statistical boys their heads in areas of your responsibility. Make no bones about it. You know more about your operation than they do. And if they are intelligent, they'll be quick to admit it. The thing to do is to be in on data collecting and processing decisions that affect your area right at the start and on every step of the way. That way you'll have a better chance of seeing a system developed that serves your interests rather than one that overlooks it or works against it.

Delegate for Results

One purchasing agent when queried about his delegation techniques replied, "I tell the steel buyer to keep on top of the distributors to see that their prices are in line with the market. I tell the supplies buyer to be sure we're getting the right quantity discounts. And I tell the subassembly buyer to insist on tight conformance to delivery schedules. So long as the buyers do it the way I've set it up, I don't bother them from one week to the next."

Is this delegation? Well, it's something like it. But it's far from a complete picture. The purchasing agent here is delegating certain *tasks* to his subordinates. And along with these tasks he's prescribing *how* they should be performed. What he hasn't done, however, is to delegate a *responsibility for results*. Without doing this, the purchasing agent may find his subordinates going through the motions in accordance with his plans but failing to achieve the kind of results intended. It is much better for the purchasing agent, or for any manager for that matter, to spell out for his assistants just what he wants in the way of accomplishments. If he places his emphasis on these results, he can devote less of his time to laying out methods, which, after all, may not be as effective as those devised by his subordinates.

For instance, the purchasing agent might say to his steel buyer, "Your goal is to provide the plant with the desired quantities and quality of steel at the lowest prices consistent with deliveries when we need it. As specific targets, I'll expect that (1) unavailability of raw stock in the plant will never be the cause for production delays, (2) 99.7 per cent of all incoming steel will pass specifications established by our metallurgist, (3) average price paid per ton will be within 3 cents of the average weekly market as published in *American Metals Market,* and (4) inventory level should not exceed $50,000."

Delegating for results this way implies a freedom for a subordinate to choose his own way of securing them. Obviously it would be wasteful for your assistants to ignore your know-how and advice. And in many instances it is absolutely necessary that prescribed channels be followed—either for legal purposes or for the sake of organizational harmony. But in the main, delegation should mean a shucking off, not only of responsibilities for certain results, but also of the prerogative to prescribe how to go about securing them.

Sharpen Your Observational Powers

When you have spun off a stack of your responsibilities to others in your organization, your next big problem is to know at any time what's going on. Even with a sensitive reporting and control system, you may find yourself in the dark between reporting periods. While this has its advantages in that in the absence of danger signals from the system you can assume that all's going according to plan, it doesn't obviate the need for sensing the "climate" of progress or retrogression.

Controversial, but perceptive Vice Admiral Hyman Rickover made such a point a few years ago when criticizing manufacturers of basic equipment who failed to meet their promised deliveries to nuclear and missile projects. He rebuked management for being too willing "to sit in plush offices . . . far removed mentally and physically from . . . manufacturing and engineering areas, relying upon paper reports for information about the status of design and production in the plant." His belief was that top management had become too prone to rely upon administrative systems to do its work for it.

Another way of looking at this is that delegation doesn't free a manager from his responsibility for continuing personal contact with his organization. Delegation and the practice of management by exception should not make management remote or mechanical. It should make management more available for relaxed, day-to-day coaching and communication.

What is needed is for a manager to increase his perceptive powers. By intelligent listening, by careful looking, and by stepping up his sensitivity to human behavior, he can supplement formal reports with his own feel of what's going on. For instance, regular housekeeping reports may be telling the works manager that his plant is spic and span. An occasional tour of the works which takes him into overlooked nooks and crannies may give him a different, and more accurate, impression.

Take the case of a company president who was disappointed with his company's failure to get its share of a growing market in household appliances. Examination of various trends furnished him by the controller indicated the trouble lay in not having enough sales coverage at the consumer level. He changed his opinion about this after attending a string of district sales meetings. While he neither asked nor answered questions, he overheard enough of the shop talk among the district managers to realize that their experience indicated a need for more advertising in local newspapers rather than additions to the sales force. The district managers had not offered this opinion in their regular reports because it seemed foolish to turn down extra manpower if headquarters was inclined to provide it.

In still another way, sharpened perception enabled the research director of a large chemical firm to detect impending trouble

*months before it might have shown up in a regularly conducted
employee attitude survey.* Instead of resting on his convictions between annual studies, he made a habit of discussing technical problems daily with each of his project managers. While his interest was
overtly directed toward scientific matters, his true purpose was to
provide a communication channel in which his subordinates had
confidence. As a result, a serious misunderstanding about pay policies among technicians was brought to his attention, and corrective
action taken, before the inferred inequality could stir up wide-
spread sentiment for unionization of engineers.

The point to bear in mind is that observation of the state of
business affairs should not be left entirely to an administrative system. Each executive should sharpen the perceptive powers of all
his sensory elements—hearing, sight, smell, touch, and even taste.
Only a few of us are psychologically blind in these senses. A spokesman for Arthur D. Little industrial research laboratories has observed, for instance, that even keen skills in differentiating taste can
be taught to almost anyone who wants to develop it.

Finally, it should be stressed that in-between-reports observations
by managers practicing management by exception should not constitute snooping. Such oversupervising would work to destroy the
advantages gained by the exception technique.

Use Management by Exception to Develop Subordinates

You can do this any number of ways. You can do so in the obvious
way by delegating certain of your tasks in a typical division of responsibilities. But you can accomplish even more by assigning subordinates to help you in any of the stages of management by exception. For example:

In the Measurement Phase. A plant superintendent could ask his
department managers to furnish him with an additional measure of
their operations, such as compressed air consumption, number of
jobs moved ahead of schedule, or amount of rework attributable to
tool failure. Or he could assign a work-sampling study to a general
foreman as a special project. Or he might temporarily swap jobs
between a production department head and a standards engineer in
the industrial engineering section in order to give the line manager
direct experience in measurement.

In the Projection Phase. A sales vice-president might ask his product managers to plan for the year ahead, not only sales volume but also advertising, promotion, training, and other cost budgets. Or he might switch a promising salesman over to market research for a year in order to give him forecasting experience.

In the Selection Phase. A manager of product development could ask an engineer in training to make an A-B-C analysis of product components that caused the greatest number of customer complaints. From this determination of the "vital few," he could develop a schedule of design specification criteria for quality control (see pages 93–98).

In the Observation Phase. A company president might use as a rotating training assignment the position of assistant to the president. Such an assistant could act as a special observer to verify the accuracy of data collection and assimilating systems.

In the Comparison Phase. A production or sales supervisor could be assigned to the product design department to analyze and interpret test results. Or a task force in the production department might periodically review progress reports and make recommendations to the plant manager.

In the Decision-making Phase. Any executive can ask a subordinate to draw up a schedule of alternative courses of action in the event of deviations from programmed results. Whenever time permits, a manager could refer an exception report to his subordinates and ask for recommendations. He could do so either as a case example to be profiled against a past decision, in which it would be only a "dry run," or he could use the technique in an actual situation to collect ideas for his own decision. In both cases subordinates would be learning a little about management by exception without the risk of their making decisions in an actual situation.

Invite Enough Participation

All along the way, management by exception provides good opportunities to invite participation. Since the exception principle is aimed not only at attaining corporate goals but also at measuring how well members of the organization perform, acceptance of the system will greatly depend upon how much participation has been built into it.

At the measurement stage, each manager affected should be checked to get his opinion of the accuracy of past observations. He should also be polled at the forecasting stage so that he understands, if not agrees with, the standards selected and the goals chosen. He should have a chance to comment upon the data collections and reporting system so that he will view it as constructive rather than punitive. And at the analysis stage the system should enable each manager to verify the raw data where he doubts them and to offer his own interpretation in addition to those made by the controller. And finally, when the action taken to handle variables is going to affect him materially, he should be invited into the decision-making phase of management by exception.

Expect Some People to Call You Lazy

There will come a time after you've delegated away a good part of your responsibilities and are stimulating participation from others in the organization when you can expect to be the target of un-justified criticism. You'll find the slings and arrows coming from three directions. First, you can assume that many of your subordi-nates will figure that it's all a dodge for them to do the work you're paid to do. While they won't vocalize this attitude to you, they will to others. Secondly, if you've done such a good job of preparing for management by exception that you have opened some free time in your own schedule, some of your management associates will be downright envious. Such envy may take the form of good-natured needling, or it may cause some of your more aggressive peers to resort to petty politics and undercutting. Lastly, you can even ex-pect your boss to be critical, especially if he's a do-it-himself type of individual. In this case you'll be forced to adopt a middle-of-the-road position that gives an optimum amount of freedom to your subordinates yet permits a degree of self-participation that satisfies your superior. On the other hand, if management by exception is truly working for you, you may be able to demonstrate by your own results that the *appearance* of being a "let-George-do-it" type isn't preventing you from getting good results.

Discriminate between "Big" and "Little" Jobs

One secret of management by exception—perhaps of management itself—is the ability to discriminate between the work you should do yourself and the work you should expect others to do for you. Actually, delegation isn't intended to give you time to call your stockbroker or to run errands for your wife. Its purpose is to strip you of routine work and to force you to earn your higher salary by doing high-priced work. Those who criticize you for being lazy or infer that you're passing the buck miss the point. Executives *should* be busy. But they should be busy doing important things—like planning, listening, analyzing, and using their creative resources. To maintain the impression of great importance by rushing about performing tasks that a high school boy can do is merely foolish.

There are few hard-and-fast rules that will help you separate the important work of management from the trivial.

One good test is this: Can anyone else on my staff perform this part of my work nearly as well as I can? If so, you probably shouldn't be doing it.

Another test is: Does it utilize my most recently acquired skills? If so, chances are it's a job you should do and your juniors shouldn't.

Still another test: Does it involve a sophisticated management function, like planning to a very large degree? If so, that job is probably for you.

Another increasingly apt test is: Could this work be done by a machine? If so, it has a strong routine element that tends to put it in the bailiwick of your subordinates.

There's still another question. Its answer won't produce a decision, but it may help you avoid a major pitfall in delegating: Am I doing this kind of work not because it requires high-level attention, but because I'm already skilled in it or because I like to do it? If the answer is in the affirmative, you may be penalizing your overall effectiveness by hanging on to a job that is comfortable, but not suitable.

Don't Be an "Over-the-shoulder" Supervisor

Driver training schools do a thriving business because many a husband can't stand the agony of teaching his wife to drive. He may put her behind the wheel and give her the keys, but the temptation to tell her when to let out the clutch, how hard to step on the accelerator, and when to signal a turn is simply too great. In some ways it's miraculous that there are thousands of couples who are happily married despite the fact that the husband will not ride in a car while his wife is driving. In some ways managers who have a hard time managing by exception demonstrate a similar frustration.

Jack Black, for instance, the executive vice-president of a meat packing firm, divided up operational responsibility between four product-divisions assistant vice-presidents. On the advice of a management consultant he surrounded himself with five functional managers heading up corporate personnel, engineering, public relations, finance, and legal affairs. He also set up a planning and control section headed by a controller. Instead of gaining from this reorganization, the company slipped badly, and Black, who formerly had been considered one of the top men in the industry, became completely ineffective. The trouble lay in the fact that Black couldn't resist over-the-shoulder supervising. His defection showed itself in a number of highly demoralizing forms:

1. He'd offer well-intended suggestions to those who were in charge of the divisions. Rather than permit his assistant vice-presidents to learn anything from experience, Black regularly would issue a string of advice and cautions. To the division managers it had the effect of making them feel that whenever they made an independent decision that didn't work out well, Black would be in a position to say, "I warned you against that."

2. He'd demonstrate impatience with the control system itself. Daily he'd pester his controller for interim reports. Often he'd call the divisions directly to have them put together a separate batch of figures or to verify data that had him worried. As a result, the assistant vice-presidents gradually began to bypass the control system.

3. He'd anticipate suggestions from his functional staff. Instead of waiting for them to analyze monthly reports and to make recommendations, Black would come to his own conclusions first. Frequently he'd send his plans directly to the divisions before checking with the corporate staff specialists.

4. He'd jump into crisis problems before being invited. Black had an extremely keen mind. His business judgment was a proven commodity. When he sensed a crisis or the system turned up an exception, more often than not he would initiate action before his division managers could follow their own decisions.

Black typifies the competent executive who "buys" the management by exception idea *intellectually* but who is *emotionally* incapable of abiding by it. His reactions, of course, were exaggerated. But almost every executive can find real difficulty in submerging some of his own talent in order to strengthen the overall effectiveness of his organization. In a smaller company, such one-man direction can, and does, work. But as businesses become larger and more technically complex, the man who can anticipate all the problems and know all the answers is in the minority.

Avoid the "Organization-man" Attitude

System is of great advantage to management. Uniformity and consistency are virtues that are often synonymous with low costs. But too much conformity is fraught with management pitfalls. Once the administrative system overrides the common sense of the organization, the organization is inviting trouble. And when the organization itself becomes an inflexible stricture rather than a living organism, the trouble will come fast.

I recall one of the world's largest companies in which every procedure was spelled out in a huge set of policy manuals. Even such exceptions as what to do when a secretary spilled a bottle of ink on her dress were covered in specific detail. Among members of the staff the policy manual was a joke, of course, even though it was rigidly followed. Over the years this policy-orientation on the part of management worked a process of natural selection on the part of the organization. Those men who were natural conformists stayed on. Men with ideas moved out to other companies. Managers with a punitive attitude toward controls rose to the top. Managers who regarded controls as guides to action were discouraged. Gradually the management structure of the company atrophied. Competing companies surged ahead. It took a long period of poor profits and a decline in the market value of the stock before a major reorganization was made. It is noteworthy that today this company is a leader, and is pursuing management-development programs aimed at making its executives more creative.

The responsibility for avoiding too rigid a conformity lies with the executives at the top of the organization. Subordinates tend to initiate the actions and attitudes of their superiors. Consequently, a manager who practices management by exception must, by his own example, demonstrate a belief in each individual's superiority over the system. Of course he shouldn't encourage willful or irresponsible flaunting of self-interest. But he must be ready to judge each action on its merits in context with the demands of the total situation.

Actively Seek Out Exceptions

An exception is management's signal that action is needed. Such action can take one of two forms. It can be corrective, selected to bring a variance from projected performance back into line. Or it can be creative, chosen to exploit an opportunity that otherwise might have been overlooked.

Consider a military parallel. A commanding officer while inspecting his front lines may find a weak spot in the position of his troops. This exception to what is essential must be corrected immediately. The gap may be plugged by fresh troops or by moving adjoining platoons toward the center of the gap. This is defensive, or control, action. On the other hand, a probe of the front line may expose a similar gap in the enemy's position. Faced with this kind of situation the commander has an opportunity to take an entirely different kind of action. Offensive tactics of front-line warfare consist in finding such opportunities and exploiting them.

In business, the exceptional opportunities too often go unnoticed. Executives, because of their realization of the cost-control potential inherent in stability, tend to be conservative. Their tactics, consequently, are more often defensive than offensive. And, as a result, many profit opportunities, even when brought to the attention of someone in a position to act, are not seized.

In marketing and research and development, especially, and even in finance and operations, dozens of creative opportunities arise for the manager who is on the lookout for them. For instance:

In Marketing. Your salesmen may report that dealers are becoming increasingly restive about the failure of your competition to offer attractive quantity discounts or to make "deals" based upon specific conditions. This might suggest to you the adoption of a more flexible pricing policy for your own products. Or sales analyses may show that an unusually high percentage of sales of a certain product are lost because your salesmen have no medium- or low-priced alternative product to offer. Perhaps this is an opportunity to broaden your product line in order to reduce overall selling costs per call.

In Research and Development. The basic patent for DDT was developed when researchers, looking for something entirely different, reported that whenever they performed a certain experiment, the laboratory was littered with dead flies. The history of invention is full of such examples. In fact, it's a basic research maxim to be on the alert for the unusual, the unexpected, and the accidental. Such exceptions have often proved to be the key to discovery.

In Finance and Operations. One treasurer in a metal-working company noted that the unit cost for making a certain kind of part was always considerably lower than those of other gears made in greater quantity in the same department. Investigation showed that whenever this gear was made, it could be "ganged up" with other parts for machining. In a sense, it got a free ride. A committee was formed of the treasurer and the sales and manufacturing managers. They found that similar opportunities to double up parts for production existed elsewhere in the plant. By deliberately planning schedules to facilitate such doubling up, the company was able to secure a great deal of profitable subcontract work to supplement normal runs of its own product. Not only was new and profitable business turned up, but also the plant was enabled to achieve greater machine utilization.

Exceptions, then, are not only danger signals. In selected instances, they also display a green light for opportunity.

Expect to Work Harder but to Enjoy It More

Management by exception is designed to make management more effective by conserving time and attention. Paradoxically, this should not be construed as meaning that management will work less diligently than before. Conversely, you can expect to work harder than ever. But there will be a big difference in the kind of work you'll be doing. And there should be a vast improvement in the enjoyment you'll get from it. Here's why:

1. *The tasks you'll be working at will be more important.* You can't remain idle while you're waiting for exceptions to crop up, not if you're smart. You'll be seeking out jobs to do that need doing —such things as making market studies, ironing out long-term bottlenecks in production, designing a new system for order handling, or setting up a plan for the development of your subordinates.

2. *The decisions you'll be making will be more difficult.* Many solutions to performance variables will be preplanned. But those that don't fit the preconceived pattern will be real sticklers. These will be the problems for which the books don't have an answer.

These are the ones that will require searching analysis on your part, intensified exploration, and courage to move off in a direction different from what was originally planned.

3. *The assignments you'll get will be more stimulating.* Management by exception permits you to abandon much of the drudgery of administration. It provides infinite opportunities to be creative. You'll be putting yourself in new and varied situations. You'll be dealing with different and more talented people. The problems you face will be more complex and will have more variety and depth, and what's more important, they'll be more interesting.

4. *The challenges you face will accelerate your development.* As any tennis player will tell you, you don't improve your game by playing against people less skilled than yourself. And similarly, you don't get to be a better manager by handling the same old problems over and over again. Management by exception will provide you with new, different, and more challenging problems that will bring out the best in you. Solving them and continually moving on to new ones will increase your earning capacity and improve your real status in the organization.

References

1. Ernest Dale, *The Great Organizers*, McGraw-Hill Book Company, New York, 1960, pp. 76, 89.
2. *The New Yorker*, Nov. 10, 1962, pp. 92–94.
3. Henry Ford II, "Choosing a Career in Business," *The Saturday Evening Post*, Oct. 20, 1962, p. 36.

PART 2

THE SYSTEM
of Management by Exception

How to Measure
How to Project
How to Select
How to Observe
How to Compare
How to Take Action

Chapter 3

THE MEASUREMENT PHASE

In Which You Collect and Assess the Facts
of Your Total Operational Situation

In 1889, Lord Kelvin said, "When you can measure what you are speaking about, and express it in numbers, you know something about it. But when you cannot measure it, cannot express it in numbers, your knowledge is a meagre and unsatisfactory kind." More recently, Dr. H. B. Maynard, the twentieth-century management scientist who is the father of predetermined time standards, reiterated, "Before you can control, you must be able to measure what you want done." In fact, observes Maynard, "The first 30 or 40 years of scientific management were devoted to this basic effort: making measurements simple and accurate." [1]

An example of how some modern managers rely upon accurate measurements—even to an extreme—was furnished by *Business Week:*

> The night plane from New York touched down on the runway of the Tocumen Airport in Panama at 4 A.M. Among the first down the landing ramp was a craggy-faced man dressed in worn seersucker pants, a frayed sports shirt, and scuffed shoes.
> Unencumbered by baggage, he climbed into a waiting car and drove through the first glow of the tropic dawn to Las Minas Bay, 50

35

mi. away on Panama's Atlantic Coast. There, at a village store, he
rented a motorboat and bought a 20¢ roll of string and a 5¢ bolt. As
bemused bystanders watched, he carefully tied knots into the string at
6-ft intervals and attached the bolt to it as a weight. Then he set off
in the motorboat to check every nautical sounding marked on the chart
of the bay.

Such behavior is typical of Daniel K. Ludwig who, despite a net
personal worth well in excess of $500-million, remains one of the most
mysterious figures in American business today. Considered the world's
biggest individual shipowner, Ludwig was embarking on a mammoth
program of diversification and expansion.

When Ludwig flew to Panama, he was planning to build a $34-mil-
lion refinery on the shores of Las Minas Bay. His trip out on the bay
was to assure himself that reports given him were correct and that his
huge tankers would have no berthing problems there. The soundings
he took that day eventually resulted in the Refineria Panama, SA, one
of Panama's biggest industries.[2]

Admittedly, Mr. Ludwig's behavior is not typical of all businesses.
But even the coolest of them build their management by exception
decisions on the hard rock of accurately measured facts. *Time* magazine described Charles "Tex" Thornton, chairman of the phenomenal growth corporation Litton Industries, this way:

> Thornton . . . is a great believer in running things under tight sta-
> tistical control. . . . In a field where speed is a motto, he snaps out
> no instant decisions. He likes to take his time about making up his
> mind. He overcomes a problem by attacking it with dogged tenacity,
> painstakingly learning all the facts, then turning them over slowly in
> his mind many times until they fit together into a decision.[3]

What to Measure

Scientific management pioneers were primarily concerned with
the measurement of "work." The reason for so doing was that manpower was then (and still is in many industries) the largest variable ingredient of operating costs. The concept of the early measurement specialists was that work was a form of energy to be
conserved. And like the power derived from coal or other fuels,
human work could be—and must be—measured as accurately as
these were. Paradoxically, however, while Taylor, Gilbreth, Gantt,
and others recognized that human effort involved lifting, pushing,

pulling, and all kinds of related motion to overcome friction or gravity, the standard measure for human effort (for work) has evolved as a unit of time. Manpower is most often gaged by the time taken to perform a task, as measured in seconds and fractions of seconds, minutes, or "unit hours."

Management's historical preoccupation with time lapse was logical; management by exception derived from the production phase of business operations. And since time conservation forms the basis for repetitive manufacturing, many production factors relate to time. Time lapse, then, became the first common denominator for work measurement. This denominator, however, does not apply easily to other functions and phases of management.

Fortunately, the concept of work measurement broadened markedly after Taylor's days. A more common denominator for business activities was recognized. This is "condition." Management asks, What is the *condition* of our financial resources; what is the *condition* of our materials and products; what is the *condition* of our equipment; what is the *condition* of our organization? It asks these questions for good reason: management's task is to improve these conditions as time progresses. Consequently, when we speak of measuring management's achievements in altering conditions of business today, we talk of measuring management's "performance" —its performance in changing conditions (1) with respect to time and (2) in accordance with predetermined objectives. This broader measurement of performance applies to every type of business ingredient. Today, management uses this concept to measure the performance of its whole range of inputs, such as:

• *People*—hourly and clerical, skilled and unskilled, engineers and managers. Today, more than ever, we must know how well their efforts—physical and mental—contribute to the goals of the organization.

• *Money*—its productivity, flow, liquidity, and conservation. Fundamentally, management wants to know how effectively its financial resources are being used to produce goods, services, and profits.

• *Materials*—their condition, availability, convertability, and waste. The problem is to determine how economically materials are managed from their receipt, through processing and storage, to delivery.

• *Equipment*—machine utilization, capability, and productivity. The specific objects of measurement, of course, are numbered in the thousands. While this text will not go into detail here, Part 3 will provide additional listings of what to measure in several management functions.

How to Measure

To list every means of measuring each of the four fundamental business inputs would be exhausting. However, some generalizations can be made.

Performance of individuals, for instance, can be measured directly with stopwatches and indirectly by predetermined estimates of the time it takes to make certain basic physical movements; it can be measured by psychological tests and by attitude surveys; it can be measured by the tangible results achieved—and by dozens of other techniques.

Management of capital can be measured by counting the money in the till at the end of the day or by making up a balance sheet at the year's end; it can be measured by tens of ratios, too (such as the ratio of current assets to current liabilities); it can be measured by its return of profit on investment—and in many, many more ways.

Materials management measurements range from simple inspections of finished products to complex comparisons of inventory accumulation to sales or current assets; or by the length of time materials are held in process or in storage, etc.

Equipment performance is measured in terms of utilization or downtime, by its cost to operate and maintain, by simple counts of production, and by remote recording devices that detail a machine's every performance characteristic, such as temperature, vibration, and power consumption.

A "laundry list" that serves to illustrate the variety of devices, measures, and techniques available for measuring elements of business activity follows. It is by no means complete, even though it may seem exhaustive or even silly. Its value lies in demonstrating that management has dozens of readily available measuring tools and techniques at its beck and call. Management need be only imaginative and resourceful to be able to get the facts and assign values to them.

Devices, Measures, and Techniques for Measuring Business Inputs

For measuring money and finance:

accounting	income
accounts payable	interest paid
audits	inventory count
average collection period	investment in equipment, buildings, and land
balance sheet data	mortgages
bank statements	net worth
cash on hand	notes outstanding
cost accounting	overhead
cost of sales	profit
credit ratings	receivables due
current liabilities	sales volume
depreciation expense	SEC statements
dividends	stock issued
earnings	stock price
fixed assets	surplus
fixed costs	working capital
funded debt	

For measuring equipment and facilities:

acreage	power factor
assessment	pressure gages
audiometers	production counters
bay size	remote-production recorders
clearances	rents
clock recorders	return on investment
cubage	resale value
depreciation	scrap generation
failsafe indicators	signal lights
flowmeters	speedometers
fuel consumption	square footages
maintainability	taxes
maintenance cost	television tapes
malfunction detectors	throughput
mortgage payments	turn-in value
motion-picture cameras	vibration analyzers
obsolescence	visual inspection
original cost	wattmeters
oscilloscopes	

For measuring materials and products:

backorders on hand	micrometer
bills of lading	microphotometer
calipers	order points
cost of holding inventories	pressure meter
counting	purchase requisitions
customer complaints	pyrometer

delivery compliance
economic-order quantity
goods in process
handling cost
hardness tester
inventory count
inventory leakage
invoices
lightmeter
manufacturing cycle time

rework quantity
rule
scale
statistical quality control
transducers
turnover of inventory
visual inspection
waste generation
X ray

For measuring men and management:

absences
accident frequency
accident severity
aptitude tests
attitude surveys
breakeven charts
budget adherence
credit rating
customer complaints
deadline conformance
delivery performance
dividend record
Gantt charts
idle time
incentive earnings
insurance-rates variable
job evaluation
lateness
listening
machine utilization
manufacturing expense
memo-motion studies
methods studies
motion studies
new products developed

nomographs
number of grievances
number of patents acquired
performance appraisals
personality tests
predetermined time standards
profit generation
psychological tests
quit rate
ratio-delay analysis
results
return on investment
sales calls
sales expense
skill tests
standard times
stock price
stopwatches
strike frequency
time clocks
time studies
utility conservation
visual observation
work sampling

Kinds of Measurements

Generally speaking, measurements for industrial management purposes fall into three categories: basic data, ratios, and trends.

1. Basic measurements may be simply an element, a fragment of data, a point in space. Examples include the determination that a ⅜-inch bolt goes through a 0.126-inch gage and does not go through a 0.125-inch gage. Or that 75 per cent of our research assistants have M.S. degrees. Or that it takes a workman 0.045 minutes to

solder a No. 12 wire to a terminal. Or that a sales call in Los Angeles costs $12.50. Generally, basic measurements show what has happened or what is happening at a certain point in time.

2. Ratios are comparisons of one or more elements of basic data with another one or more elements of basic data. For instance, a ratio of direct labor to indirect labor might be 2:1 or 200 per cent. Or a ratio of net profits to net working capital is 10.6 per cent. Or a ratio of actual sales to bids issued is 25 per cent. (Or it could be expressed as a quotation mortality rate of 75 per cent.)

Measurement by ratio can also be more complex, such as comparing ratios with other ratios (for example, comparing the ratio of rejects to total output with the ratio of inspectors to assembly workers in order to seek a relationship between spoilage and quality control effort). Various other indices, too, can be constructed empirically or statistically by combining ratios.

3. Trends measure the movement of basic data or ratios from one point in time to another. For instance, gross sales might be $2,000,000 in 1962 and $2,200,000 in 1963—a growth rate of 10 per cent. Or indirect labor ten years ago was 30 per cent of the manufacturing dollar; today it is 40 per cent—an increase of one-third in ten years. Or the trend of the ratio of sales to inventory (turnover rate) might move from 4.7 in August to 5.2 in December. Trends are always spoken of with reference to a time lapse. For a graphical representation of the three kinds of measurement see Fig. 3-1.

Fig. 3-1. Examples of Kinds of Measurements (in This Case, Annual Labor Input into a Product)

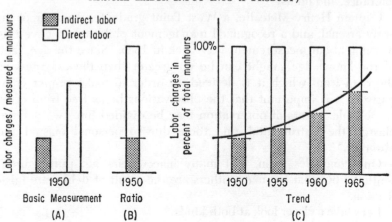

Accuracy of Measurements

Measurement is a good thing. Agreed, it is essential to the process of management by exception. But most measurements available to and employed by management should be treated with caution. Some measurements that were accurate at the time they were made become obsolete—because of the introduction of new production methods, for instance. Other measurements, blithely taken at face value by management, are simply unreliable to begin with. Sometimes this inaccuracy may be due to statistical ignorance during sampling. More often, however, it is the result either of unintentional errors that creep into the observing process or of deliberate falsification during observing, recording, or reporting. Still other measurements are accurate enough in themselves—that is, they do measure *something;* their unreliability emerges because of relationships to other factors which management assigned to them although these relationships either no longer exist or never existed.

Noted cost-control expert Phil Carroll calls our attention to an observation made by John Perry in his book *The Story of Standards* Perry points out that "In our own century in Brooklyn, New York, there was a time when the city surveyors recognized as legal four different 'feet'; the United States foot, the Bushwick foot, the Williamsburg foot, and the foot of the 26th Ward." [4]

Carroll goes on to say that "there is no such thing as absolute accuracy once you leave 2 × 2 arithmetic. Everything else has error, tolerance, and limits."

Captain Henry Metcalfe, a West Point graduate, manager of an army arsenal, and a recognized management philosopher, gave this warning about measurement way back in 1885. "Since the accuracy of the knowledge sought can be no greater than the exactness of the data from which it is derived, in order to make proper comparisons it is important that the observations be as free from error as possible. Errors of observation may be divided into two general classes; the instrumental, and those due to personal bias of the observer." [5]

One concludes, then, that many inaccuracies are purely unintentional but that too many others are the result of deliberate falsification.

Let's take a closer look at both kinds:

Unintentional Errors. These are often due to:

• Simple mistakes in observation. A workman reads a counter and forgets to multiply the setting by a calibration factor.

• Laziness. An accountant closes his books early every day and thus transfers late afternoon business to the following morning.

• The "halo effect." An observer or reporter is impressed by only the high spots (or low points) in his data and throws out other readings as nonrepresentative.

• Nonrepresentative reporting. A sales manager, for instance, is furnished a cumulative record of sales calls that masks what would be shown by a detailed breakdown of calls by days or by individual salesmen.

• Loss during transcribing. Observations may be correct, but in the transfer and tabulation of data, errors creep in as figures pass from clerk to tab operator to clerk. For example, an accountant might accidentally add the March inventory figures twice into a year's total.

• Misunderstanding of the system. A production-control clerk reports as "late" only those deliveries one week overdue, when management is trying to identify *every* late shipment.

Accidental and unintentional errors in measurement can be reduced, if not eliminated, by more careful design of the observing, collecting, and reporting system itself. The measurement process needs cross-checks, just as accounting systems do. And the people employed in the system need adequate indoctrination and continual training. Time-study authorities have long recognized this latter need and have done much to improve the situation by conducting "leveling" sessions, for instance, to avoid halo effects.

Deliberate Falsification of Measurements. This takes place more often than industry likes to recognize. It takes place for a variety of reasons, such as:

• To improve individual earnings. Traditionally, workmen have tried to beat piece-rate systems by cheating on their production counts.

• To conceal poor performance. A workman, or a supervisor, may report higher output or less waste simply to avoid looking bad.

• To cover up for others. If the company president has insisted that salesmen increase their sales calls from five to six a day, the sales manager may report that the increase has taken place even though his salesmen may be reporting differently to him.

• To imply progress. A plant superintendent holds back production from one week to the next in order to show an upward trend in output.

• To divert attention. In one company, maintenance costs were unreasonably high on a certain pump. Investigation showed that there was nothing unusually wrong with the pump. What was happening was that maintenance men who finished a job too late in the afternoon to start on a new one were having their time charged to that pump so it wouldn't appear on the master mechanic's report as idle time.

• To make you feel good. "Yesmanship" applies even to data collection. A lot of figures are carefully selected annually for a simple reason—to confirm the boss's preconceived notions.

Curtailment of deliberate falsification is hard to achieve. It is deeply rooted in motivational causes. Men at all levels of the organization must be convinced that measurement is something that benefits them before they can be fully relied upon to avoid bias. And, of course, they must embrace the concept of what Peter Drucker and Douglas McGregor call "self-control"—as opposed to the belief that measurement is a punitive device which higher management uses to undercut them.

Measurements Out of Context. Measurement of business conditions may be undependable for still other reasons. Almost any single measure is influenced by, or inseparable from, other measures. Any engineer knows, for example, that a pressure reading is not truly significant unless a concurrent temperature or volume reading attends it. This is a matter of scientific fact as proved by the general gas law (Boyle's law and Charles's law) which states that (pressure) × (volume) = (temperature) × (a constant). Most students of economics feel that business indicators, too, are related by natural laws—if not by simple ones, then by inscrutably complex ones. Consequently, an executive must look not only at a fact, but also behind it and around it to determine its context. An obvious example of shortsightedness would be to accept without further inquiry the fact that a plant's production capacity is 1,500 units per day. What does this figure, by itself, mean? Not very much. To give it meaning we have to know how many employees are needed to support this capacity, whether equipment will run on one or two shifts—five days or seven days a week, etc. Similarly, a sales report for last year may show that a machinery company's sales in New

York City averaged $1,538 per sale. To an astute manager, this would be inconclusive unless he also knew who the salesmen were, the nature of the competition in that area, the amount of advertising support, the concentration of prospects, and a dozen other conditions.

The fact is that measurements may be accurate in an absolute sense and still be misleading. Before judging the worth of measurements for use in managing by exception, an executive should consider a number of other factors that might influence their present and continuing representability. These factors include the following considerations:

- Seasonal influences
- Equipment condition
- Extent of direct and supporting labor
- Operational methods in use
- Materials used
- Product specifications
- Nature of the organization and its staff
- Extent of competition
- General economic conditions
- Growth rate of the company
- State of employee morale
- Presence of a union or not
- Production rates
- Market conditions and growth rate
- Technological acceleration
- Product mix
- Company's financial position
- Company or plant size
- International harmony or discord, such as war, cold war, or peace.

The list could be expanded, of course. One example, however, that occurs among many companies might serve to demonstrate the point. The *cost* of maintenance of plant and facilities, for instance, is related to the extent of maintenance performed, to the condition of the equipment, and surely to the extent to which equipment is kept operative. During the Great Depression, many companies indulged in "deferred" maintenance. Plant and equipment were permitted to fall into disrepair. Maintenance costs during those years were understandably low. When World War II came along, management was surprised to find that the cost of maintenance rose sharply. The obvious fact is that prewar maintenance costs and wartime maintenance costs, while bearing the same label, measured different things. They were certainly not measuring maintenance *effectiveness*.

One other serious factor affects the validity of business measurements. It is the matter of proper definition. "Overhead," for instance, means one thing to accountants in Company A and another to those in Company B. Most executives are aware of this. What does not catch their attention is that frequently, in their own organization, definitions and interpretations of overhead differ significantly. Comparisons of management effectiveness made on this basis, consequently, are frequently misleading. Key measures should be carefully defined—and a number of examples furnished—in order to obtain consistence of comparisons in any one company or situation.

Cost of Measurement

The cost of measuring and of measurements is a limiting factor in the practice of management by exception. While ideally it would be desirable to have as many measurements to project from as possible, most organizations can afford only a relatively small number in each critical area of management. Too often, however, executives tend to be penny-wise and pound-foolish in making their selections. This is due to a mistaken impression about the cost of securing a certain measurment, a shortsightedness in appraising its potential worth, or—surprisingly enough—ignorance of its availability.

If one were to provide a gage for estimating the relative cost of obtaining various measurements, a table something like Table 3-1 could be developed.

In addition, it is fairly safe to generalize that the measurement of money, materials, and machinery is considerably easier and cheaper to obtain than that of men and management. The former three lend themselves to solutions by established scientific methods and available technology. The latter usually do not.

Another rule of thumb is that it is generally cheaper to accumulate measurements when they can be collected during the normal and essential administrative routine of the organization (as opposed

Table 3-1. *Relative Costs of Measurements*

Lower-cost measurements	Higher-cost measurements
TANGIBLE QUALITIES: products made, machine performance, material usage, cash on hand, etc.	INTANGIBLE QUALITIES: attitudes, morale, loyalty, potential
SIMPLE TASKS: assembly, clerical, unskilled, etc.	COMPLEX TASKS: scientific work, troubleshooting, management, etc.
ROUTINE SITUATIONS: mass production, volume sales, repetitive work, etc.	VARIABLE SITUATIONS: small lots, special projects, engineered jobs, diversified products, etc.
NEARBY LOCATIONS: centralized operations: concentrated areas, big plants, etc.	REMOTE LOCATIONS: field sales, branch plants, etc.

to separately and independent of normal routine). For instance, customer orders, engineering specifications, shop schedules, payroll sheets, invoices, etc., can all be used as media for measurement or the collection of measurements.

A further estimate of measurement costs according to various functions might be looked at this way:

Financial measurements from profit-and-loss and balance sheets are relatively simple and are readily available. Measurement of the value of investments, such as rates of return by the MAPI formula or the "investor's method," are relatively complex to make and require a great deal of fact gathering.

Material measurements of product quality, inventories, and waste are increasingly essential to business management, although they are far from inexpensive to obtain. Measurement of the costs of product movement and handling in the plant is technically difficult, and while promising high returns on the effort, is performed in less than 10 per cent of all manufacturing establishments.

Equipment performance data can be obtained with ease, but at relatively high cost, from all sorts of meters, downtime recorders, and equipment maintenance records. However, management's utilization of such techniques, even in the face of a national industrial repair bill of $10 billion per year indicates there is still much opportunity for savings in this area.

Measurement of men and management, while generally difficult and costly, varies according to what is under observation. Physical skills, and some mental ones like the ability to handle figures, can be measured accurately and at relatively low cost. Knowledge of an individual's aptitudes for some work, such as assembling, clerical jobs, and selling, comes a little harder. Executive potential and scientific creativity are probably the most difficult human qualities to measure, and it's costly to obtain even unreliable measures. Conversely, measurement of executive *performance* based upon results is relatively easy and straightforward and can be integrated with normal company accounting.

In an interview with *The Wall Street Journal* a Clark Equipment Company executive complained that when he walked through a drafting room in his plant, he had no way of knowing whether a designer gazing out the window was thinking creatively or merely daydreaming.[6] A technique developed by the Hughes Aircraft Corporation to measure the activities of engineering and scientific personnel, and rather unfortunately called "PACE"—Performance and Cost Evaluation was challenged the same year by a labor union on twenty-one different counts—mainly to do with the inability of the company to verify the accuracy of its measurements. These two examples seem to illustrate the dilemma management faces when trying to gage human activity accurately.

Sources of Measurement

Measurements may be classified as (1) those available from external sources and (2) those generated within your own organization in the course of operations (internal sources). These two broad categories can also be subdivided according to whether they represent (a) past history or (b) current performance. A further breakdown of external measurements might be to consider (c) those generally in the public domain and (d) those available only from private sources. Internal measurements can also be classified according to (e) whether they are collected in the normal course of assembling data for accounting purposes or (f) whether they represent data specifically collected to aid in the planning, operation, and control of the business by the practice of management by exception.

External Sources of Business Measurement. These can be found in every field and range in scope from very broad-gage economic indexes (like the Dow-Jones stock price averages published in many daily newspapers) to specialized minutiae (such as in a textbook that pinpoints the time for a foundryman to strike a mold).

A representative but not all-inclusive list (in rough order of general availability and frequency) is furnished below:

1. Publications such as:

• Daily newspapers—for stock prices, government indexes, and fragments of local business information, such as quarterly earnings, the opening of sales territories, and contracts let.

• Daily business papers—*The Wall Street Journal, Oilgram Price Service, The Journal of Commerce,* etc.—for more detailed information and measurements, including price movements.

• Weekly business and trade papers—including broad-coverage ones like *Business Week* and narrower ones such as *Iron Age, Chemical Week, Baker's Weekly,* etc.—for interpretation and evaluation of business indicators. In this category are also newsletters, such as *Kiplingers Washington Letter, Nucleonics Week, Standard & Poors,* etc.

• Monthly trade papers—like *Factory,* with its monthly manufacturing production figures; its index of maintenance costs; surveys of manufacturing trends in costs, methods, manpower, etc.; plus case histories reporting measurements in specific plants. Another example is *Dun's Review and Modern Industry,* which publishes indexes of failure rates and other measurement ratios for various industries.

• Journals of professional, technical, and scientific societies—such as those of the National Association of Accountants and the American Society for Production and Inventory Control. There are hundreds of sound organizations publishing reliable, serious data, although much of their information is highly specialized or relatively narrow in application potential.

• Publications of the United States government—especially those of the Department of Commerce, the National Bureau of Standards, and the Department of Labor. It's unfortunate that so many reliable data, although often impractically broad in scope, are used so infrequently by businessmen.

• Research and survey reports of various universities—such as those from the Massachusetts Institute of Technology and Iowa State University.

• Special reports—such as the F. W. Dodge reports of construction activities, Dun & Bradstreet reports, etc.

• Industrial and business books—in almost every field of endeavor, there are hundreds of texts that provide a reliable source

1. Cost, not only the first cost of obtaining data, but also the cost of obtaining it on a repetitive basis. For instance, it's not unusual for a company to undertake a survey in a good profit year and discontinue it the following year because of insufficient funds. The test should be: Do we want these data badly enough to make gathering them a permanent cost of doing business?

2. Potential value to management in controlling operations and in producing profits. Management must determine if this factor is significant as an indicator of performance. As Drucker says, "The real difficulty lies indeed not in determining what objectives we need, but in deciding how to set them. There is only one fruitful way to make this decision: by determining what shall be measured in each area and what the yardstick of measurement should be. For the measurement used determines what one pays attention to. . . . It makes things visible and tangible. The things included in the measurement become relevant; the things omitted are out of sight and mind."

3. Time-lapse period between observations. An executive should answer questions like these: Is this measure something that must be logged with great frequency (such as hourly rate of sales in a department store) in order to be representative? Is it a measure that has such a long frequency interval (like an annual appraisal of managers) that it might permit a situation to get out of control between check points?

4. Availability of the measure, or access to the element to be measured. A fairly accurate indicator readily at hand, such as the payroll record of the number of employees charging their time against a certain project, is often nearly as useful as a highly accurate one, such as a time study of the project, that can't be gotten without special effort. And while it might be invaluable to know the manufacturing cost of a competitor's product, it is nearly impossible to come by such information.

5. Statistical soundness of measurements. This is something many managers are surprisingly naïve about. They seem to be looking for single-case proofs to justify "one-fact" management. In almost any business conversation, you can hear conclusions drawn from and ostensibly substantiated by citation of data that are not statistically reliable, reproducible, or valid. Hundreds of texts have been written about this branch of mathematics, and businessmen should

make certain that those who are charged with measurement read some of them. Many happenings in business are the result of literally dozens of influences that come together to produce an event. Mathematical formulas have not yet been devised that can describe these events reliably. The danger to management lies in simplifying the data (making assumptions about those things you might know nothing about, such as climate, attitude, impulse, etc.) in order to make the data fit an existing formula. In any event, management should insist that when numerical results are referred to them for examination, some indication of their limits of accuracy also be supplied.

Need for Vigilance

In any system set up for obtaining measurements, the existence of a measurement maintenance program is absolutely necessary. For instance, in the manufacture of bearings to a high degree of specified accuracy, Timken Roller Bearing Company operates a tool-control laboratory that is a wonderland of measurement accuracy. Accuracy of all tools, which are themselves measuring devices in a way, is verified against the most rigid absolute measures, each of which in turn is verified against those of the National Bureau of Standards. One measuring standard, for instance, can be deflected an inch or more simply by touching one's hand to the base plate on which it rests. Management yardsticks are just as sensitive to the myriad of fluctuating business influences.

Industrial engineers long ago learned that the drift of variables into an existing time standard is inexorable. A task that was measured last year at 0.12 minute may be reduced by a resourceful operator (or by a change in tooling, jigs, materials, finishes, tolerances, etc.) to half of that this year. Consequently, maintenance of standards to prevent runaway rates is a major function of a well-organized industrial engineering organization. The same vigilance must also be applied to every measure in management's tool kit.

References

1. H. B. Maynard, "Past, Present, and Future of Work Measurement," *Factory,* August, 1959.
2. *Business Week*, Nov. 23, 1963, p. 88.

3. *Time*, Oct. 4, 1963, p. 105.
4. John Perry, *The Story of Standards*, Funk & Wagnalls Company, New York, 1955.
5. Henry Metcalfe, *The Cost of Manufactures and Administration of Workshops*, John Wiley & Sons Inc., New York, 1885, p. 17.
6. *The Wall Street Journal*, Jan. 8, 1963.
7. *The Public Pulse*, no. 16, Elmo Roper Associates, New York, December, 1962.

Chapter 4

THE PROJECTION PHASE

In Which You Carry Forward Past and Present Data to Forecast Future Conditions and to Set Goals, Prepare Plans, and Revise Organizational Structures

It has become routine to advise businessmen to plan ahead. But trite or not, those companies which follow this advice prosper while those which ignore it are left behind. Take the examples of several companies that have succeeded. Here's how they incorporate forward planning in their practice of management by exception:

To Provide for Growth. A & P, with sales in the $5 billion range, still deliberately holds its profit margin at about 1 per cent. Its objective, obviously, is to attain growth by stimulating sales. American Machine and Foundry Company, on the other hand, takes the view that growth in a field where technology is advancing rapidly is better assured by systematic investment in research and development. In 1960, for example, AMF set up its first central research staff—and then budgeted 4 per cent, of total sales for R & D.[1] Still another approach is illustrated by E. I. du Pont de Nemours, Inc. Chairman Crawford W. Greenewalt projects the company's growth trail not through increasing sales but by increasing the percentage of dollar return on total investment. To do so, du Pont continually

55

drops older, low-profit margins from its line and adds newly developed, high-profit items.[2]

To Stimulate Profits. Genesco, Inc., directs each of its operating companies to forecast monthly its expectations of income for the balance of the year and for the next month, along with comparisons of results for the preceding month and the projections made at that time. Furthermore, the corporation sets as a target for each company a net earning on capital (after taxes) of 12 per cent. Executives' incentive earnings are based on this target. Only exceptional managers whose divisions earn more than 12 per cent become members of Genesco's "Par Busters Club." [3]

To Improve Communications. General Electric Company has attained its leadership in the field of employee and public relations largely through look-ahead planning of communications objectives. For instance, the company first predicts areas where misunderstanding about corporate intentions are most likely to occur. Then GE provides a list of opportunities and activities open to its various plants for overcoming or forestalling such misunderstandings. For instance, a major hysteria theme is misunderstanding about automation. Accordingly GE makes a point of (1) contrasting old and new production methods and their effect on physical effort, cleanliness, and safety; (2) contrasting old and new products according to cost, quality, and convenience for the customer; and (3) informing employees ahead of time about possible job changes resulting from process or product improvements.[4]

To Meet Competition. Executives of the ABC Television Network speak of "Goldenson's miracle." When Leonard H. Goldenson, ABC president, took over he found a TV network with affiliates covering only one-third of American television homes. Worse still, ABC could claim only 13 per cent of the prime-time viewers and collected less than 10 per cent of the sponsor money spent each year. Looking into the future, Goldenson had to choose one of two ways to put ABC into stiff competition with the two major networks. He could try to match program quality with artistic efforts, or he could plan for a broader base with mass appeal. He chose the latter approach. And he not only expanded ABC to competitive stature, but to quote *TV Guide,* "set into motion what might be called TV's Laws of Elementary Economics: (1) Filmed programs in prime time tend to drive out live programs, (2) Mass appeal tends to drive out minority appeal, and (3) The more common tastes tend to drive out the more selected tastes." In a "root hog or die" struggle, Goldenson's plan filled a viewers' void (an exception verified by market research). Whether morally defensive or not, it secured for ABC 90 per cent of the prime-time viewers and about 25 per cent of the advertising dollars in 1962.[5]

To Rebuild a Sick Company. The venerable Railway Express Company operated for nearly a century as a virtually nonprofit organization. Its owners, sixty-seven railroads, underwrote annual deficits as large as $38 million. On the brink of liquidation in 1958, Railway Express was rescued by William B. Johnson, a young president who believed in the essentials of management by exception. His beginning move was to find out for the first time what the company's actual costs were. By examining historical records he evolved an out-of-pocket figure that could be projected as a cost goal for company income to exceed. REA Express (the company's new name) then contracted to buy transportation from railroads at that figure. By 1962, the company was able to release an income statement that not only made sense, but also showed a modest profit of $4 million on a gross revenue of $384 million. Along the way Johnson also had to reorganize the management staff to fit the new concept and the new goals. For the first time, middle and lower management got incentives, authority, responsibility, and a yardstick to judge how well they were discharging the latter.[6]

Individual and corporate planning *does* separate the sheep from the goats. Just as companies like Inland Steel, Macy's, and Sears Roebuck have become leaders because their managements have been astute in defining corporate purpose and in putting their resources to the chosen end, so companies like Montgomery Ward and Packard Motor Car have become sad examples of companies that lost sight of their purpose somewhere along the way.

Objectives of Management Planning

In making projections and forecasts and converting them to goals, managers perform one of their most important functions. Perrin Stryker, when he was with *Fortune* magazine, found in a survey of executive practices that executives in great numbers confirmed this opinion. Of 115 duties (identified by 100 executives) classified by Stryker in ten categories, that of "setting policies and objectives" ranked second only to "achievement of those objectives" and was far ahead of "leading," which ranked seventh, and "decision making," which ranked ninth.[7]

Planning targets, themselves, cover a wide spectrum. At the board level, objectives are likely to be abstract and involve projections of from one to five years or longer. At the operational level, plans are procedural and detailed, although these plans may extend up to five years also. Below that level, however, plans become predominantly short in duration and increasingly specific.

Goals at the Board Level. Initially, the president, his staff, and the board of directors may be called upon to set objectives that vary according to the state of development of the business. For instance, the first objectives might be any of these:

• To set up a new company to produce an old or new product or service.

• To expand an existing business by (1) securing a larger share of the existing market, (2) increasing the market, (3) adding products, (4) acquiring new companies, (5) improving quality or decreasing cost of present products or services, or (6) extending operations to new areas or to other countries.

• To strengthen a slumping company by (1) rebuilding its organization, (2) defining new goals, (3) improving customer relations, or (4) creating better management-labor relations.

Stated in the broadest possible terms by Carlos Efferson, organizational specialist for Kaiser Aluminum and Chemical Corp., planning at the top level of the organization is usually directed at three basic objectives:

1. Efficiency—improving the ratio of output to input
2. Survival—of the organization in its movement toward its objectives
3. Morale—of members of the organization

Naturally, broad-brush concepts such as these are reflected in generalized, rather than overly specific, statements of objectives. It is probably desirable to keep them this way in order that operational management may have opportunity and range of choice in drawing up its plans to reach these objectives. One should not infer that corporate-level objectives should be vague. They should be stated clearly and concisely, of course. The statement of the Atlantic Refining Company sets an excellent example to follow:

> The basic objective of the Atlantic Refining Company is to engage, as an integrated company, in the various phases of the petroleum

business, striving for such balance between phases as may achieve a reasonable profit for the company. In carrying out its basic objective, the company will make the most effective use of capital, people, and other resources, and will:

1. Explore for and develop sources of crude oil, natural gas or other petroleum product raw materials (in those areas where these materials can be made economically available) and produce in maximum quantities consistent with economy and sound conservation.

2. Manufacture petroleum products and by-products at the lowest cost consistent with quality that will assure public acceptance.

3. Market, with the maximum economy of distribution, petroleum products and by-products and related merchandise; [and] provide associated services.

4. Operate, or secure the use of, all facilities necessary to meet company transportation requirements; utilize to the best advantage any excess of such facilities.[8]

Goals at the Operational Level. While there is a great deal of imposing literature advocating the practice of long-range planning at the operational level, there is still considerable doubt about its immediate value. Probably its best purpose is to keep the sights of divisional managers on the uncertainties of tomorrow so that they become accustomed to looking for exceptions and are prepared to meet them. As a matter of fact, however, much of what happens in business that operational management must deal with occurs on a day-to-day basis. If nothing else, activities at the operational level are distractingly variable and dynamic. Long-range plans at that level may serve to keep management from becoming too expedient in its decisions, but that's about all they serve. On the other hand, short-term goals need to be specific. There is little excuse for them not to be so. The forecasts upon which they are based can be more reliable. After all, most of the measurements involved are internal rather than external, and more of the variable factors are within the control of the organization. Figure 4-1 shows an example of well-planned objectives very specific in content, for management at a rather high operational level.

Goals at the First Level of Management. The difference between goals here and those at higher levels is in the degree of specificity. At the foreman level, especially, it is essential that goals be within reach and embrace only those targets over which the foreman has adequate control of ways and means for attaining them. An example of a pinpointed monthly target for supervisors is shown in Fig. 4-2.

Fig. 4-1. Example of Operating Goals

Next year's goals for an operating division:

1. Strengthening of management staff by realignment of the organization to improve (a) communications, (b) controls, and (c) utilization of scarce skills
2. Raising of divisional profits to 17 per cent before taxes
3. Extending markets to include the "Inner Seven" countries
4. Construction of new office building on leased land north of building No. 6; total cost not to exceed $675,000
5. Follow-through on a well-planned advertising and sales promotion program for product lines A and F
6. Negotiation of a labor contract with Local 137; settlements not to force price increases in our products
7. Completion of standard cost system to cover all products in our line
8. Consolidation of territorial sales personnel west of the Rockies into one work unit
9. Improvement of manufacturing methods and costs in small-lot area of our business, where 75 per cent of orders now occur
10. Development of all personnel through existing training program; plant supervisors to attend forty hours of training in product quality control

---

Responsibility for Setting Goals

No one in the entire range of management organization should be excused from entering into the planning activity. It should be made clear to everyone, from the president's level to the third-shift foreman of the labor gang, that projecting, forecasting, and goal setting are functions that he must be prepared to perform in the line of service. Variations in degree and in time spent on these activities, of course, will be marked. But all plans—repeat, all plans —should be built on the principle of integrating the views of every member of the management organization. There is also a very good case for carrying this philosophy and practice all the way down the line to include each employee. Douglas McGregor and others believe that in many circumstances failure of organizations to reach their logical goals can be traced directly to employee and group resistance arising out of the failure to secure their participation in goal setting.

In emulating the military, many companies have gone overboard in designating planning staffs and have lost the greater part of the responsibility for goal setting to the specialists. There are advantages and disadvantages to this practice. In large, complex organizations, the mere logistics of data collection, analysis, and detailing can be overwhelming. Someone other than key executives should perform this work, or the bulk of it. On the other hand, the ability to forecast reliably and to choose goals that are both attainable and desirable is one that the important executives must have and exercise. To completely delegate this activity would be to dissipate the organization's greatest strength.

In any event, those in whose hands lie the destinies of the organization (as defined in its goals) ought to be carefully chosen. The higher up in the organization the goals are to be set, the more care should be used in the choice of the planners as well as the executives. Carter L. Burgess, president of American Machine and Foundry Company, makes a forceful statement on this subject:

> In business, unfortunately, there seems to be no apt phrase to describe the successful planner, as there is, for example, to describe the successful gardener. The good gardener is the man who has a "green thumb."
>
> Others can follow his instructions to the letter, yet fail to get the same results. In cooking, a young housewife can follow precisely the recipe of her mother, yet her dish somehow lacks the same savor. One of our most successful businessmen once said that the art of making

FIG. 4-2. EXAMPLE OF OBJECTIVES FOR FIRST-LINE SUPERVISOR

Area of measurement	Last year's record	Next year's goals
1. Ratio of jobs completed on schedule to total jobs worked	85% average, 92% highest, 65% lowest in June	90% average, minimum acceptable 75%
2. Percentage of job costs held within 3% of standard costs	91% average, 95% highest, 75% lowest in June	90% average, bring up low figure to 87% or better.
3. Rejects and rework....	Less than 1% rejects. Rework averages 7%	Keep rejects to less than 1%, but cut rework to 3%.
4. Labor stability........	Two quits, one transfer	No quits of employees with over three years service
5. Absences, latenesses....	5% absences, 7% latenesses	5% absences, 2% latenesses
6. Overtime.............	Only on jobs OK'd by sales department	Only on jobs OK'd by sales department
7. Accidents.............	No lost-time accidents. 37 calls to dispensary for minor ailments	No lost-time accidents. Reduce number of dispensary visits

money was an isolated skill that bore no traceable relation to any other attribute, learning, or ability. Perhaps so. About all that can be said about this indefinable sixth sense, when it is applied to planning, is that it seems to consist of an instinct that senses future requirements and combines with a sense of timing to make some men and companies succeed immeasurably above most others. All of which means that the human element is important and that sound plans must be based upon the capacities and special abilities of a company's people.

Planning has intuitive as well as analytical aspects, and both are related to experience.

Planning involves decisions and action, and both are related importantly to timing.

Successful planning requires, above all, people—the right kind of people.[9]

Despite all the difficulties, there are some rules of thumb that can guide a manager at any level in handling his planning obligations. For example:

1. Delegate to the next lower level of management all planning responsibilities that can better be handled at that level than at your own.

2. Delegate to your own staff those functions of planning that are most routine, such as making projections and comparing the adequacy of existing plans with newly set goals.

3. Integrate into your own plans the plans and ideas from all levels subordinate to yours.

4. Check with the plans of your associates to determine the need for coordination of their plans with your own.

5. View all goals submitted to you by your staff or by your subordinates as recommendations rather than as decisions.

6. Reserve for yourself alone the finalizing of goals for your organization.

Other Considerations

The ingredients of planning form a curious mixture. Planning involves, in unequal amounts, facts and fables, hopes and hunches, statistical reasoning and a sixth sense. It is full of paradoxes.

Later in this chapter we shall attempt to dissect planning into its many components, and each will be discussed separately. But first, let's take a closer view of some factors which in themselves seem only incidental but which must be taken into account as parameters in blocking out the planning process.

Time Period of Forecast. At first blush, most executives would declare that the most important kind of planning is that done for long range. These long-range objectives give an organization a fix, an azimuth, a North Star to guide it. Unfortunately, forecasts upon which long-range objectives should be built are woefully undependable. Happily, in practice, the most frequent kind of planning is of the what-shall-we-do-tomorrow species. Forecasting for such short-range planning is relatively simple and reliable. What is essential in short-range planning is that expediency should not corrupt or obstruct monthly, annual, or five-year goals.

The fact is that both short- and long-range planning involve essentially the same management functions. These functions differ only to the degree to which time permits their employment.

Time Interval between Forecasts. As indicated in the previous paragraph, there is a distinction between the time period and the time interval. Consideration of the latter is needed because there is a tendency on the part of many managers to believe that once a budget has been set, the organization must become like a locomotive charging down a pair of steel rails. Such a concept is dangerous. Business affairs are much too fluid to permit this single-mindedness. The setting and attaining of goals should be "progressive."

The exception principle is designed to alert management to the need for reexamination of its goals. The more often this opportunity is provided, the better. Each time an exception is reported, management must answer this question: *Should I bring this factor back into line with my preset objectives, or is this an indication that my objectives need modifying?*

Many organizations establish a system of progressive planning which periodically (monthly, quarterly, or annually) reviews attainment of objectives (1) as compared with original objectives and (2) with a view to making a new forecast in light of the additional experience. A sales quota, for instance, may have been set at $3 million for the year. If by May, however, only $1 million has been booked, it is time to restudy the sales objectives. Perhaps the objectives need revising. Or perhaps there's need for changes in pricing, sales effort, advertising support, and the like.

The Du Pont Company, for instance, makes four forecasts a year

—of sales, cost of sales, earnings, and investment. The first forecast is for the period January through December. The second forecast comes out in April for the period April through March of the following year. At the same time, the calendar-year forecast is corrected by inserting the first three months' actual. The third and fourth forecasts repeat this process in July and October.

Rigidity of Goals. The degree of flexibility maintained in organizational goals will depend upon a balance between personal inclinations and the nature of the business. A utility, for instance, because of its long-term financing, will have more rigid objectives than a department store, which must respond more sensitively and quickly to the consumer market. A manufacturing company, on the other hand, must achieve some sort of stability in order to secure operating efficiencies from its investment in plant and equipment; however, it must be supple enough to make adjustments in objectives as economic factors fluctuate.

In most organizations, despite what often appears to be rigid operational commitments, the determining factor in flexibility is the attitude of each executive. Some men like to remain personally uncommitted, constantly alert for challenge and opportunity, with their resources poised to respond. Others like to make thorough, considered planning decisions and then hold to the course (somewhat like Admiral Perry when he said, "Damn the torpedoes!") come what may. There is much to be said for both approaches. The simultaneous presence of extreme adherents to both concepts in a single organization, however, is likely to cause trouble. Harmony in these matters is highly desirable.

Safety Factors. In making predictions and projections, statistical mathematics does much to minimize risks due to false assumptions about data reliability. Nevertheless, projected goals can be made securer by applying safety factors, or by planning for "pull-back" points. Safety factors, of course, are applied most often in inventory control. If, as a matter of calculated policy, a company wants to be able to fill 75 per cent of its orders from stock, it can predict exactly what the risk of a stock-out will be.

In broader areas of projection, safety factors are less applicable. But almost all planning should incorporate some relatively safe retirement position which the company can fall back to if it fails to meet its goals. For instance, the airlines after World War II went all out to capture passenger service from rail and waterways. However, in their planning, few companies, if any, anticipated the tremendous productivity jet airplanes would provide. The result was a general overcapacity which troubled the industry by 1962. William A. Patterson, president of United Airlines, commenting on the problem said:

> Enthusiasm grew beyond all relation to reality . . . the overenthusiasms were contagious. Air line managements caught expansion fever and it spread to the government regulatory agency that was supposed to apply checks and balances. . . . Looking back, it seems clear that the regulatory agency was making forecasts and awarding routes in terms of piston engine operations. Apparently there was no consideration of the tremendous productivity of jet aircraft. The increased speed and capacity of the DC-8, for example, made its potential output in passenger miles equivalent to three and a half DC-7's.

Another mistake, said Patterson, was the failure to anticipate the extent to which coach travel would be upgraded in terms of speed and comfort. "Most of the growth in coach use," he said, "came from former first-class travelers, not from persons who never flew before." [10] Apparently, in business as elsewhere, the best-laid plans go awry.

Management must be prepared for failure or half-success as well as for complete success. To quote the tongue-in-cheek wisdom of "Murphy's law": "If there is any chance of something going wrong, you can be sure it will." Another pertinent adage is: "Expect the best, but prepare for the worst."

The Projection Process

When it comes to defining just what a projection is, there are lots of hairsplitters among us. Not only that, but there is also keen disagreement about how accurately projections can be made. Statesman Edmund Burke said, "You can never plan the future by the past." Politician Patrick Henry said, "I know of no way of judging the future but by the past." Management authority Peter Drucker says, "We have adequate concepts only for measuring market standings. For something as obvious as profitability we have only a rubber, yardstick, and we have no real tools at all to determine how much profitability is necessary. In respect to innovation and, even more, to productivity, we hardly know more than what ought to be done. And in other areas—including physical and financial resources—we

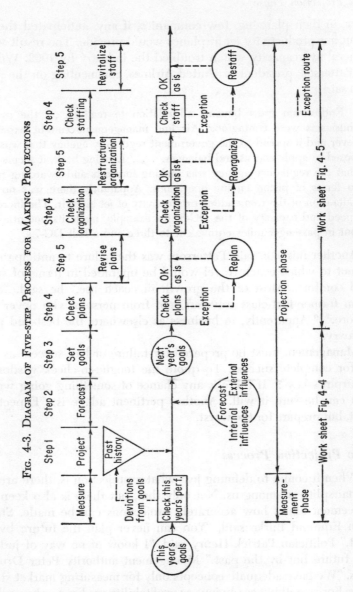

FIG. 4-3. DIAGRAM OF FIVE-STEP PROCESS FOR MAKING PROJECTIONS

are reduced to statements of intentions, rather than goals and measurements for their attainment."

This author does not share Drucker's dim view. Neither does he intend to debate with Edmund Burke or Patrick Henry. This we know: businessmen *must* look into the future. They must plan for it in the best way they can. If the tools are vague, elastic, and inaccurate, that is the way it is. Management in a dynamic economy can't afford to intellectualize like the philosophers or procrastinate like the academicians. Managers must make do with what's available.

Rather than delve too deeply into the semantics of definition, perhaps it would be more useful to look at the plan-ahead process as a series of steps:

First, we can take our measurements of past events and then in relation to their time occurrence project (extrapolate) them into the future.

Second, we must make a guess at what hasn't happened before, or recently, and try to forecast the chances of its happening in the future. For our purposes in this chapter and in selected places in this book we shall draw a distinction between a projection and a forecast.

Third, we've got to figure out in what way these new happenings will change the projections we made in the first place. These projections, modified by the forecasts, we can call "goals."

Fourth, at this point we shift attention to our existing plans (which were set up sometime in the past to attain our previous goals) to determine whether they're now adequate. Now we're aggressively looking for exceptions. What's in line, we'll let alone. What pops up as a weakness or a strength means we'll alter our plans.

Fifth, we're finally ready to do three things:

1. Alter existing policies and procedures to fit the projected goals.

2. Improve existing organization structure to serve the new goals and the new plans.

3. Check the adequacy of existing staff (and its assignments) for attaining the new goals and to carry on the new procedures within the new organizational structure. Understaffed or weakly staffed positions will need to be taken care of; overstaffed positions and overqualified incumbents will need reassignment.

In order to better visualize these steps, the reader may now want to check the projection process flow diagram (Fig. 4-3) and planning

Fig. 4-4. Work Sheet for Establishing Performance Objectives

Account	Last year's performance	This year's goals	This year's performance	Exception report	Projected goals for next year	Forecast of new influences		Final goals for next year
						Internal factors	External factors	
Sales volume.........	$1,000,000	$1,150,000	$1,100,000	Sales increased as forecast, but prices slipped badly.	$1,200,000	Will eliminate sales promotion cost of $25,000 next year.	Market continues to grow at steady rate.	$1,200,000
Net profit..........	$120,000	$138,000	$110,000	Company cut prices to secure volume.	$96,000	Manufacturing economies will increase (see machine utilization).	Price position improving as inventories fall.	$144,000
Ratio of profit to sales	12%	12%	10%	Manufacturing economies couldn't overcome price squeeze.	8%	Will gear current policies to attain this goal.	Brown Brothers Company dropped out of our market.	12%
Ratio of direct/indirect manufacturing labor	300%	290%	290%	Installation of labor-saving machinery cut direct labor, indirect steady.	280%	Centralization of engineering and tooling departments will cut indirect force.	Survey shows engineering salaries to rise 5%, labor settlements at 7 cents per hour.	285%
Machine utilization (average)	68%	70%	71%	Sales volume helped. Also sold surplus standby equipment.	74%	Sales volume up; plant continues to weed out obsolete equipment.	Nothing significant.	74%
Cost of materials of manufacture per unit produced	$0.250	$0.263	$0.265	There were general increases in raw material markets.	$0.280	Materials conservation program begun in September is saving now at rate of $3,000 per month.	Materials market forecast is expected to level out and remain steady for the next twelve months.	$0.260

work sheets (Figs. 4-4 and 4-5). We'll repeat the five steps here in detail.

Step 1. Making the Projection

In its simplest form, the concept of projection can be demonstrated this way: Take a series of numbers recorded sequentially in the course of ten years—8, 8, 10, 9, 10, 11, 11, 10, 12, 11. Based upon these ten numbers, you can arrive at a projection for the eleventh year by using simple arithmetic. If you add the ten numbers, the figures yield a total of 100. Dividing by 10 yields an average of 10. So 10 could be your projection. Another way would be to plot the numbers as points on a chart and then draw a smooth line through the numbers that best fits it. See Fig. 4-6 for a demonstration of how results would vary. A straight line would indicate that the projection would be 12. If you drew a curved line, the projection might be 14 if the sequence of numbers were rising, 7 if the sequence were falling. Still another approach would be to ask a statistician to examine the past series of numbers. Using a technique that depends upon measuring how far each number is removed from either the average or from the straight line or from the curve, he can tell you the degree of confidence you could place in the projection derived from each technique.

The point is that most projections involve a process of *moving* past history forward into the future without first considering the effect of new influences. (The U.S. Weather Bureau, incidentally, can issue a forecast with a high degree of confidence, based upon the simple technique of predicting that tomorrow you'll have the same weather you had today.)

In projecting past or present data into the future, an executive ought to have an understanding of some basic statistical concepts, even if he is not fully able to make the computations himself. Among the more important concepts are:

Probability. This expresses the chance a certain statistic has of occurring again. (Statisticians define probability as "relative frequency.") If you were to put 27 balls in a bag (3 white, 18 black, and 6 red) the probability of your pulling out a white ball would be 3 in 27, or 3/27ths. If in a shipment of 100,000 vacuum tubes, 57 were known to be defective, the probability of a customer's getting a defective tube is 57 in 100,000, or 0.057 per cent.

FIG. 4-5. WORK SHEET FOR REPLANNING, REORGANIZING, AND RESTAFFING

Account	This year's performance	Next year's goals	Adequacy of this year's plans for next year's goals			Adequacy of this year's organizational structure			Adequacy of present staff		
			OK as is	Exception	Recommended action	OK as is	Exception	Recommended action	OK as is	Exception	Recommended action
Sales cost per sale	$258	$240		Promotion and training program ineffectual. Salesmen averaged only 5 sales per 25 calls.	Revise training materials. Add space coverage in vertical trade publications.	OK		None		Short-handed in the training department.	Add staff assistant to the sales promotion manager. New man works on promotion and training.
Annual cost of inspection	$375,000	$245,000		Shop performed 100% inspection but still missed 8% of defects. Many customer complaints.	Install statistical quality control program. Cut inspection labor 35%. Catch 99% of defects.		Need centralized control of quality with clearer lines of responsibility.	Form SQC department with responsibility for sampling, test, and inspection. Report to works manager.		Need SQC manager, one statistician, one clerk.	Fill vacancies at once. SQC manager to be hired from outside company, others promoted from within.
Minimum cash position at monthly closings	$52,000	$70,000		Three key accounts were habitually late in payment.	Step up collection period on these accounts.		Sales manager has been making final decisions on key-account credit.	Assign final decision to assistant treasurer.	OK		None

70

FIG. 4-6. EFFECT OF SEQUENCE PATTERNS ON PROJECTIONS

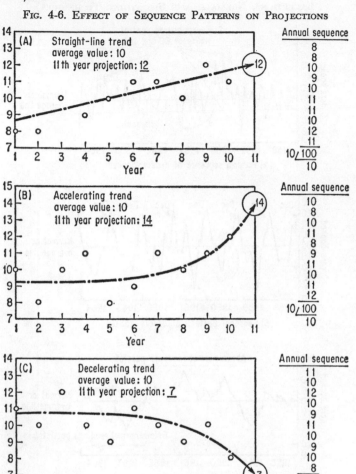

In *A*, *B*, and *C* the numerical average for the ten-year period is always 10. The annual sequence patterns vary, however, indicating projections for the eleventh year of 12, 14, and 7.

Precision. This is a measure of how great a variation from an average figure any one figure is likely to be. (Statisticians define precision as the "standard variation of the variable," where standard variation is a method of squaring to determine the variation. The smaller the deviation, the greater the precision.)

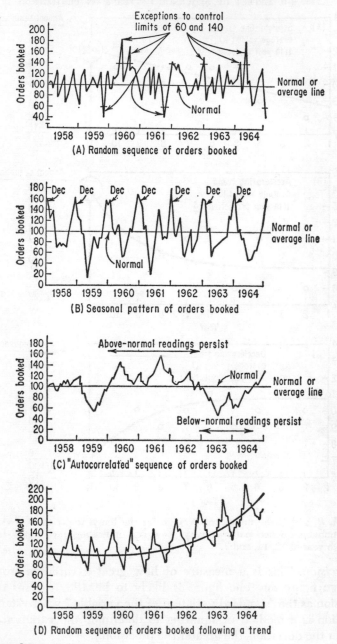

(A) Random sequence of orders booked

(B) Seasonal pattern of orders booked

(C) "Autocorrelated" sequence of orders booked

(D) Random sequence of orders booked following a trend

Adapted from Robert G. Brown, *Statistical Forecasting for Inventory Control*,
McGraw-Hill Book Company, New York, 1959, pp. 15–19.

Confidence. This is an expression of the chance that a certain figure will occur in a sequence of numbers.

Correlation. This is a statistical measure of the degree to which two observed variables move in some sort of harmony. A typical way to get an indication of correlation is to plot on a chart two sets of simultaneously observed data (such as a series of department store daily sales versus daily mean temperatures). If the points plotted indicate a straight line that approximates a 45° angle, the correlation is high. If the points cluster in a circle, form no pattern, or indicate a horizontal or vertical line, the correlation is slight or nonexistent.

Significance. This term is used to indicate the degree to which the result, or measurement, varies from the normal, or assumed normal, more than can reasonably be attributed to chance errors in sampling.

Sensitivity. This expresses how well a certain measurement can detect deviations.

Sample. This is a group of figures or measurements removed from a larger group that is referred to as a "universe." The accuracy of most projections and forecasts depends upon the degree to which samples were chosen "at random."

Smoothing. This describes a technique for ironing out nonsignificant deviations from normal (average, mean, etc.) in a series of measurements taken over a period of time. The purpose of smoothing is to remove from consideration nonsignificant variables (often called "noise") and/or significant ones (such as seasonal fluctuations) that mask underlying trends. Figure 4-7 shows how such smoothing can be done graphically. Smoothing, of course, can be done arith-metically or statistically.

One of the simplest methods for smoothing out noise and seasonal influences is to use "moving totals." Businessmen most frequently use moving *annual* totals in a manner illustrated by this example: Take a series of data for twelve consecutive months ending in May, 1963. When the 1963 data for June comes in, June, 1962, is dropped from the total and June, 1963, added in. This moving total is plotted for consecutive months, continually dropping the oldest and adding the newest. Figure 4-8 illustrates this technique.

Cycle. This refers to the repetition of peaks and valleys in some sort of periodic fashion. Seasonal cycles are one example. Business cycles with periods longer than a year are another example.

FIG. 4-8. EXAMPLE OF DEVELOPMENT OF MOVING ANNUAL TOTAL FIGURES AND CHART

Monthly safety record

		D	J	F	M	A	M	J	J	A	S	O	N	D	J	F	M	A	M	J	J	A	S	O	N	D	J
No. of accidents	Current	0	2	2	6	3	1	6	3	4	9	11	6	5	12	4	7	6	7	7							
	M.A.T.												57	60	70	68	72	77	78	82							
Hours lost	Current	0	5	3	1	31	2	10	5	3	2	20	3	4	10	2	6	2	5	6							
	M.A.T.												96	95	104	103	78	78	73	69							
M.A.T. 100– 50–	Number of accidents																										
20 10																											
M.A.T. 100– 50–	Hours lost																										
20 10																											
Month		D	J	F	M	A	M	J	J	A	S	O	N	D	J	F	M	A	M	J	J	A	S	O	N	D	J
Year		1962	1963												1964												1965

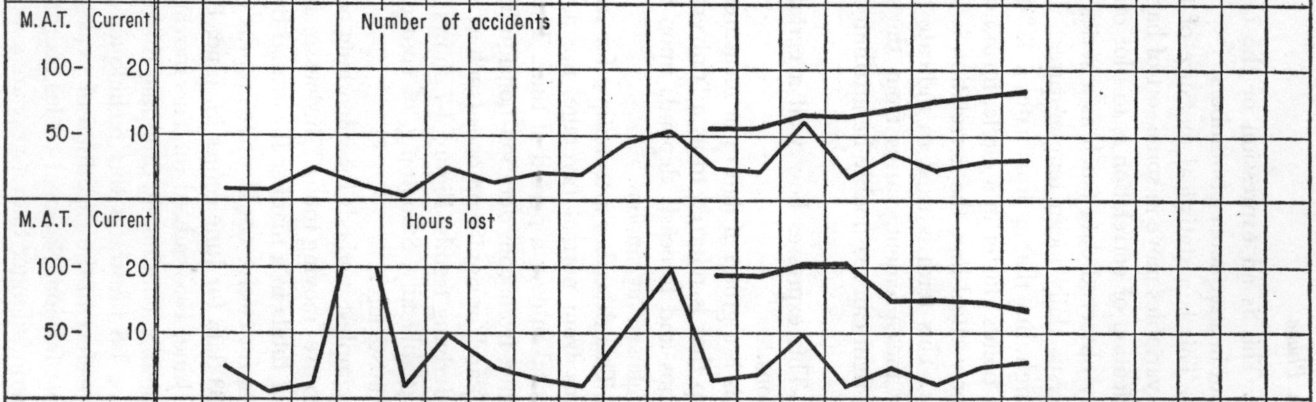

SOURCE: T. G. Rose and Donald E. Farr, *Higher Management Control*, McGraw-Hill Book Company, New York, 1957, p. 68.

Crystallizing the Projection. In finalizing his projections, the planner has a choice of three basic alternatives:

1. Conditions will continue as they are now. In other words, a straight-line trend, whether up, down, or on a level course, will persist at its current rate. If a company is adding ten new accounts receivable each year, it might be expected that it will add ten next year. Similarly, if it were losing accounts in that number, the losses would persist. And if the company had shown no growth in the past three years, chances are no growth would be expected in the next three (Fig. 4-9, Chart 1).

2. The current trend, if up or down, will either accelerate or slow down. The former is called "peaking"; the latter "flattening out," or "plateauing." For example, suppose costs of manufacturing have dropped 15 per cent in 1960, 14 per cent in 1961, 11 per cent in 1962, and 8 per cent in 1963. After the fourth year, the next cost reduction attainable (if production rates are stable) will level out at 6 or 7 per cent (Fig. 4-9, Chart 2).

3. Current conditions or trends will be dominated by cyclical factors of greater period than the period of the projection. In other words, if it has been observed that sales fall off six months after the appearance of a bull market, and conversely rise six months after a bear market, the projection would expect sales to fall off by spring, regardless of current trends, if the stock market in October was dipping badly (Fig. 4-9, Chart 3).

Step 2. Making the Forecast

The Weather Bureau often draws irate abuse from the citizenry when its forecast goes awry. More often than not, the cause for the poor forecast is far beyond the control of the weatherman. It is the *new* climate factors introduced—and the extent to which they distort projected weather patterns—that upset his predictions.

To carry the analogy further, the forecaster may know from past measurements that a storm bringing rain to Chicago will, in twenty-four hours, be dumping rain on New York. He may examine charts that demonstrate the physical state of the air mass from the earth's surface to 60,000 feet. He may also know the direction and strength of various air currents which appear to control the sphere of the storm. And he certainly knows the topographical features of the New York area. Based upon either simple arithmetical extrapolation

FIG. 4-9. EXAMPLES OF THREE KINDS OF TRENDS

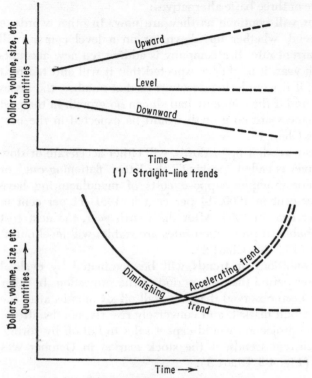

(1) Straight-line trends

(2) Diminishing or accelerating trends

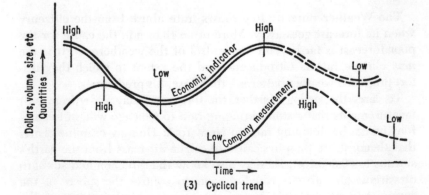

(3) Cyclical trend

of all these data or upon complex formulas integrated and solved by a computer, he issues a forecast for rain in New York tomorrow. If the forecast proves right, it's taken for granted. If an unanticipated influence crops up, or if an anticipated one varies from its predicted intensity, it may not rain in New York and the forecast will fail. Citizens shrug this off, quite correctly, as a vagary of the weather. But the weatherman must keep right on making projections, forecasts, and predictions 365 days a year, year in, year out.

Now what's the connection of all this to business management? Every executive must fully understand that economic forecasting has just as many vagaries as the weather. Careful measurement and analysis can make projections fairly accurate. No amount of analysis will ever make a business forecast completely dependable.

In making a forecast, the problem is one of examining projections from two viewpoints:

1. Should we be satisfied with projections as they are? In other words, do our finalized projections represent what we really want to attain, or should we try to improve upon them?

2. Will these projections remain unaffected by new influences coming up in the future? If not, how will they react?

In answering the first question, we reach over a little bit into the area of goal setting. But in responding to the second question, we're still pretty much in the realm of forecasting, although some of the information we use will be the result of goal setting, especially by organizational elements at lower levels. We often need their estimated goals before we can make a forecast of their effect on projections at higher organizational levels.

Data from Internal Sources. In forecasting, an executive should first examine the potential effect of changes he knows are taking place, or will take place, inside his organization. For instance, through internal sources he may be able to gain knowledge of:

• Release of a new product development to production
• A breakthrough in a critical manufacturing process
• Acquisition of laborsaving equipment
• Introduction of new materials permitting improvement of product quality
• Institution of methods program directed at reduction of indirect costs
• Development of an improved inventory-control program

• Impending labor negotiations with expectations of wage increases or work stoppages

• Changes in key managerial personnel which will affect operation of certain phases of the business

In a nutshell, investigation of impending changes within the company's control should alert the planner to (1) possible impairment of projected efficiencies or (2) potential improvement in projected efficiencies. The forecast impact of these changes should be used to modify present projections.

Data from External Sources. Outside the company a manager has recourse to three general forms of information that can help him detect changes that might influence his forecast: (1) Surveys conducted by or for his company, or surveys conducted by other agencies but which are pertinent to company operations, (2) movement of general economic indicators which might show some correlation with company operations, and (3) personal hunches regarding the external business climate and its effect on routine projections.

Surveys. It is surprising to discover how few mature companies know anything statistically definite about their markets. For example, a company that has been making air-conditioning equipment for over twenty years only recently made a determined effort to find out how many square feet of un-air-conditioned space there is in industrial buildings. Their case was not atypical.

Reasons for not finding out more specifically about market potential are numerous. Surveys, for instance, are expensive. Data are often unattainable. When information can be acquired, it rapidly becomes outdated. Frequently, statistical or average data are of little immediate use to a sales department, which is more interested in specific leads to follow, with names and addresses. Furthermore, surveys are often misleading, especially when they are joint ventures or have been conducted for someone else or for another purpose. And since surveying is a form of measurement, it suffers from definition problems. Respondents may not understand the questions; there may be interviewing bias (introduced frequently as a result of the incompetency or disinterest of the interviewer).

In spite of all these objections or weaknesses in survey technique, it would be foolish for management not to make surveying or survey utilization a regular part of forecasting.

The term "survey" may also be used broadly to include surveys of business literature and technical journals. This enables you to find out what knowledgeable people in your field are predicting and what new factors in reseach, design, materials, and methods could be introduced by your company or by its competitors. Such information may be in the form of reports, news stories, interviews, and statistical research conducted by trade papers, professional societies, and trade associations.

Economic Indicators. Somewhere along mahogany row in most large corporations you're likely to find a captive economist, or at least an upgraded statistician, who interprets for management the impact of business trends upon the company's future. These specialists, if they are hardheaded and business-oriented, are valuable assets to the organization. But a company need not despair if it has none. Economic forecasts are a dime a dozen. Most of them issued by sources like the National Industrial Conference Board, *The New York Times,* McGraw-Hill Publications, national banks, investment houses, and the like are fairly reliable. The difficulty lies not in the inaccuracy of their forecasts so much as in your interpretation of what these forecasts mean to your business. More often than not, economists are looking at present indicators and are projecting them six months to a year ahead. For this reason, a businessman may be puzzled because the economist he reads is predicting an upswing next year when he knows that his business right now is sick. The explanation is that the economist has studied a number of indicators which, in the aggregate, tend to make him believe that general economic conditions must improve. For instance, in the fall of 1962, while manufacturing companies were still feeling a tightening profit squeeze, economists were seeing an upturn in 1963. They had this vision because inventory levels on a national scale were relatively low, consumer spending in department stores was rising, the gross national product for all American industries was also rising, and corporations were committing themselves to an increase in capital spending for the following year. Taken as a whole, these factors represented pressures being built up now that would force a pickup in business activity before too long a time. (See also Chapters 10 and 12.)

Once an executive is aware of the existence of indicators, his next step is to find out how to use them. In the absence of a staff economist or statistician, the executive may have to draw his own conclusions. He can do so rather easily by plotting (or by having his secretary or someone on his staff plot):

1. The trend of those indicators which seem logically related to his operations—on the same chart on which he plots

2. Trends in operational data (raw or weighted data, ratios, etc.) of his own operation

Simple inspection will show whether the cycles of the business indicators bear any relation to the cycles of his own data. Sometimes the relationship will be positive; that is, upturns in the indicator will be matched by upswings in operational data. Other times the relationship may be negative, in that upswings in the indicators will be matched by downturns in operational data. Rarely will these relationships be in phase; that is, it is more likely that one movement may tend to lag or lead the other. Also, the amplitude (extent of upward or downward movement) of the swings will probably differ. And sad to state, often there will be no apparent relationship between the indicators and what's happening in your company.

Some other variables in the business climate that may plague you and often need your attention are:

• The attitude or spirit of the people: if they're optimistic, business may improve; if they're pessimistic, anything can happen.

• The truly unforeseen, like wildcat strikes, work stoppages among your suppliers, rain that slows construction projects, snow that deflates consumer buying.

• The political health of the nation, anticipated legislation, reaction to the current administration, etc.

• The state of international affairs—war, cold war, or peace, and international growth and competition.

Intuition. There obviously comes a time in the making of a forecast when an executive must abandon the warm, reassuring world of reason and firm data and make a good old-fashioned guess. Some executives call this a hunch or the use of intuition. For too many executives it's neither; it's only a hope, which their better judgment might warn them against. Carter Burgess states the proposition wonderfully:

> Logic and reason must be blended with "anticipation" and "instinct," the latter having been sharpened by experience. The two go together. Call them, if you will, the rational and the psychic elements that combine to make planning successful. I certainly don't claim them as a new philosophy of planning. But I know that my own experience has

taught me how true they are—and how much better guideposts they are than many of the procedures and programs one finds in the rule books.[11]

Your objectives in all this analysis of external conditions is to discover new factors that might cause an exception to your present projections. If you find none, then your policy should be to let well enough alone—that is, after making necessary adjustments for internal changes. On the other hand, if you *do* discover relationships between an external indicator and your own operational data, this can be used in either of two ways:

It can be followed and held as a guide to making future projections, or it can be tentatively interpreted as a new factor, forecasting impending changes and a resultant exception in your present projection. If so, it should be used immediately to adjust the projection of the specific operating data to which it bears a relationship.

Step 3. Setting Operational Goals

If steps 1 and 2 (projection and forecast) have been properly completed, goal setting becomes a simple pinning-down procedure. It is simple in concept only, however. For most managers it is the moment of truth so far as the future is concerned. A manager must at this instant weigh a host of variable influences and then *make up his mind*. (This, of course, is a decision-making function, of which more will be said in Chapter 8.) When pinning down future objectives, an executive should consider some or all of these factors:

• *Nature of the Decision.* That is, is he setting a goal that is designed to exert control or to exploit an opportunity?

• *Duration of Effect.* Will the new goal represent a permanent trend, as the executive now sees it, or is it essentially a stopgap measure until internal or external factors become clearer?

• *Degree of Financial Involvement.* Will the new goals require long- or short-term financing, for instance, or placing the company's stock before the public, or a departure from traditional profit goals?

• *Degree of Organizational Change.* Will new units, such as research and development, have to be added? Will the company need radical restructuring, such as from a decentralized to a more unified control?

• *Degree of Technological Change.* Will new goals mean moving away from familiar areas of know-how to new ones involving strange materials or complicated processes for which the present staff is unsuited?

• *Effect on Marketing Policy.* Will new goals require revision of long-standing pricing and discount practices, shifting from distributor marketing to your own sales force, etc.?

• *Utilization of Present Facilities.* Will new goals be attainable with current equipment capacities and capabilities, or will they require new or expanded facilities?

Most of these questions can be answered factually. An astute manager may even be able to assign numbers and weights to the various factors. But in almost every case, the accountable executive must bring his own mental computer to bear on his decision. And the decision will have a good chance of being a wise one if (1) he has been able to marshal enough significant information and if (2) he has carefully weighed the influencing factors.

In the short history of modern management, one can recall many momentous decisions regarding revised goals. Some turned out to be good, others not so good. The Ford Motor Company, for instance, did an incredibly comprehensive planning job before introducing the Edsel. The Edsel turned out to be a monumental flop, partly because the forecasting of market trends was terribly wrong and partly because there were long operational delays in bringing the new car before the public. On the other hand, George Romney of American Motors, working more on intuitive hunch and keen observation of public tastes than on historical data, brought out the compact car at about the same time with amazing success. These examples attracted national comment. The millions of other goal-setting decisions, made at both high and low levels of management, usually go unnoticed except for the few vitally concerned people close to the impact. However, the quality of the day-in, day-out decisions probably determines the value of the big decisions that are made only once à year or once in a lifetime.

Harry Arthur Hopf, heralded by CIOS * as founder of a concept called the "science of the optimum," urged in 1935 that corporate goals represent an optimum balance between size, cost, and human capacity. Hopf carried the original ideas of scientific management forward when he stated: "Optimology has as its principal task the analysis and measurement, by scientific means, of all facts, experi-

* Le Comité International de l'Organisation Scientifique.

ences, techniques, processes, and trends in any field of human effort and their classification and codification, with the objective in view of defining for a given enterprise the level of optimal relations to which it should aspire, and of providing it constantly with reliable data through the use of which the progress made in realizing and adhering to the optimum may be determined." [12]

Of course, Hopf was anticipating the development of the electronic data-processing computer. But the principle of a balanced objective that represents a harmonious optimum is one for every executive to keep in mind when finalizing his goals.

In any event, the revised (or new) goals of an organization become the standards against which each organizational function and each individual is measured.

Step 4. Determining Adequacy of Present Plans

In this text, we have purposely tried to draw a distinction between goals and plans. While in practice this distinction is often nonexistent or blurred, it should serve to emphasize that a statement of objectives does not necessarily imply the ways and means to that end. Once new targets have been chosen (or if you will, while the new targets are being set up), the manager must thoroughly review his existing policies, procedures, organization, and personnel to see if they will, as they are now constituted, bring about the ends desired. This process is basically one of measurement. The executive holds up each existing management element to the strong light of the new goal, much as a farmer holds an egg to the candle. If in this new light the manager sees no flaw, he sets the element aside, assured that it can remain in its present form. If, however, the element, when measured against this new standard, shows a weakness, it is an exception which calls for a change from standard operation procedures. (See worksheets, Fig. 4-5, for a graphical demonstration of this step.)

Step 5. Replanning for New Goals

Measuring adequacy (step 4) will isolate those soft spots in present plans that need adjustment. Adjusting to meet these new goals can be broken down into three areas—planning, organization, and staffing.

Revising Plans to Support New Goals. While the term "planning" encompasses both the function of setting future goals and the determination of procedures for attaining them, for practical purposes it is helpful to separate the two activities.

Celanese, for instance, in a 1963 advertisement, made this distinction: "In our view a projection is an educated guess at what may happen. A plan is a specific program of action to make as sure as possible that the right thing does happen."

Once performance standards have been set (acknowledging here that properly set objectives must anticipate ways and means), it is time to turn your attention to the more detailed phases of planning. Since this book makes the assumption that most readers are not starting their operations from scratch, the term that we think fits better is "replanning." After all, policies and procedures (written or not) exist in every functioning organization. For management to think in terms of replanning serves to alert it to the fact that new plans almost always imply that changes will be imposed upon existing procedures. Replanning, consequently, should also take the impact of change into consideration.

When organizational plans are revised, management should consider the need for action in four major areas:

1. *Policy.* Perhaps it's splitting hairs again to distinguish between objectives and policies. But if you envision a policy to be a guide for current action rather than an end to be reached, the distinction is justified. As an example, a corporate goal for next year might be to reverse a downward trend in market position. A related policy might be developed to include such principles to follow as:

a. Pricing policies will continue to be in accord with those established by the U.S. Department of Justice and with ethical standards of business competition.

b. The policy restricting sales bonuses to a maximum of 50 per cent of the previous year's income will be lifted.

c. A new policy of marketing management will be established to encourage greater authority at the product management level.

2. *Procedures.* These are the natural outgrowth of policies. Either formalized in writing or simply as a body of understanding, procedures dictate *how* things will be, or should be, done (see Fig. 4-10). Procedures may regulate channels of organization through which certain information must flow; procedures may spell out in meticulous detail how to perform a laboratory test; they may map

the flow of paperwork needed to process a customer's order; they may also prescribe how to handle an employee grievance.

Those procedures which are written are at once easy to examine and revise. But they are also deceptive in that they may have little relationship to the way things are actually being done. Consequently, in revising procedures, it's wise not to take them too literally. Personal observation and investigation will probably be needed to put them into proper perspective.

Since more procedures are of the everybody-knows-that's-how-we-do-it variety, management can get a liberal education from a survey which asks various people in the organization how any specific problem is handled. The American Brake Shoe Company designed a simple questionnaire to find out what its supervisors knew about the guarding of management prerogatives while dealing with unions. The diversification of opinion as to what was the proper way of dealing with this problem was astonishing enough to launch the company on a long-term program of management education in this area.

Another aspect of procedures is that they may be taken too literally as the *only* way a task may be performed. Obviously, this rigid concept implies a perfect procedure, of which there are only a few. McGraw-Hill, Inc., guards against this concept of the inflexibility of procedure with this statement in its *Personnel Procedures Manual:*

> It cannot be too strongly emphasized that, in a company as diverse and as complex as ours, no set of policies and procedures can cover every situation. There are bound to be exceptions that fit none of the procedures set forth. For this reason you will find references in these chapters to methods of handling exceptions. *It is the responsibility of every manager and supervisor to request exception procedures in cases which they are convinced warrant such treatment.*

For an example of a typical procedure statement see Fig. 4-10.

3. *Communications.* The design of operating procedures, while a tedious process, does not constitute management's big problem in replanning. The real problem is one of getting those people involved prepared for change, willing to accept its value to them, and eager to make the new policies and procedures work. Company files are packed full of sound, workable procedures which are ignored by those for whom they were designed. The fault lies, not in the procedures, but in the failure of management to plan for their acceptance. For this reason, many companies invite participation in estab-

FIG. 4-10. EXAMPLE OF PROCEDURE FOR REVISING PAPER WORK SYSTEM

When the Procedures Division receives a request for service or when an employee of the division has an idea that a particular assignment should be undertaken, the matter should be discussed with the division manager and a "project" established.

One of the following priority classifications will be assigned by the manager:

"A"—all assignments which are believed to be urgent in order to protect company assets or income or for some other reason or which are believed to be high in potential cost reductivity;

"B"—all other assignments.

As analysts become available for assignment to projects, the manager will review his "project book" and determine, according to the relative urgency of the unassigned jobs, which project would next be assigned and to whom.

Whenever a choice is possible, the analyst's preference for a project will be given consideration.

When a project has been assigned, the analyst will confer with the manager, at which time all known information concerning the project will be discussed and a tentative date set for completion of the assignment.

An appointment will then be made for the analyst to meet with the head of the department in which the project is located and begin the analysis.

SOURCE: Earl R. Strong, *Increasing Office Productivity*, McGraw-Hill Book Company, N.Y., 1962, p. 74–75 by permission of the publisher.

---

lishing procedures, even if it means settling for something less than perfect. Other companies make a point of keeping managers, and all employees, informed of impending procedural changes and the reasons for them. A few companies, with unusual deference to reality, invite continual feedback from operating people after procedures have been changed. There are many texts devoted to the subject. Most of these point to the need for keeping those on the receiving end of procedural changes in the know and those on the handing-out side aware of how well these procedures are working out.

Restructuring the Organization for New Goals. Your logic ought to go something like this. If everything is going according to plan, then the present organization must be okay. But if exceptions are cropping up—especially those which call for revised plans—then your organization needs a critical assessment. In auditing this area, ask yourself whether the present organization provides:

1. *A properly designated management activity to deal with the exceptional problem.* In one company, a lag in putting newly developed products into production caused sales to fall behind quotas.

What was needed was a liaison group between product design and the manufacturing operation to synchronize start-up tooling and to provide engineering modifications as their need was discovered.

2. *A suitable authority to deal with the problem.* A multiplant chemical company was irritated by the size of its demurrage charges on railroad tank cars. Forceful instructions from headquarters to the traffic managers at the various plants did not materially improve the situation. Finally the problem was solved by setting up a centralized traffic department with authority to coordinate interplant shipments.

3. *Adequate support by communications for measurement and control.* A Midwestern department store was plagued by periodic dips in its working capital. While the treasurer's plan for control of funds was sound, he was unable to implement it until he appointed a one-man control officer to analyze buying activity and sales figures daily—and to report exceptions to projected trends to him each day.

4. *A means of avoiding gaps between organizational functions.* A home appliance manufacturer found that its inventory of materials in process was becoming a disturbing cost factor. Investigation showed that the purchasing department was ordering an advance in deliveries of subassemblies to conform with production schedules but that no one function was charged with the responsibility of inventory control. The company solved the problem by setting up a materials management department designed to control materials inventories from purchase, scheduling, in-process production, and through to shipment.

5. *Minimal duplication of effort.* Another company detected a persistent rise in indirect charges. Study of the organization showed that three manufacturing departments each maintained their own clerical accounting group and that almost half of what was reported represented duplication. A solution was brought about by centralizing clerical work for these departments.

Not every executive worries too much about duplication—especially as it might be indicated by an organization chart. Hertz's board chairman, Leon Greenebaum, says, "I'd rather have two guys going after the ball and maybe run into each other than have everybody think it's somebody else's play." [13]

Revitalizing Staff for New Goals. If a company's system of management by exception and its organization for carrying it out appear to be sound—and yet results are disappointing—then there's a good possibility that the trouble lies in the staffing of the organization. H. Ford Dickie, manager of manufacturing services for the International General Electric Company says "It's a rare company that can rightly assume (in a management by exception situation) that no news means good news. Systems just won't provide that kind of foolproof control for you. What is needed above all is adequate motivation, discipline, and self-control throughout the entire organization." To achieve these ends, management must ask and answer these questions:

• *Has the staff been selected with regard to its ability to grasp the concept of management by exception and carry it out?* The self-control required is something many men cannot generate in themselves. Others cannot conform to the requirements of an unemotional administrative system. Still others don't have the cold courage to enforce the discipline of the system on others.

• *Has the staff been motivated to make the concept work?* Ford Dickie emphasizes that few production schedules will be met unless the goal is one agreed upon beforehand by both executive and subordinate. Unless there is some mutuality of agreement at this stage, defectors will always be able to conjure up excuses. Of course, it should go without saying that an essential motivational instrument is the relating of financial rewards to results attained. Genesco's "Par Busters Club" nicely combines with recognition a salary incentive program for executives.

• *Has the staff been properly trained?* Especially if the system is new, it is better to proceed gradually from modest to more rigorous objectives so that the staff can acquire know-how through experience. In addition, managers should be schooled in the techniques of evaluation and appraisal interviewing during performance reviews. Also often overlooked is the need for instruction in the more technical aspects of projection, forecasting, statistical quality control, operations research, linear programming, etc. And attention should be given to familiarizing managers up and down the line with the company's communications, reporting, and control system.

• *Have staff assignments been made judiciously?* There's nothing like the occurrence of an exception to provide the opportunity for trying a manager on a different job. Men who are floundering in a dynamic situation—say with a growth product—may provide a stabilizing influence in a situation that needs a steadying hand. Or an executive who has proved to be a good problem solver can be transferred from a project he has brought under control to another that is going haywire.

• *Has the staff been properly disciplined in the ways of management by exception?* Management by exception implies a reward-and-punishment system. Those managers who meet objectives receive raises, promotions, praise, and choice assignments. Those who fail to get their operations in line are on the receiving end of less pleasant treatment. After being given an opportunity to improve, after being furnished proper motivation and training, they should stand or fall on their results. When they fail repeatedly, their fate should become one of transfer or discharge or, at the very least, curtailment of salary increases.

The danger in such discipline lies not so much in the punitive aspects as it does in encouraging overstatement or understatement of goals. Let's take understatement of goals first. This has the more debilitating effect. Shrewd or timid managers become overcautious in setting their targets. Everyone is familiar with the sales manager who understimates quotas either (1) to be sure he can reach the goals or (2) to make it easy to exceed them. When this practice prevails in an organization, the entire company will suffer from a lack of aggressiveness, and growth will be hampered.

Overstatement of goals, especially when forced on a manager from his superior, can also have a deleterious effect. If goals are unrealistic, if problems are too difficult, or if managers are overmatched in their assignments, permanent damage can be done to individuals as well as to the organization. The case of the electrical manufacturing company executives (from Westinghouse, General Electric, Allis-Chalmers, and eighteen other companies) who acted in defiance of the law (and of emphatic company policies to the contrary) to fix prices is a tragic example of this. The root of their defection lay not in their lack of morality, but simply in their inability to find a legitimate way to deliver expected profits in the face of overproduction and heavy price cutting in the electrical industry at that time.

References

1. Melville C. Branch, *The Corporate Planning Process,* American Management Association, New York, 1962, p. 58.
2. "The Attack on Short-run Production," *Factory,* November, 1962, p. 94.

3. Mason Haire, *Organization Theory in Industrial Practice*, John Wiley & Sons, Inc., New York, 1962, p. 61.
4. W. V. Merrihue, *Managing by Communication*, McGraw-Hill Book Company, New York, 1960, pp. 296–297.
5. Thomas B. Morgan, "ABC's Decision Makers," *TV Guide*, Dec. 8, 1962, p. 6.
6. "Profit Motive to the Rescue," *Business Week*, Dec. 8, 1962, p. 60.
7. Robert T. Livingston and William W. Waite, *The Manager's Job*, Columbia University Press, New York, 1960, p. 121.
8. Louis A. Allen, *Management and Organization*, McGraw-Hill Book Company, New York, 1958, p. 29.
9. Carter L. Burgess, "Planning," in H. B. Maynard (ed.), *Top Management Handbook*, McGraw-Hill Book Company, New York, 1960, p. 251.
10. *Chicago Daily Tribune*, Nov. 15, 1962, p. 7.
11. Carter L. Burgess, "Planning," in H. B. Maynard (ed.) *Top Management Handbook*, McGraw-Hill Book Company, New York, 1960, p. 251.
12. Harry Arthur Hopf, paper presented at Sixth International Congress for Scientific Management, London, July, 1935.
13. *Fortune*, October, 1963, p. 121.

Chapter 5

THE SELECTION PHASE

In Which You Select Those Vital and Economically Available Measures That Will Best Indicate the Organization's Progress toward Its Objectives

We tend to think of decision making as something that we do at one point in time. Of course, this is not what happens at all. Many, too many in fact, of our decisions are ones that are forced upon us simply because of action taken, or commitments made, in the past. And these actions and commitments lead us inexorably down a path the end of which is often not of our present choosing.

Three Kinds of Criteria

To minimize an empirical predetermination of our decisions, we must consciously try to cast our decisions way back in the planning stages of an activity. We do so by carefully selecting the criteria (or measurements) which will best enable us to control future actions.

Industry-wide Criteria. History has established many go–no-go gages for success or failure in any number of industries. For instance:

• In a department store, the climate as measured by temperature, rain or snow, or amount of sunshine, will enable management to plan its newspaper advertising volume, ordering, etc.

• In mining, operators judge as a poor investment a coal seam that has an "overburden" ratio of more than 15:1. That is, if the seam is 4 feet thick, the maximum amount of dirt and rock (overburden) that can be stripped economically to surface-mine it would be 60 feet (15 × 4 feet). Mine experts have drawn this rule of thumb, although careful analysis will show variations in any single instance.

• In steel manufacturing, old-timers will figure that for every operating shift added above the normal rate for a rolling mill, there will be a 1 per cent reduction of product yield. In other words, if the manager expects an 88 per cent yield from a mill operating at an optimum of eighteen shifts per week, pushing it to nineteen shifts will drop the average yield to 87 per cent. Newly hired engineers or by-the-book cost estimators are hard put to realize that uncontrollable variables such as mixed crews, men fatigued by overtime, deferred maintenance, and off-grade ingots scraped from the slab yard introduce inefficiencies that only industry experts can anticipate.

• In banking, one of the first inquiries a banker would make for an index of a bank's profitability trend would be about the rate of cash turnover.

Functional Criteria. Similarly, specialists in almost every established field have come to agree on certain basic measurements as being reliable criteria for decision making regarding their particular specialties. For instance:

• Production control managers will gage performance in their area of specialization according to the percentage of total orders that are shipped on time.

• Sales managers will closely watch the number of sales proposals rejected as a measure of sales-force effectiveness.

• Controllers will judge a credit operation according to its on-time collection record.

Personal Criteria. Then there are the hundreds of other "hunch" criteria which, while statistically difficult to verify, develop in an individual's mind through experience. For instance, a purchasing agent we knew thirty years ago used to be guided in his buying activity by the ratio of "jobs wanted" to "help wanted" ads in his daily paper. Today, curiously enough, there is an index published based upon just such measurements. Other hunches are less scientific, but nevertheless they play a big part in establishing criteria upon which executives base their decisions.

Desirable Characteristics

Regardless of whether the criteria have an industry, functional, or personal base, the fact is that in each area there are dozens and dozens of possible choices. It is because of the plethora of possible criteria that an executive must make his first critical decision if he is truly to practice management by exception. He must select those performance criteria, in advance, that (1) most directly relate to profit and loss in his business, (2) are available economically, (3) can be collected and assimilated promptly, (4) are acceptable to his associates and subordinates, and (5) are most easily understood and acted upon by the executive himself.

Interrelationships

Since the time of Frederick W. Taylor, management has sought, with no success, the magic single criterion that would integrate all the influential measurements into one index of profitability. While the criteria needed for success seem to be interrelated, even the most advanced statisticians have been unable to formulate this relationship. So you must learn to live with, and forever keep in mind, the reality of the interdependence of the various criteria—and also to remain uncertain which is cause and which is effect. For example, see Fig. 5-1 which demonstrates some of the more obvious relationships between a number of commonly used criteria that must be weighed when finalizing performance budgets.

The Vital Few

One of the best ways to narrow down the choice of criteria is to apply the principle of the "trivial many and the vital few." This principle, recognized by economists and others down through the ages, has had its most frequent application in inventory control. But the principle can be applied to *any* control problem. An explanation of its application to inventories, however, will make its use in the selection of performance criteria easier to grasp. H. Ford Dickie of the General Electric Company calls the technique "ABC

Fig. 5-1. Interrelation of Various Profit or Loss Factors as Considered in Budget Preparations

	Sales	Finished goods inventory	Work in process inventory	Raw materials inventory	Production requirements—units	Direct labor requirements	Direct material requirements	Indirect manufacturing expenses	Nonfactory departments expenses	Capital improvements	Cost of goods manufactured	Cost of sales	Other income and expenses	Prepaid expenses and accruals	Purchases	Accounts payable	Loans payable	Payroll	Accounts receivable	Cash	Profit and loss statements	Balance sheet
Sales		X			X							X							X		X	
Finished goods inventory	X				X						X											X
Work in process inventory				X	X			X			X											X
Raw materials inventory					X		X								X							X
Production requirements—units	X	X	X	X		X	X	X														X
Direct labor requirements					X													X				
Direct material requirements				X	X										X	X						
Indirect manufacturing expenses													X	X		X		X			X	
Nonfactory departments expenses										X			X	X		X		X			X	
Capital improvements																X	X			X		X
Cost of goods manufactured												X										
Cost of sales	X	X																			X	
Other income and expenses														X		X	X		X	X	X	
Prepaid expenses and accruals													X		X	X		X		X	X	
Purchases							X									X						
Accounts payable							X	X	X				X	X	X					X	X	X
Loans payable										X										X	X	X
Payroll						X		X	X	X											X	X
Accounts receivable	X												X	X						X		X
Cash			X	X									X	X		X	X	X	X	X	X	X
Profit and loss statements	X									X		X	X	X		X	X	X		X		X
Balance sheet		X	X	X						X				X		X	X	X	X	X	X	

source: Herman C. Heiser, Budgeting, Principles and Practices, The Ronald Press Company, New York, 1959, p. 80, by permission of the publisher.

analysis." In any inventory, he has demonstrated, there are three kinds of items: "A" items are those few major ones that tie up most of the inventory investment. "B" items are of secondary dollar importance. "C" items are the numerous but inexpensive items that make up the minor part of the inventory investment.[1]

Figure 5-2 shows a typical inventory curve obtained by plotting the *number* of parts against the *value* of parts. Expressed in terms of percentages, these relationships are typical not only of inventories but also of almost any other kind of business data you collect.

Note that A items account for 75 per cent of the total inventory value, but comprise in number only 8 per cent of the items carried. B items equal 20 per cent of the value and 25 per cent of the number. C items account for only 5 per cent of the value but add up to 67 per cent of the total number of items carried.

Fig. 5-2. Analysis Shows up the Inventory Spots where Concentrated Control Will Do the Most Good. "A" Items Are the Few Parts that Cost Most, Need Closest Control. "C" Items Are the Parts that Cost Little. "B" Items Are in between

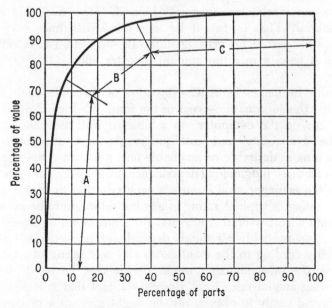

source: H. Ford Dickie, "Six Steps to Better Inventory Management," *Factory*, August, 1953, copyright McGraw-Hill Publications, New York.

To apply this principle to the selection of performance criteria, you can begin by assigning a value rating for each of the possible criteria. Take the example of a company making relatively inexpensive watches that can be sold in drug and variety store outlets. The sales manager may consider a list of 32 possible criteria (Fig. 5-3). But a considered analysis will show him that in actual practice he makes use only of a portion of these. Many he rarely examines, and if he does, he places small reliance upon them.

As a first step in deciding which criteria to request and use, let him assign an A (high), B (medium), or C (low) rating to each according to how reliable and meaningful it has been in the past in guiding his action. Note in this example that he scored fourteen indicators as high-dependence and only eighteen as medium or low. The relatively high frequency of A scores is because instinctively he has already screened out several dozen other possible criteria that night have been included in a more comprehensive list. Now he might stop here and make a plea for each A (and many B) items because he "needs it" or "couldn't manage without it." The trick is not to give in to this reasoning and to force at least two other value judgments before making this decision.

So now our sales manager asks himself, "How available is this information?" That is, can it be assembled with only very little effort on the part of his existing staff, salesmen, etc. (an A rating)? Or will it need a medium amount of extra effort (B)? Or much (C)?

Thirdly, he makes an ABC evaluation of the additional cost of obtaining this information—cost in the form of added clerical help, more time on the computer, an additional staff assistant, etc. In both the "availability" and "cost" judgments, an A rating makes the criteria a more desirable or justifiable one, a C rating the opposite.

With all three judgments (dependence, availability, and cost) declared, the manager now examines each criterion to assign a final priority rating. A triple-A rating of any indicator naturally will shake down into a final, overall A priority. But some of the A *dependence* ratings, and probably all the B dependence ratings, may still be modified according to the *availability* and *cost* rating of each. For instance, the sales manager might decide that he needs item 7, the moving annual sales total, despite the fact that it is somewhat difficult and costly to obtain. But he might give up a pet favorite, the "late report" (item 17) because its value isn't worth its cost

Fig. 5-3. Assigning Priorities to Observational Data in Selecting Vital Performance Criteria

	Dependence (Need)	Availability Time, (ease)	Cost to obtain and report	Priority
Sales $ Volume versus Budget:				
1. This month	A	A	A	A
2. This month last year	A	A	A	A
3. This month for last five years	A	A	A	A
4. Total for year to date	A	A	A	A
5. Total, year to date last year	A	A	B	A
6. Total, year to date for last five years	B	A	B	B
7. Moving annual total this month	A	B	B	A
8. Moving annual total this month last year	B	B	B	B
9. Moving annual total this month last five years	C	B	B	C
Inventory Levels (Dollars):				
10. This month	A	A	A	A
11. This month last year	B	A	A	B
12. This month last five years	C	B	B	B
13. Moving annual total this month	A	B	B	A
Inventory Turnover $\left(\dfrac{\text{Inventory end of month}}{\text{Sales for month}}\right)$:				
14. This month	A	B	B	A
15. Last month	B	B	B	B
16. This month last year	B	B	B	B
Late Report:				
17. Dollar sales volume from closing date	B	C	C	C
Sales Analysis Breakdown (for current month):				
18. Dollar volume in five price ranges	B	B	C	B
19. Dollar volume, men's and women's products	C	B	B	C
20. Dollar volume in ten style lines	C	B	B	C
21. Dollar volume in eight territories	A	B	B	A
22. Dollar volume for seventy-five salesmen	B	B	B	C
Sales Call Reports Analysis (for current month):				
23. Number of sales calls for month	A	A	A	A
24. Number of calls per each of seventy-five salesmen	C	B	C	C
25. Number of new installations per salesmen	C	A	A	C
26. Percentage of stock replacement per territory	A	C	C	B
27. Discontinued installations per salesman	C	A	A	C
Backorders at End of Current Month:				
28. Dollar total	A	B	B	A
29. Number of orders	C	A	A	C
Trade Indexes:				
30. Department stores sales	A	A	A	A
31. Consumer income	B	A	A	B
32. Bank deposits	C	A	A	C

Dependence: How much do you depend upon this figure? A—A lot. B—Some. C—Very little.

Availability: How much additional effort is needed to get this information? A—Very little. B—Some. C—A lot.

Cost: How much additional clerical help, etc. is needed to get this information? A—Very little. B—Some. C—A lot.

and difficulty. And while items 25 and 27 are easy and cheap to obtain, their dependence value is so small as to obviate their worth in building up a control report.

It may appear that going through this process is just a rigmarole to make difficult what to many managers comes naturally. Perhaps. But the desirability of systematically assembling and selecting the data upon which your decisions will depend can't be overemphasized. Furthermore, it prevents accountants, controllers, auditors, etc., from arbitrarily—albeit innocently—making this decision for you.

Tables of criteria from which to select your decision-making controls abound (see Part 3), but their applicability to your business, your organization, and your inclinations will vary. For example, suppose the sales manager in our illustration wasn't selling inexpensive watches to retail consumers. Suppose, instead, that he were selling heavy compressors to fewer than 5,000 manufacturing companies. Immediately we can see that many of the items rated A in the charts would fall to B or C for him. Conversely, he might, for instance, place a high dependence rating upon other criteria (not considered by the watch company sales manager) such as delivery-delay periods, sales orders received versus sales bids made, sales progress reports, in-process (rather than final) inventories, and indexes such as factory production and number of new orders for machinery.

Setting Exception Indicators

A company treasurer walks urgently into the president's office. "We better begin trimming inventories right away," he says. "Our cash balance has been declining steadily for three weeks now." He hands the president a sheaf of reports. The president studies them for a minute or two, then hands them back to the treasurer. "I think we can sit tight for a couple of more weeks, Charlie. It would be a mistake to cut back on production when there's such a good chance we'll need that stock desperately later on. But if this trend continues into March, take whatever steps you need to stabilize our cash position."

This anonymous company president remained calm and collected under pressure because he had already decided what he would do in this situation. He had faced up to this decision the previous

November, when he drew up his projections for the coming year. He had used a technique of management by exception to predetermine his course of action.

The gist of this technique is that for every projected goal (criteria of performance versus time) you must also establish limits of tolerance. In its simplest form, an executive predecides, for example, that he can—and will—tolerate for four weeks an inventory 5 per cent over projected levels (specifically in the spring, just before summer sales accelerate). An inventory versus time figure beyond this becomes an "exception indicator." When inventories exceed 5 per cent for four weeks running at that time of year, he will automatically delegate corrective authority to his production-control manager, for instance. If this corrective action is not effective within another predetermined time limit (or if inventories build, say, beyond 7 per cent of expected) the president will again automatically, place the problem in the hands of the executive vice-president—who has also been given the necessary authority to correlate production cutbacks with intensified sales efforts. Finally, if the problem persists or intensifies—either in degree of variation from normal or in its time dimension—the president himself will step in. In other words, up to a certain preestablished tolerance threshold, no action is indicated. But from that level to the next preestablished tolerance level, the action responsibility will automatically fall into the hands of a preselected individual. In this manner, successive exception-indicator levels are chosen to match (1) the degree of tolerated variation from expected performance to (2) the capabilities of the executive from whom action will be expected.

Such preestablished exception indicators help a key executive to decide in advance of crisis which problems may be delegated and which problems will require his personal attention. He can also decide beforehand to whom the problem will be delegated at each increasing step of difficulty. And, when a problem is anticipated to be of sufficient stature to warrant it, he can map out in advance various alternative plans of action.

So in the selection-making phase of the practice of management by exception, there are four prime elements to be considered and planned for: (1) the degree of variation from projected performance, (2) the duration of the variation, (3) the level of authority and responsibility necessary to deal with the problem defined by observing the previous two, and (4) the predetermination of the course(s) of action to be taken—or reviewed—whenever an exception indicator lights up.

Determining the Tolerable Degree and Duration. Decisions regarding (1) how much of a variation from normal (your operation) can stand and (2) how long you can stand it may be based upon past experience, statistical analysis, and calculated judgment. Many of industry's rules of thumb are based upon irrefutable historical fact. If men's summer sport shirts, for instance, have not been cleared from a department store's shelves by July 1st, the buyer knows he has cause for worry. Experience with seasonal wear has proved this to him. And if the shirts are still on the shelf in great number by July 15th, he knows that he will have only a week or two more to move them without drastic price reductions. If they remain after August 1st, chances are the veteran buyer will place ads in the daily newspaper announcing a 40 per cent price slash on men's summer shirts. Similar exception indicators exist in almost all businesses. They are derived from either formal or informal accumulation of experience.

When this past experience can be reduced to numbers—and sufficient data have been accumulated—then statistics can be brought into play. Using a statistical technique (see page 135), the standard—or expected—deviation can be calculated. This figure helps a manager to identify with a great deal of certainty those variations from standard that are truly exceptional rather than to be misled by those that are merely random.

Many companies establish only two guides: (1) standard or satisfactory performance levels and (2) unsatisfactory performance levels. Figure 5-4 illustrates what these two bench marks might look like for a typical manufacturing company.

But the manager, preferably at the time he makes his prognostications and forecasts, must add another ingredient to that which he has learned from historical data and the advice he receives from statistics. In presetting the exception-indicator ranges, he must also integrate with these two his own personal knowledge—knowledge based upon observations, inclinations, and hunches of his own. Frivolous prejudices are to be avoided, of course. But the executive is at least partially wrong if he abandons the exception-indicator level-setting task to arithmetic. In any event, past data usually in-

Fig. 5-4. Example of Financial Bench Marks for Action
for a Typical Manufacturing Company

Factor	Problem indicated	Usually satisfactory
Net profit after taxes on net worth............	Under 8%	12 to 15%
Net profit after taxes on net sales.............	Under 4%	4 to 6%
Net sales per dollar of net worth..............	Under 2	2 to 4
Net sales per dollar of total assets............	Under 1.25	1.5 to 2
Cost of sales per dollar of inventory...........	Under 4	5 to 8
Net sales per dollar of depreciated fixed assets..	Under 3	3.5 to 5.0
Current assets to current liabilities...........	Less than 2 to 1	2 to 1
Cash and receivables to current liabilities......	Less than 1 to 1	1 to 1
Cash and equivalent to current liabilities.......	Less than 0.6 to 1	0.75 to 1
Funded debt to net working capital...........	Over 80%	40 to 60%
Inventories to net working capital.............	Over 85%	60 to 80%
Net fixed assets to net worth.................	Over 60%	30 to 50%
Current liabilities to net worth...............	Over 50%	30 to 40%
Current and long term liabilities to net worth...	Over 90%	50 to 70%
Reserve for depreciation to original cost of fixed assets.................................	Over 60%	45 to 55%
Break-even point (per cent of capacity)........	Over 90%	50 to 75%
Average collection period....................	Over 40 days	20 to 40 days

source: H. B. Maynard (ed.) *Top Management Handbook*, McGraw-Hill Book Company, New York, 1960, p. 410.

clude many imponderables which introduce options and alternatives that must be reconciled by executive decision making.

Delegation: Matching Problems with People

Generally speaking, the greater the magnitude of the exception indicator, the more difficult the problem it uncovers. Consequently, it appears logical to assign higher-ranking exception-indicator problems to executives with proportionately higher authorities and responsibilities. In other words, a first-level indicator would be assumed to be within the scope of foreman or department manager, a second-level indicator within that of a division chief, and a third-level indicator that of the top executive.

However, in thinking through this rationale, it is wise to consider the *nature* of the problem as well as its intensity. Is it one, for instance, that could be better handled by a staff man than by a line manager? Is it part of a newly introduced program for which little past experience exists? (If so, perhaps even a low-magnitude problem should receive the early attention of a highly placed official.) Or is the problem one that, while minor, will ripple through the entire organization rather than just nicking a single segment? (If so, then it might best be brought before a committee of managers who can work out solutions that are mutually beneficial.)

Another approach would be for the higher-level executive to retain the action prerogative in *any* event, but to use the exception indicator to automatically call for study, advice, and recommendations from preselected subordinates—either line or staff.

Another factor to consider is the personality and work habits of each executive. Some middle- and lower-level managers are best qualified to coordinate and motivate in routine, relatively trouble-free situations. Problem solving under pressure is not their forte. Conversely, there are others at all levels who are at their best only under pressure. It would help, then, to identify those problems that will call for the most vigorous action under pressures of time and to point them toward those executives whose visceral makeup is most suited to them.

Looking at the system from an individual point of view, each executive must set up his exception-indicator screen in such a way that he is gainfully employed to the best of his particular qualifications—but is not overwhelmed by a multitude of problems that can better be handled by his subordinates and associates.

Preplanning Action Alternatives

Most of the great military plans of history were worked out years in advance of the war in which they were used. Each of those battle plans was drawn up only after considerable analysis of the anticipated situations and a forecasting of the various ways in which the vagaries of battle would cause them to unfold. Consequently, World War I had its two Von Schlieffen plans, the Battle of Bataan its Red and Orange plans, and the Battle of France its Operation Overlord and Operation Anvil. These plans were thought through in advance in great detail and extended downward from supreme headquarters through the various levels of command. And contrary to what might be supposed by laymen, the lower the echelon of command, the more numerous the alternatives and the greater the opportunity for independent action. In managing by exception, management, too, must have ready one or more alternative modes of action.

The noted multimillionaire oil financier J. Paul Getty, speaking of business adversities, says, "All factors in the situation must be examined with meticulous care. Every possible course of action must be weighed. All available resources—cerebral as well as financial, creative as well as practical—must be marshaled. Countermoves must be planned with the greatest care and in the greatest detail —yet with allowances for alternative courses in the event unforeseen obstacles are uncovered." [2]

Alternative Courses for Control Action. Let's take a relatively simple problem: control of maintenance cost per unit of output in a manufacturing plant. In preplanning courses of action, management is aware of several constants: Maintenance costs tend to have a strong "fixed" quality when related to buildings, grounds, and facilities upkeep; maintenance costs of production machinery are directly related to time (usage); maintenance costs can be manipulated rather easily by deferring routine upkeep—in effect taking a chance that important machinery won't break down or the roof won't leak; and maintenance costs are on the rise owing to the increasing complexity of new machinery.

At the first threshold of critical maintenance deviation, management might leave the responsibility for bringing costs back into line in the hands of the maintenance manager. And he might anticipate any of the following alternative plans of action: (1) cut out overtime arbitrarily, (2) transfer maintenance workers to a production department, and (3) assign excess maintenance workers to capitalized construction projects so that their time would not appear as an operating cost.

In the first alternative, the maintenance manager will have to draw up preventive maintenance schedules in conjunction with production departments so that machinery is available for inspection and repair on weekdays. In the second alternative, he will have to prearrange with personnel, production, and perhaps the union a plan for transfer that conforms to existing seniority agreements and company practices. In the third alternative, the maintenance manager will have to backlog such construction projects in advance so that they are available when needed.

Now suppose these maintenance costs rise (owing to a further cut in plant output) to the next exception-indicator level. This, according to plan, would now place the problem squarely in the lap of the works manager. In forecasting this kind of problem, he may calculate that short-term deferred maintenance is the lesser of evils and plan a layoff to cut down this overhead. Or he may feel that maintenance is the one function that cannot be penalized by rising costs and decide to permit this item to continue out of control. Or he may lay out a plan whereby he will allow attrition to deplete the excess manpower in the maintenance force and also resist enlarging the force in the future by contracting out excess work.

Now suppose the works manager chose the course of permitting maintenance costs to remain out of control, and this degree of exception eventually put the problem up to the executive vice-president, also according to plan. This executive will have saved himself a lot of anxiety if he has previously reviewed this possibility and said, in effect, "I will permit this cost to stay out of line *unless* it affects (1) our cash position, (2) money available for extra sales effort, or (3) our research program. If any of these three occur, I'll order *first* a slash in spare parts inventory, and *second* a general cutback in employment."

This example demonstrates typical, logical, and fairly easily derived courses of action. They relieve each level of management from performing routine research and analysis under pressure of time. They also permit an advanced basis from which to develop fresh ideas if and when the problem actually arises.

Alternative Courses for Creative Action. Now let's take a more difficult case—one which offers an opportunity for exploitation rather than control. While the figures here have been altered to conceal the identity of the company, the incident is true.

The sale of a new-model auto was projected in August to sell at the rate of 10,000 per month by January of the following year. When January arrived, the model was doing very well indeed. It was selling at the rate of 14,000 per month and giving no indication of topping out. Faced with this news, the general sales manager checked his more optimistic alternatives chosen the previous August. These were (1) step up selling efforts and continue to back-order until this plan is vetoed in Detroit, (2) use this opportunity to develop the sales of new dealers while holding older dealers in check, (3) shift the sales effort to other models in the line and discourage sales of the "hot" model.

By February, however, this booming trend continued and sales rose to 15,000 per month, which would outstrip factory production for the year. This brought the executive vice-president into the picture. His preplanned choices included (1) reduce sales expenditures in order to increase immediate net profit, (2) relax quality control in order to step up factory output, (3) institute more subcontracting and use of marginal manufacturing facilities, and (4) cut back on advertising expenditures for the new model and transfer funds to promote older models.

The trend persisted, however, and the company president had to take over. He called together his board for advice regarding the following alternatives:

1. Authorize lease or purchase of new manufacturing facilities and continue to press for sales, hoping that production will catch up before year's end

2. Offer discounts on other models while "loading" the hot model with extras that would boost income

3. Set in action a plan for exploiting this model next year rather than this year

4. Maintain a conservative position, putting a check on back-ordering and swinging production facilities from old models to new

Upon the board's advice, the president selected alternative number three, and it turned out to be a good choice. Customer interest in the model was sustained, and with proper time allotted, an effective, coordinated plan of production and marketing was worked out.

In the first example, management by exception invited negative, or control, attention. In this second example, it offered management an opportunity for positive action and to move ahead.

The Place for Policy

Establishing exception indicators and preplanning for action can also be looked at another way. They can be described as the process in which policy is crystallized and procedures mapped out. A company's policy may be "to encourage the greatest freedom of judgment at every level of management." Exception indicators pin down this ideal to firm commitments. Similarly, a company may declare its policy as one that "offers the highest-quality product commensurate with price." An exception indicator quantifies this by calling for attention when quality digresses too far from standard, and at the same time it prescribes an approach to be followed in bringing the variance back into line. The military parallel would be likening this process to the linking of strategy to tactics.

Centralized versus Decentralized Controls. One of the key decisions to be made when establishing policy is the extent to which control will be centralized or decentralized. Centralized control tends to provide greater assurance that top management goals will be achieved. Decentralized controls—especially when they apply broadly to profit responsibility—present four difficult problems. First, they are costly to administer. Second, they require a tighter, more complex information system. Third, they depend upon a more highly qualified middle management staff. Finally, there is always the danger that the lower-echelon managers will not be motivated, or act, in the best interests of the company.

Weighed against these disadvantages are the greater resilience, balance, and diversity that a decentralized system can develop and maintain. Ralph J. Cordiner, former chairman of General Electric, says, "I am a strong believer in decentralization, and it is my conviction that the natural aggregate of many individually sound decisions made as nearly as possible to the point where action is needed, will be better for the business, the customer, and the public than centrally planned and controlled decisions." [3]

Alfred P. Sloan, Jr., says, "In 1921 I started with the principle that 'a decentralized organization is the only one that will develop the talent necessary to meet the corporation's problems.'" [4]

America's "Iron Commander" of World War I, General John J. Pershing, famed for his autocratic personality, nevertheless broke the back of the German offense with what he called "open" warfare. He described it this way: "Open warfare is marked by . . . irregularity of formations . . . comparatively little regulation of space and time by higher commanders . . . the greatest possible use of the infantry's firepower to enable it to get forward . . . variable distances and intervals between units and individuals . . .

brief orders and the greatest possible use of individual initiative by all troops engaged in action." [5]

The point is that at this stage of policy-procedure determination, it would be wishful thinking to believe that the management-by-exception process will operate automatically. In fact, whenever push-button thinking creeps in, the system is at its weakest. Management by exception provides a framework in which judgment can be applied most systematically, with the least emotional involvement, in the greatest haste, and with the least dependence upon good fortune to decide a company's destiny. Stated another way, the more policy, the less original decision-action brainwork. But the more policy, the fewer crises, the smoother and less costly the operation.

References

1. H. Ford Dickie, "Six Steps to Better Inventory Management," *Factory*, August, 1953.
2. J. Paul Getty, "The Businessman at Bay," *Playboy*, September, 1963, p. 124.
3. Ralph J. Cordiner, "The Nature of the Work of the Chief Executive," paper presented to CIOS, New York, September, 1963.
4. Alfred P. Sloan, Jr., "My Years with General Motors: Our Strategy Works Out to a T—and the Model T Goes Under," *Fortune*, November, 1963, p. 167.
5. Laurence Stallings, *The Dough Boys*, Harper & Row, Publishers, Incorporated, New York, 1963, pp. 125–126.

Chapter 6

THE OBSERVATION PHASE

*In Which You Periodically Observe and Measure the
Current Condition of Critical Performance Indicators*

In 1962, Frank S. Capon, vice-president of Du Pont of Canada, reorganized his information reporting and control system. He set up three new and independent departments:

1. *Finance and accounting*—to provide bookkeeping and cost records for the company as a whole

2. *Planning and control*—to coordinate information for both corporate and division managers

3. *Data processing*—to integrate the mechanical, clerical functions of both the accounting and control departments

Du Pont's planning and control department is chiefly concerned with day-to-day operations. Its primary goal is to reduce the amount of detail in reports to successive management levels. This, in Capon's words, "allows us to be concerned only with deviations from agreed plans and to use the management by exception principle." [1]

Instead of stressing a *system* to support management by exception activities, Henry Blackstone, president of Servo Corporation of America, puts much of his faith in an executive's ability to observe and compare on his own. In what he calls "managing by differences," Blackstone acknowledges the need for a formal measuring, observing, and reporting system. He says:

108

Reliable information is required for every step in the managing process. First it is used to establish objectives. Second, it is used to direct the attainment of these objectives. Third, to complete the cycle, it is used to measure results.

But he also likens the executive role in this process to a computer:

In our modern world of printing and data processing, there is a freight-car load of chaff for each single kernel of valuable and usable information. The successful executive must have a highly developed, fast-sorting and weighing faculty to bypass tons of chaff. He must have a conceptual and linking capability to perceive and visualize the association of ideas which interrelate data and information into a clear and distinct pattern. One happy payoff (for such a man) is that eventually the islands of data and information begin to fit together to form new continents of broad patterns and basic philosophies.[2]

Both Du Pont of Canada's highly sophisticated information-handling arrangement and Blackstone's reliance on the personal factor typify modern trends in managing by exception. The mass of data that must be transformed to meaningful information is becoming increasingly unwieldy. Management must depend upon complex, ultrafast systems to collect, sift, and rationalize it. But on the other hand, management has long since come to the conclusion that the best system in the world must be supplemented by the keen perception and analytical mind of its key executives.

Observing Performance and Gathering Data

Observation and measurement are nearly synonymous. Both functions employ sensing devices—human senses in the former and mechanical or electronic sensors in the latter—to find out what machinery, money, materials, or men are doing or have done. While there is a tendency to refer to the human activity as observation and the mechanical function as measurement, the distinction is neither clear-cut nor necessary.

Automatic Observation. In recent years, the development of mechanical sensing devices (sensors) has broadened the scope of and speeded up the management by exception process. X rays permit nondestructive testing (measurement) of steel, on-line chemical analysis, and volume control of high-speed canning and bottling lines. X-ray emission gages are capable of analyzing six elements simultaneously in liquids, slurries, and powders. Gas and liquid flow can now be accurately measured by a weighing process. Electronic "leak detectors" can "sniff" critical leaks in such "closed" operations as the manufacture of aerosol products.

Honeywell, for example, has developed a vertical scale indicator unit for installation in process control centers. These 3- by 9-inch units provide continuous measurement of temperature, pressure, valve positions, and any number of process variables. Each indicator unit has the control index (the expected or standard position) set at a fixed centerline on the chart. When a number of indicators are mounted in a row, these center-line indicators form a highly visible, optically continuous "clothesline" for an operator to watch. When a variable deviates from a central point, a vivid orange pointer appears above or below the fixed set-point line of indicators. A quick glance shows the operator which variables are off the control point. He doesn't have to stop and study each indicator to observe when an exception is occurring.[3]

General Electric has developed an electronic hotbox detector which inspects wheel bearings of railroad trains as they move past it along the track. The Southern Railway uses such detectors to inspect passing trains along its entire right of way. All data gathered are transmitted automatically to a central observation facility in Atlanta. From there, direct radio communication to the train warns an engineer of developing trouble.

Eastman Kodak Company uses speed, temperature, and timing devices to measure machine performance for maintenance purposes. By connecting these sensors to records, plant management is able to detect breakdowns promptly and to more accurately determine the causes of failures.[4]

More and more companies are using some sort of automatic reporting device to relay operating information from shop or plant to a data-gathering center. One such device (Telecontrol) gives an almost instantaneous comparison between actual and standard times to perform a task. It signals delays for immediate correction. And it will even print out cards that summarize and price a job at any point in the work sequence. In a second type of reporting mechanism, the operator punches in production data from a collecting station on the shop floor.

An old standby for relaying information is the pneumatic tube, still widely used today. Other plants relay information by telephone, either directly to an operator or to a tape recorder. Some companies use two-way private-channel radio to transmit information from sales people, field repairmen, and truck operators. Others use closed-circuit television to monitor all kinds of operations, to serve as a substitute for watchmen, and to transmit data. In an unusual demonstration of the use of closed-circuit television during the 1962 season, the Dallas Texans of the American Football League played back an instantaneous TV tape recording for examination by the team's coach after each play. Score in that game? Dallas Texans 41, Buffalo Bills 0.

Union Resistance. Inevitably, in this trend toward automatic observation, labor unions must protest. A Telecontrol system had not long been installed at Cutler-Hammer's Milwaukee plant before management was confronted by an officer of I.A.M. Lodge 1061. He charged that workers were saddled with an "electronic spy system" and demanded 21 safeguards to protect workers from abuse. However, an AFL-CIO spokesman observed that worker opposition to electronic production-monitoring devices was the exception rather than the rule. He offered some sound advice: "If the workers believe the measuring or control devices will interfere with their own control over incentive works systems, they're pretty certain to object. But if labor-management relations are favorable and the devices have been shown to reflect management's legitimate interest in getting information that will not hurt working conditions, then there's no problem." [5]

The fact is that most workers like such automatic measuring devices. First, such controls help stabilize employment by permitting better planning of labor requirements. Secondly, records tend to be more accurate than when the foreman or a shop clerk maintains them. Thirdly, the worker doesn't have to go hunting for a foreman when trouble occurs on his job. A flip of a switch summons him. This speed assures the worker of full credit for his downtime since the foreman can acknowledge the interruption automatically by inserting a master key in the worker's control box.

Reliability of Observers

In these days of electronic data processing, it is a temptation to dwell too long on the infallibility of the system and to understate the importance of the individual. Harold Smiddy, formerly vice-president of the General Electric Company and later dean of the

Academy of Management Sciences, warns that such preoccupation with systems often stems from managers whose preference is for top-down command decisions. Noting that such a viewpoint runs counter to much of our latter-day research in human relationships, Smiddy observes, "A precisely opposite approach is equally possible, namely to carry out research to produce organizing, managing, and information-system principles which, while employing the most advanced concepts of information technology, can be used to avoid centralized planning and decision-making, and can consequently be used to get the planning and deciding done directly at the work place to an ever increasing degree." [6]

Captain Metcalfe, perhaps anticipating the trend toward decentralized observation and data transmission, cast some doubts on the practicality of a bottom-up approach. Speaking eighty years ago, he said:

> Foremen, as a class, are necessarily among the most intelligent of men and are quick as any to appreciate the advantages of a good tool. Direct methods suit them best; they like to work as a dog digs a hole, disposing immediately of present necessities and throwing what they have accomplished behind them, out of sight and mind. They do better and more trustworthy work when not required to record their own performances, and are all the better able to appreciate the efforts of others who can classify and arrange their results for future reference. [7]

Apparently there are at least two viewpoints regarding the wisdom of letting lower-echelon people get into the observe-compare-report act. A sampling of some actual cases may help you to develop your own point of view. Consider these three examples involving salesmen, foremen, and rank and file workers:

Salesmen. International Business Machines Corporation is reluctant to ask salesmen—and field sales managers—to become too deeply involved in the observation process. Herbert W. Keith, director of IBM's marketing services, says, "The field sales manager is the key figure in this whole reporting system. He is close enough to the market to know what kind of information the salesman can get and close enough to management to know what kind of information it needs. But there are no very good yardsticks to tell us how good a job the field sales manager is doing in keeping management accurately informed." Mr. Keith reports that the attitude of sales people to reports is typified by such comments as, "It's just one more administrative job that keeps me tied to my desk"; "It keeps me from doing the number one job I am paid to do, which is to manage salesmen and meet quotas"; "Headquarters is always checking up on the field. If they would just let us alone we would have more time for selling"; "If I call the shots as I see them and tell them what I hear, they will tag me as a negative thinker"; "I always present the rosiest picture to the people upstairs."

In view of these attitudes and in order to be realistic in its demands for information from the field, Mr. Keith advises management to examine its requests critically. He suggests you ask these questions:

1. Is the information really necessary?

2. Is there a better source for this information? Might we get it more readily through some "pick and shovel" research in government reports? Would we be better off to call in a consultant?

3. How quickly do we really need the information? Will it seem as urgent tomorrow as we think it is today?

4. How frequently shall we require the report? Is it to be a one-time request, or must we have it for periodic check-ups?

5. Are we making the reporting job as easy as we can by minimizing the amount of paperwork involved? [8]

Foremen. In most plants timekeeping has been centralized for years. Arthur Young & Company, however, cites an interesting example to show that centralized timekeeping doesn't always jibe with the need to help foremen control labor costs. In this 1,000-man plant, many of the foremen's duties in the area of planning and control had been turned over to leadmen, timekeepers, and department clerks. To cut costs, the company set up a centralized call-in recording unit in the office. Surprisingly, the result was an increase in costs. What was wrong? The central timekeeping unit issued daily reports on each labor operation that showed a significant variance. Good managing by exception? Apparently, but it was not quite good enough. Here's why. The reports were too informal and were incomplete in terms of total departmental performance. Top management got only a monthly report comparing actual dollar cost and standards for each labor operation. Information on them was always ancient history. The reports were massive and showed far too much detail. Labor cost was shown in dollars only, not in hours.

To overcome this situation, the company set up a procedure that refocused the measurement responsibility on the foremen. Now each foreman personally issues all work assignments for his crew.

He's responsible for planning and scheduling their work in advance. Each time an assignment is completed, the foreman computes the actual labor cost in hours and compares this with the standard. Right then and there he investigates any significant variance. He prepares a daily summary showing total variance from standard for each worker and for his department as a whole.

Under this new system, the plant superintendent and top management receive a weekly summary report for each department, showing actual, standard, and variance hours for direct labor and actual indirect-labor hours by category. "No longer burdened with volumes of meaningless details on individual labor operations," says the Arthur D. Young Co., "they can finally manage by exception." As a result, improvements were impressive. Plant-wide efficiency went up to 20 per cent. Overall costs went down $40,000 a year. Paperwork volume was cut 70 per cent, and nine clerical jobs were eliminated.[9]

Rank and File Employees. At Collins Radio Company, management felt it would be too difficult and costly to set standards for a number of indirect jobs. But it was persuaded to try to accomplish this objective by letting workers set their own standards. Using a "participative" approach, employees now perform three essential steps in setting standards. First, they describe in step-by-step fashion the work elements they perform and estimate their frequency— daily, weekly, or monthly. Next, utilizing an hourly recording sheet prepared by the standards section, employees tally the number of occurrences of each element during the day. (The standards department then computes the time allowances for each element, using a combination of stopwatch times, predetermined time standards, and worker estimates of time taken.) Finally, the employee keeps a daily record of the number of times he performs each of the standard elements so that he can compute his earned time credits at the end of the day. His records are then posted by the standards department to a master indirect-labor-utilization report for management. This program, initiated in a 9,000-man plant, covers indirect jobs in manufacturing, marketing, service, purchasing, sales, quality control, and product development. Savings in indirect labor topped $1 million in 1961.[10]

Managers as Observers. When it comes to making observations in support of management by exception, each manager has the opportunity to be his own best friend. He can accept what the information-handling system delivers to him as being representative, or he can supplement the system by seeing for himself at first hand.

Two incidents that took place in the Pacific during World War II and required on-the-spot observations by an important military leader to clarify a situation come to mind. The first incident took place just before the fall of Singapore, too late to save what was supposed to be an island fortress. For years the British had believed Singapore to be impregnable. And it was—from the sea, where traditionally the enemy was expected. It was woefully weak, however, when attacked from the north, by land. The vital weakness lay in the inability of the island's heavy guns to reverse direction and fire at Japanese troops advancing down the Malay Peninsula. What is incredible in retrospect is that all Britain, including its military chiefs and Winston Churchill, was blissfully unaware of this fateful flaw. It was not until General Sir Archibald Wavell was appointed supreme commander of the Southwest Pacific area that the general himself, on a last minute inspection of the island's preparedness, discovered that Singapore had no landward defenses. Wavell cabled Churchill immediately. Churchill berated his chiefs of staff as follows:

> I must admit to being staggered by Wavell's telegram of the 16th of January. . . . It never occurred to me for a moment that the gorge of the fortress of Singapore, with its splendid moat half a mile to a mile wide, was not entirely fortified against an attack from the northward. . . . How is it that none of you pointed this out to me at any time when these matters have been under discussion? More especially, this should have been done because . . . I have repeatedly relied upon this defense of Singapore against a formal siege.

Churchill's recognition of an inadequate reporting system was too late to save the island. The British abandoned the Malay Peninsula on January 23 and surrendered Singapore to the Japanese land troops on February 14.[11]

The second incident involved American troops, who, because of intensive top-level observation, turned a rout into a great moral victory.

When Japanese troops invaded the Philippine Islands in 1941, American defense forces made military history by their stubborn holding action on the Bataan Peninsula. General Douglas MacArthur directed this heroic defense from his stronghold in the Malinta Tunnel on Corregidor. He was able to maintain an objective viewpoint far from the bitter jungle fighting because he was following a long-established plan of defense of the Philippines known as War Plan Orange–3. WPO-3 was a classic example of military planning —with all the logistics and alternative moves mapped out years ahead of time. However, the strategy would not have worked out so successfully if it weren't for the efforts of MacArthur's second in command, General Jonathan Wainwright. Wainwright was a firm believer in the need for firsthand observation by the military commander himself of the ebb and flow of battle. In the Bataan holding action, Wainwright's on-the-site observation and interpretation of the tactical situation enabled MacArthur to modify his preestablished plans to take advantage of unexpected opportunities or to recover from unforeseen disasters.

Decision making for management by exception depends upon a similar combination of (1) alternative preplanned decisions and (2) up-to-the-minute action based upon intimate observation and analysis of the unfolding business situation.

Your Personal Observations

Henry Blackstone, the executive who likens the company president's job to that of a human computer, says he receives his information from two sources—internal and external. Information from the first source flows upward toward him from his own organization; the second kind flows into his organization from the outside. The intelligent executive, Blackstone insists, must not be passive in this process. He must actively make many of the observations himself. There are, for example, more than a dozen ways you can improve your own observational powers:

1. *Beware of the halo bias.* This its the danger that arises from permitting your emotions to prevail over cold-headed logic. Literally, you see in a situation what you want to see. You've launched a pet project, for instance, that never gets off the ground. But you keep reading favorable signs into what are actually discouraging results. Or conversely, you overemphasize the importance of a few negative results in a program that hasn't won your support. That's one of the big advantages of putting a numerical value on any kind of observation; it's hard to argue that 2 plus 2 equals anything but 5.

2. *Interview for facts.* Rare is the organization that can afford

enough data on any single problem area. The best you can expect is that the information system will provide you with recognizable danger signals. As a result, digging up detailed facts will often be up to you. Logically, a good way to obtain such follow-up information is to interview the specialists or administrators closest to the problem. They are most likely to provide you with additional details or to reveal clues about what's wrong. Sometimes they will be able to put their fingers quickly on a key fact. But more often such people stand too close to the cloth to see the pattern.

Interrogation can be a nasty word—and it may get little valuable information for you if you act like a district attorney. A better approach is to fill in your subordinate with the facts that seem to indicate an exception. Then turn him loose on the subject with minimum interruption from you. He may seem to wander and waste time, but if you give him a chance to express himself without criticizing him or cutting him off, he's more likely to turn up some useful data or an opinion for you. And, of course, if he does come through—and *he* appears to be the one at fault for the variation—you'll want to be tactful in your criticism. If you jump down his throat, he won't be a good source of facts the next time around.

3. *Listen for latent facts.* One study shows that while most management people spend 45 per cent of their time listening, they actually *hear* only 25 per cent of what has been said. This is because we have a tendency to "phase out" of a conversation as we begin to form our next thoughts in reply, or while we reflect upon what we have just heard. Your ear *will* become muscle-bound if it operates nearly half of your waking hours filtering the deluge of sound that assaults it. But you can actually sharpen your perceptivity by purposely alternating listening with talking. The principle is somewhat similar to that of a tennis game in which one player strokes the ball and then carefully observes how his opponent returns it. By asking a question, by contradicting, by furnishing a direct reply, your ear will be better attuned to perceive what the speaker says. On his return of the conversational ball, you can look beneath the surface of his reply to assess his true meaning and the worth of what he says. Listen, for instance, to his choice of words, his confidence or aggressiveness, his objectivity or prejudices. These reveal the emotional content of his speech that words alone do not betray.

4. *Observe to fill in gaps.* Hard-to-measure qualities, like the state

of morale, rarely show up with any comprehensiveness on exception reports. A few companies do insist that key executives follow the trend of accidents, absences, grievances, and the like. This is helpful and should be done more often. But these measures are only symptoms of more serious conditions that lend themselves less easily to measurement. Consequently, the executive who has set as an objective a favorable state of organizational morale will need to provide most of his own measurements. These are the measurements he will make with his own eyes and ears as he talks with all kinds of people—not just in his office or in the executive dining room, but also in the men's room, out on the production floor, and at recreational activities.

5. *Beware of "selective inattention."* That's the psychiatrist's term for a fascinating device that the mentally ill—and many normal people—employ. These people fail to hear or observe things that are painful, inconvenient, or too strongly challenging to them. The principle of deception is exactly the same as in a delusion except that in the case of selective inattention, the alternative is provided from among competitive fragments of reality rather than by the subject's imagination.

6. *Try your own hand.* When an exception report shows that trouble is brewing, say in the production scheduling department when too many orders are being shipped short, spend an hour or two actually working with the production expediter. By performing the same duties, facing the same problem, and listening to the same excuses from purchasing or from manufacturing, you may be able to discover important facts that do not show up in the variance report.

7. *Sample routine paper work.* Too much objectivity can be a dangerous thing. That is, an overdependence upon reports prepared by your own staff would represent a naïveté on your part. While a report occasionally will be constructed to mislead you deliberately, the real danger lies in abstract reports failing to give you the feel of the situation. From time to time it's good practice to look personally at original documents as they flow through your organization. Check a work order, for instance, to see how accurately it's prepared. Glance down a page of ledger entries. Open the morning mail. Or pick a particular order at random and follow its flow through the paper network in your organization. Such action on your part demonstrates to your staff that you respect detail and tends to

keep them on their toes. And it will surely give you a more intimate grasp of your operations.

8. *Make calls with salesmen.* Whether you are a sales manager, a supervisor of product design, or a manufacturing superintendent, you'll benefit from getting firsthand customer reactions. Watching your salesmen in action will tell you whether or not they are stressing features you feel are important. You can get an idea of how hard they are selling price advantage, product quality, or fast deliveries. You may find that they place emphasis on characteristics different from the ones you stress when setting budgets or inspection standards. Customer resistance to your products, requests for extras like special engineering service, custom finishing, and the like can also be checked against in-company standards.

9. *Participate in professional meetings.* Whether you sit on the dais or in the audience, there's much to be learned at professional conferences about what's going on in management circles. If you accept a speaking engagement, you'll force yourself to get a fresh grasp on some phase of your activities. If you're a member of the listening audience, you'll inevitably expose yourself to qualified people who see things differently from the way you do. Talking with participants at lunchtime or during breaks between sessions will also give you a chance to tune up your observational powers. You are almost certain to return to your own operation with greater objectivity toward your own operations.

10. *Attend trade shows.* Few things are more factual than the hardware of your industry. While knowledge of other elements, such as market conditions and competitive activity, is essential, new products are literally something an executive can get his hands on. At a show, not only can you learn much about product trends in your own field, but you can also get an idea of process developments by the nature of the production machinery offered to your industry.

11. *Make off-the-cuff inspections.* Unless you frequently visit the work place of your subordinates, your office in mahogany row will subtly be cut off from the realities of the operations you're responsible for. Regular inspections, announced in advance and accompanied by a retinue of associates, will not break down this barrier for you. Random surprise visits will tell you a more accurate story of day-to-day conditions. Informality, modified by a sincere desire to understand operating problems, should be your attitude—not that of snooping, spying, or checking up.

12. *Sit in on group meetings at your own plant.* If you've delegated a responsibility to a committee, you won't want to interfere with their prerogatives. But attending an occasional session will give you a chance to observe the trend of their thinking. You'll be able to sense where their direction is confused and where they are at odds with objectives already set. Before exceptions turn up on reports, you may be able to anticipate them and be prepared to deal with them expeditiously. Or your observations may lead you to revise present objectives immediately and to put a crash program into effect to achieve them.

13. *Modulate your reading.* "Modulation" is a word used by Mr. Blackstone to indicate the value of selectivity in business reading as opposed to the attainment of mere reading speed. Some documents require intense concentration, careful study, and rereading in order to be fully understood. Others require only a rapid scanning to get the gist. But most written materials that cross an executive's desk aren't worth any more of his attention than is needed to determine they are insignificant.

14. *Maintain objectivity.* General Somervell, when he was president of the Koppers Company, regularly used to remove himself from everything but emergency contact with the corporation's executives. He would remain in his home, sometimes for a full week, studying the month-end control report. Far away from the distraction of minor disturbances and the influence of personalities, he would gain the perspective he needed for reliable and objective judgments. While few managers would be permitted to indulge in this practice, the principle is a sound one. It can certainly be followed to some degree. You can gain objectivity by finding a few hours' seclusion in a library, a long drive to work, a train ride, or some other reasonable escape to solitude.

References

1. "The Information Revolution," *Plant Administration & Engineering*, December, 1962, page 30.
2. Henry Blackstone, "Gathering Information," in H. B. Maynard (ed.), *Top Management Handbook*, McGraw-Hill Book Company, New York, 1960, pp. 203–205.
3. Honeywell advertisement, April, 1963.
4. Fred H. Sill, "Monitoring Your Maintenance," *Factory*, June, 1961, p. 118.
5. "Electronic Monitoring—Tool or Tyrant?" *Factory*, December, 1961, p. 92.

6. Paul M. Dauten (ed.), *Current Issues and Emerging Concepts in Management*, Houghton Mifflin Company, Boston, 1962, p. 318.
7. Henry Metcalfe, *The Cost of Manufactures and Administration of Workshops*, John Wiley & Sons, Inc., New York, 1885.
8. "Field Sales Management," Experiences in Marketing Management, no. 1, National Industrial Conference Board, New York, 1962, p. 35.
9. L. B. Mullinix, "Should You Give the Foreman Back His Pencil?" *Factory*, September, 1962, p. 120.
10. Ernest Schleusener, "Workers Set Own Indirect Standards," *Factory*, December, 1962, p. 60.
11. John Tolland, *But Not in Shame*, Random House, Inc., New York, 1961, p. 224.

Chapter 7

THE COMPARISON PHASE

In Which You Make Comparisons between Actual and Expected Performance in Order to Identify Exceptions, Analyze Causes, and Report the Need for Action to the Appropriate Authority

The problem of identifying exceptions to performance standards is seen by different people in different ways. For instance:

A company president:

I want to be able to know when we should stand pat and when we should be prepared to move. Bother me only when action is needed.

A manufacturing manager:

The longer the plant can operate continuously on a single product, the lower our costs. I'm plagued each spring by the question of how much inventory build-up we can handle before we get into trouble.

A comptroller:

Daily variations from our expected collections are misleading. But we can't wait until two days before our monthly closing to tighten up our credit policy.

122

A sales manager:

Nothing destroys a salesman's faith in management like headquarters crying wolf about billings, when at year's end we are in good shape.

A statistician:

It's a simple mathematical matter of separating nonrandom variations from random variations. Only the former are significant.

The statistician states the problem succinctly—and abstractly. It is one of comparing actual performance with predicted performance —and then determining which variations truly mean something. If the statistical history is broad enough, a statistician *can* tell management, quickly and easily, which deviations have a statistical significance. And he can also measure the *degree* of this statistical significance. What he can't do very well (or at least he can't do it very well without your help) is to tell management which deviations are significant in solving the practical problems posed in the previous paragraph. And one thing he will never be able to do is to tell management which course of action is best to take to correct the variation.

Making Comparisons

The comparison stage of management by exception is the bridge between the measuring, planning, selection, and observing stages— and final decision making. As such, comparison incorporates a little of each of the former four to set up a situation for the decision maker's action. And as each stage of the management by exception process requires decisions from management, so does this one. These decisions, unlike most that management must make, should all be made beforehand. Chronologically, they are made concurrent with projections, forecasts, and the review of plans, organization, and staff. All are interdependent. If this seems complex to you, it is. And it's one reason the management job so often calls for high intellect. And, of course, it's a big reason why the introduction of the computer has been welcomed in so many circles.

Comparing, in itself, is an uncomplicated process. All it takes is an objective eye (or ear, or nose, or sense of touch) to discern whether or not (and how much) a condition varies from a standard

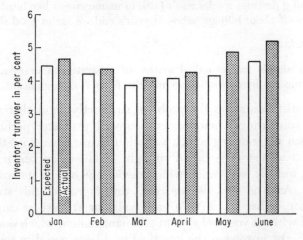

condition. A coffee taster, for instance, is rarely a connoisseur. He merely has been trained to discern when the taste of a coffee sample is different from the standard taste of a particular brand. In like manner, detecting off-standard numerical measures is something a sixth-grader can do. The difficulty lies in assessing the significance of the variation. That calls for judgment, ideally applied before the variation is detected and reported to management.

Let's look briefly at the simpler part of comparison—detecting the variations. Most of the time, management deals with measures to which a numerical value has been assigned. In these cases, the comparison will be made either directly or in graphical form.

Direct numerical comparisons are of (1) one number and a standard number or (2) a table of numbers and a standard table of numbers. This is what accountants have done for centuries.

In graphical comparisons, the numbers are converted to proportionate lengths or shapes in order to make it easier for management to visualize variations and trends. The most common graphical measure is the bar chart (see Fig. 7-1). A trend chart, the most vital of management by exception's visual tools, is nothing more than a series of bars placed alongside each other chronologically upon a common footing. In making trend comparisons, one series of bars represents projected standards, the other series represents current performance.

Highlighting Variances. Deviations, when viewed either numerically or graphically, take a number of forms:

• In comparing single numbers, a particular variation is either above or below normal (see Fig. 7-2).

• In comparing tables of numbers, the sequence of variations (or the pattern they form) is as important as the fact that any of the variations are above or below standard (see Fig. 7-3).

• In comparing trends of numbers graphically, current data may form a line or curve (1) that slopes parallel to the standard line or curve but is removed a distance above or below it, (2) that converges with the standard curve at a slight or acute angle, (3) that diverges from the standard curve at a slight or acute angle, (4)

Fig. 7-2. Example of Variance Report for a Single Month*

VARIANCE REPORT

Analysis of Performance	Department: Month:	Sales Billing January
1. Earned standard hours		3151
2. Special assignments		28
3. Total hours of work earned		3179
4. Regular hours attended		3420
5. Overtime hours		24
6. Total scheduled hours attended		3444
7. Scheduled hours (over) or under hours of work earned		(265)
8. Performance percentage		92%
9. Unattended hours paid (vacation, holiday, illness, etc.)		40

Analysis of Dollar Cost Variance

A. Scheduled hours attended		3444
B. Salaries paid for scheduled hours attended (exclusive of overtime premiums)		$6888
C. Average hourly rate of pay		$ 2.00
D. Salaries paid for scheduled hours attended (including overtime premiums)		$6912
E. Value of hours of work earned (C x 3)		$6358
F. Dollar cost (over) or under hours of work earned		($ 554)

* Variations between actual performance figures (items 6 and *D*) and standard performance figures (items 3 and *E*) are reported in hours (item 7) and dollars (item *F*).

SOURCE: F. Ray Friedley, "Clerical Cost Reduction and Control," N.A.A. Bulletin, Section 1, October, 1953, p. 182.

FIG. 7-3. EXAMPLE OF VARIANCE REPORT FOR YEAR*

(Record of Departmental Budget Variations, New York Sales Office)

Original item	Jan.	Feb.	Mar.	Apr.	May	June	July	Aug.	Sept.	Oct.	Nov.	Dec.	Total
Original Annual Budget projected in January:													775,800
Salaries	(250)	1750	1750	1750	1750	1750	1750	1750	1750	1750	1750	1750	19000
Newspaper advertising	2000	(22000)	2000	2000	2000	2000	2000	2000	2000	2000	2000	2000	—
Supplies	(1000)	(1000)	(1000)	(1000)	(1000)	(1000)	(1000)	(1000)	(1000)	(1000)	(1000)	(1000)	(12000)
Monthly Variance: under or (over)	750	(21250)	2750	2750	2750	2750	2750	2750	2750	2750	2750	2750	
Year-to-date Variance: under or (over)	750	(20500)	(17750)	(15000)	(12250)	(9500)	(6750)	(4000)	(1250)	1500	4250	7000	7000
Total Expenditure for the Year													768,800

* Monthly comparisons facilitate study of variation pattern.

SOURCE: H. G. Oberlander. "Working Papers for Operating Budget," N.A.A. Bulletin, October, 1951, p. 194.

that does any of these three—randomly or significantly—over a period of time.

Statistically speaking, whether you compare numbers as such or numbers in graphical form, there are three variables that will affect your interpretation of them. These are (1) the degree to which the variations are not accidental (nonrandom), (2) the absolute value of the variation from standard, and (3) the pattern of the variation with respect to time.

Descriptive Comparisons. A third kind of comparison is that which is done without the simplicity and convenience of numbers. Measurements that have not been, or cannot be, reduced to numerical quotients—primarily measurements of attitudes, inferences, "feel," morale, and similar intangibles—suffer from deficiencies in description and identification. How often we find stated in a set of management objectives such phrases as "to maintain high morale." We ask that research workers develop "initiative," executives demonstrate "resilience," employees become more "responsible." A few progressive companies have developed numerical indicators for these qualitative measures especially in the area of attitudes and creativity) but most authorities are quick to concede their limitations (see page 224). Consequently, many comparisons must take a narrative form or depend upon careful verbal qualification. Such standards are described with words, not numbers. Deviations must be expressed with adverbs and adjectives, not numbers.

Visualizing Exceptions

In visualizing exceptions, three kinds of charts are commonly used. They are the Gantt chart, the break-even chart, and the action-demand chart. All three demonstrate the principle of (1) showing the progress of work (or conditions) accomplished, (2) as compared with work (or conditions) scheduled (3) on the same chart, and (4) in relation to time. Comparison and control depend in each instance upon planning done prior to current accomplishments. And inherent with each are decisions made at the time plans are made— decisions about the significance to management of any variation from plans.

The Gantt Chart. Henry L. Gantt developed this chart during World War I for use in production scheduling, stores keeping, cost recording, and bonus computations. It is designed for management

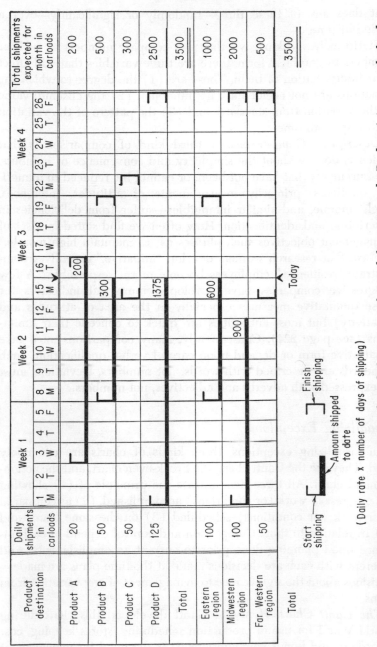

FIG. 7-4. SHIPMENTS TO REGIONAL WAREHOUSES. EXPECTED SHIPMENTS VERSUS ACTUAL (AS OF CLOSE OF BUSINESS ON MONDAY, FEBRUARY 15) FOR MONTH OF FEBRUARY

Example of Gantt chart for comparing planned shipments with actual shipments made. Product A is one week ahead of schedule. Products B and D are right on schedule. Product C is one week behind schedule. Shipments to Eastern region are on schedule. Shipments to Midwest are two weeks behind schedule. Shipments to Far West should have begun a week ago but did not.

by exception because it brings to the attention of the executive the facts about his operation that are most urgent—and then holds his attention until he takes action and sees the results. While the Gantt chart resembles a bar chart in some ways, it differs from a bar chart or a trend-curve chart in that the latter two are used more frequently for historical analysis; the Gantt chart is used for relatively short-term planning and for controlling everyday operations.

In its simplest form, the Gantt chart consists of a sequence of horizontal boxes in which a notation appears of the amount of work to be done in the period of time indicated by the length of the space. As work progresses, a light line is drawn from the left side toward the right of each box. Its length, compared with the length of the box, represents the proportional amount of work actually done as compared with the total scheduled. Thus for each time period the manager can tell at a glance whether the accomplishment is better or worse than predicted. A heavier line is drawn continuously from the lefthand box toward the right, showing the cumulative amount of work done as compared with the cumulative scheduled work as indicated by the total production-period space. Figure 7-4 shows a Gantt chart for controlling shipments to a regional warehouse.

The Gantt chart can be used for any number of operations or conditions. It is commonly used to show (1) machine utilization, (2) incentive workers' performance against standards, (3) progress of work through various operations, (4) construction and design project progress, and (5) loading of production machinery according to time reserved on the machine for scheduled jobs.

PERT, critical path method, and other network or arrow diagramming techniques are, in the eyes of many, simply computer-oriented, 1960s versions of the Gantt chart.

Another variation of the Gantt chart is the EvE chart.[1] Developed by Charles E. Anderson of the Hazeltine Corp., it relates *efforts* to *events* (see Fig. 7-5). The horizontal axis of the chart indicates dates upon which a certain event should take place (such as the shipment of a special order, completion of a preliminary phase of a project, etc.). The vertical axis indicates (usually in man-hours or dollars or machine time) the effort forecast to make that event take place. Effort is recorded cumulatively so that an observer can tell at any point how much has been put in, how much should have been put in, and whether or not the event is occurring on schedule.

The Break-even Chart. This is a device that graphically shows

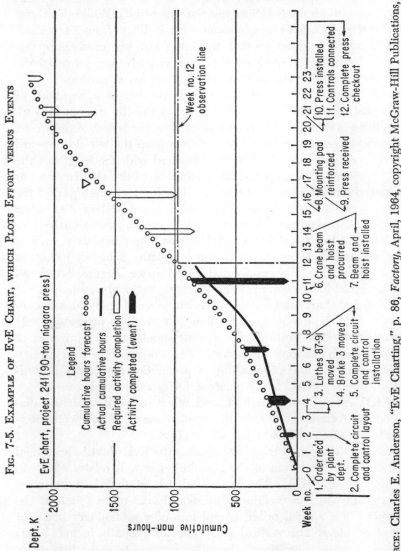

Fig. 7-5. Example of EvE Chart, which Plots Effort versus Events

Dept. K

EvE chart, project 241 (90-ton niagara press)

Legend

Cumulative hours forecast oooo

Actual cumulative hours ——

Required activity completion ▷

Activity completed (event) ◀

Week no. 12 observation line

Cumulative man-hours

Week no. 0 1 2 3 4 5 6 7 8 9 10 11 12 13 14 15 16 17 18 19 20 21 22 23

1. Order rec'd by plant dept.
2. Complete circuit and control layout
3. Lathes 87-9) moved
4. Brake 3 moved
5. Complete circuit and control installation
6. Crane beam and hoist procured
7. Beam and hoist installed
8. Mounting pad reinforced
9. Press received
10. Press installed
11. Controls connected
12. Complete press checkout

SOURCE: Charles E. Anderson, "EvE Charting," p. 86, *Factory*, April, 1964, copyright McGraw-Hill Publications, New York.

management the relation between sales volume, costs, and profits. For the average business, this relationship forms the single most important factor in planning profits. Figure 7-6 shows a typical break-even chart. Note that it shows the interdependence between dollars of costs and numbers of units sold. In the example (Fig. 7-6), fixed cost for the period of the chart is $20,000. The company will incur this cost even if nothing is sold. The variable cost (usually the cost of manufacturing and selling) is $5 per unit. The fixed cost rides on top of the variable cost line. The sales price is planned at $10 per unit. If nothing is made and nothing is sold, both the variable costs and the sales income will be zero. If 900 units are made and sold, the variable cost will be $5 × 9,000, or $45,000, and the sales income will be $10 × 9,000, or $90,000. The fixed cost of making 9,000 units will still be only $20,000. So the profit at the

Fig. 7-6. Example of Break-even Chart, Showing
Volume-Costs-Profit Relationships

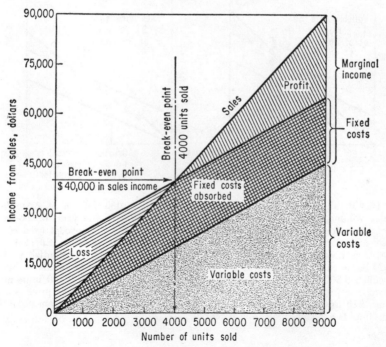

source: Herman C. Heiser, *Budgeting, Principles and Practices*, The Ronald Press Company, New York, 1959, p. 26.

FIG. 7-7. EFFECT OF CHANGES IN FIXED COSTS, VARIABLE COSTS,
OR PRICE CHANGES ON BREAK-EVEN POINT

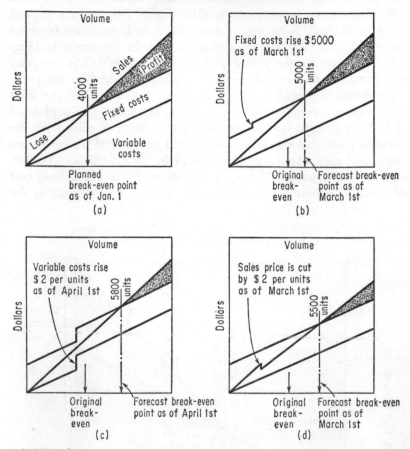

(*A*) Break-even chart from Fig. 7-6 is shown in outline form here. Assuming sales volume, prices, and costs planned at beginning of the year, break-even point was forecast at 4,000 units. (*B*) Same chart as in (*A*) except fixed costs rise $5,000 on March 1—just as sales volume hits 2,000 units. Effect is to displace break-even point to 5,000 units—and to reduce potential profit. (*C*) Same chart as in (*A*) except variable costs rise $2 per unit as sales volume reaches 3,500 units. Effect is to displace break-even point to 5,800 units and to reduce profit potential. (*D*) Same chart as in (*A*) except sales price is cut from $10 to $8 per unit on March 1. Effect is to displace break-even point to 5,500 units and to reduce profit potential.

level of sales will be $25,000. But the significant part of the chart for management is the point where the sales line crosses the cumulative line of variable plus fixed costs. In this case, the point is at 4,000 units. Profits are earned only when sales exceed that volume.

Figure 7-7 demonstrates what could happen to the break-even point in Fig. 7-6 when either fixed costs, variable costs, or prices change.

Since the break-even point depends upon the relationship between three factors, failure of management to meet standard on any of the three will affect profits and profit objectives. Conversely, profit objectives are dependent upon the planning of fixed and variable costs and sales volume. This chart is especially useful, then, in (1) determining which costs to curtail and by how much and in (2) determining what kind of action can be taken in altering price structures to conform to market situations.

When Lynn A. Townsend, for example, took over the presidency of the long-ailing Chrysler Corp. in 1961, he inherited a command that was beset with outmoded plants and a staggering fixed overhead. In one year, Townsend took some $100 million off Chrysler's production and operating costs. By 1962, Chrysler had become the comeback story of the year. The difference between huge losses in 1959 and a profit in 1961 was largely due to a reduction in break-even point. In 1959, Chrysler lost $5 million on $2.6 billion in sales. In 1961, the company earned $11 million on sales of only $2.1 billion.[2]

Action-demand Chart. Graphical identification of exceptions comes to fruition with the use of the action-demand chart. Devised by Gilbreth to relate performance variances from projected standards to the degree of action demanded from management, it is the single most valuable tool of management by exception.

A simplified version of the action-demand chart is shown in Fig. 7-8. In this instance the projected standard of performance for manufacturing costs, as measured by a percentage of sales income, is set at 60. So far the procedure is much the same as in Chapter 4. But now a vital ingredient has been added: *preplanned decisions on how far from standard present performance can stray before some sort of managerial action must be taken.* The decision in this example was that a variance of ¾ of 1 per cent, either up or down, could be tolerated passively (action-demand zone No. 1). When the exception exceeds this tolerance (point A), action is needed. What

FIG. 7-8. EXAMPLE OF ACTION-DEMAND CHART

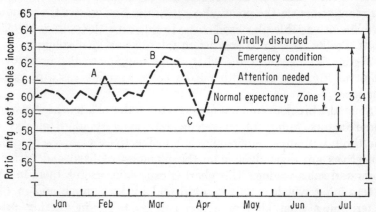

Zone 1: requires clerical attention; Zone 2: requires first-level supervision; Zone 3: requires action from middle management; Zone 4: requires top management decision.

kind of action—and by whom? That also is a preplanned decision. Typically such action is initiated by the first level of supervision— say in the controller's office. And the action might be a routine memo to the manufacturing department to cut out all overtime until the ratio returns to normal.

When the ratio measurement moves up another degree to point *B* in zone No. 3 (the emergency area), the responsibility shifts to a higher level of management. The controller himself would examine the situation and could take action without consultation, if he wished. Or together with the manufacturing vice-president and the sales vice-president, he could choose between a vigorous cost-reduction program or a step-up in sales activity.

If the action taken at point *B* brings performance back into line so sharply as to cause another exception in mid-April (point *C*), an exception in what appears to be a favorable direction (zone No. 2), it may be preplanned that the supervisor in the controller's office take action only if the tendency persists for more than a week. In this instance he would take no action.

When the ratio soars out of control into zone No. 4 (point *D*), the vitally disturbed area, planning would call for this condition to be brought to the immediate attention of the president, regardless of where he was or what he was doing. The president might call a meeting of his staff and line officers in order to assess the situation. The resulting decision could change any one of a number of operating practices, or it might result in a revision of performance objectives.

Note that as the variance becomes increasingly severe, the action demand passes into higher levels of management. And with each degree of variance, the extent to which action can be preplanned diminishes. In zone No. 1 (normal expectancy), only clerical attention—observing and plotting the measurements—is required. In zone No. 2 (management attention needed), the path of action is fairly routine and fixed. But in zone No. 3 (where conditions indicate an emergency), management action becomes more urgent. Often, complex and preplanned alternatives must be weighed before a decision can be made. Finally, in zone No. 4 (where the control is vitally disturbed), many functions of management become involved and the decision is no longer confined to consideration of control action but also to modifications in the controls themselves.

Readers familiar with statistical quality-control charts will recognize the similarity that action-demand charts bear to $\bar{X}$ and $\bar{R}$ charts used to set product inspection standards and to control quality characteristics. Shewart, who designed the $\bar{X}$ and R charts, applied the same principle as Gilbreth, but he used statistical means to determine the breadth of zone No. 1. (It rarely exceeds 80 per cent of the tolerable variation from standard. Breadth is determined by statistical formulas that resolve the extent, or range $\bar{R}$, of variations from average $\bar{X}$ and their frequency.)

The example in Fig. 7-8 was simplified. It used only current raw data and involved a straight-line projection. The same principles would hold true, however, if the technique were applied to trend-curve projections and the data leveled by the moving-annual total technique, for instance.

Action-demand charts can be used to project, follow, and control any chosen condition. For instance, a hospital is as different from a manufacturing plant as can be imagined. But Gilbreth has shown the chart is equally valuable in hospital work. According to a patient's temperature, ranging from a normal of 98.6° to a high of 104°, the action-demand zones divide themselves logically into tasks proportional to the shoulders that must bear them. Zone No. 1 (normal) is handled by the nurse, zone No. 2 (attentive) the intern, zone No. 3 (emergency) the house physician, and zone No. 4 (vital) by consultation.[3]

Because of the considerable planning input that action-demand charts require, they are usually reserved for control of major factors critically related to broad organizational objectives.

Another Visual Technique. Anyone who has worked with graphs and charts knows that even these can be difficult to work with when many variables are being compared. The Automatic Electric Company devised an unusual approach that seems worth reporting here. It used a three-dimensional chart system to compare the relationships of delays occurring in five different departments. Instead of using a series of transparent overlays, it plots each department's progress on a sheet of stiff cardboard. The chart is next cut out along the progress-profile line. (It now resembles a silhouette of a skyline.) Each chart is then inserted into one of a series of parallel slots cut into the top of a specially made chart table. What the controller now has is a series of profiles ranged one behind the other so that each can be examined independently or in conjunction with any or all other charts. Such comparisons enable Automatic to determine reasons for the delays by visual inspection rather than by complicated statistical means.[4]

Reporting Exceptions

Control reports show management what kind of progress it is making toward its objectives. Postmortems are helpful in analyzing what went wrong. But when a report is too long delayed, the opportunity to take the right kind of action may have passed its optimum.

Phil Carroll minces no words when expressing his feelings about report timing: "Speed is more vital than accuracy."[5] He observes that when you miss a train, it usually isn't that you can't run fast enough to catch it, it's because you didn't start soon enough. Reporting of exceptions, too, ought to begin in time for executives to catch and correct the cause in its infancy. Obviously, accuracy is highly desirable, but high-level accuracy, unfortunately, is costly. Even with computers, it often is time-consuming. So try to see that you and your system follow the rule of urgency first, reliability second.

Management by exception is based upon the principle that "no news should be good news." Consequently, it's the exceptions rather than routine verifications of progress that need the ultrafast handling. Information on variances ought not to wait for a final polished report. They can be rushed to the action-demand executive in rough form, by word of mouth, TV, or telegraph or telephone. On the other hand, impulsiveness is to be guarded against. An exception must be seen in its context in order to be fully understood. So the information handlers need to work up supplementary data just as soon as it's feasible.

Form of the Report. Just as there are three ways to represent comparisons, there are also three similar kinds of reports: tabular, visual, and narrative. A well-designed report should combine all three elements. Predominance of any one of the three elements should depend upon the information presented and the managers who will receive the reports.

For instance, *tabular reporting* is most suitable when data are not profuse, when the report deals with relatively small sums of cash or with items of considerable value, and when detail is needed for analysis. Managers with a specific turn of mind, like foremen, often prefer tabular reports. Accountants and financial people also find it easier to work with figures. *Visual presentation,* such as charting, is especially useful when condensing volumes of data, in covering long periods of time, and in providing the broad view. Charting appeals to engineers and scientists, who are familiar with chart interpretation, and to managers with a more general frame of mind. Charts speed up information transfer and are unusually good for presenting data to committees and larger groups. *Narrative presentation* lends itself to the reporting of intangibles, to isolation of subtle deviations, or to pointing out of variances that occur at lower levels, which are obscured in summary reports. Narrative, of course, is used to explain causes of exceptions, to assess the severity of variances, and to suggest corrective action.

Reporting Channels. As exception reports pass through the hands of successively higher-placed officials, they should contain more and more qualitative information. A variance report from a first-line supervisor to a department manager, for instance, should indicate what action he has already taken to alter current results. The department manager, in passing the report along to the general manager, ought to pin down the reason for the variance, make an estimate of how effective the corrective action will be, and indicate the need for changes in procedure requiring approval at the next higher level.

As variance reports accumulate and flow upward through the channels of management to the various action levels, the reports should acquire more and more interpretation and advice that can be used at the higher levels in dealing with vitally disturbed conditions.

In the matter of exception reporting, each executive must use judgment in determining when to short-circuit the reporting format, the reporting period, or the reporting channel. If the reporting format has been standardized on six key categories for purchasing and the purchasing agent observes that a seventh item is becoming critical, he ought to make a note of this in his report. If the period of the manufacturing report is monthly and a major breakdown fouls up schedules during the second week, the plant manager ought to make this information known to the right parties immediately. And procedure for reports to flow systematically from manager to more highly-placed manager and then to the chief executive's control assistant should never become so inflexible that the manager on the firing line can't get a key executive's ear in an emergency.

Characteristics of Good Reports. Reports are designed to convey information: management by exception reports are designed to convey exceptional information. As discussed in a previous paragraph, the form of the report should suit its audience. In addition, a good control report should have at least eight other characteristics:

Brevity. Management spends so much of its time receiving and issuing communications that the exception report should add only what is absolutely essential to this burden. The answer to the question "How much detail is necessary?" should resemble Abe Lincoln's answer to the question of how long a man's legs ought to be—"They ought to reach the ground." In preparing reports, it's a good idea to hold as many data in reserve as possible, with the implication in the report that if more are needed, "there's more where this came from."

Regularity. Sporadic reporting encourages poor control habits, or none at all. Consistency of reporting and the setting of firm deadlines help each manager to face up regularly to his moment of truth. Regularity dispels wishful thinking and vague hopes that things are going all right when they are not.

Timeliness. It's wise to fit the period of the report to the criticality of the measure. One company president emphasizes the need for a daily closing on some critical factors. He says, "Some accountants would throw up their hands if asked to make a daily closing. Yet if the operation stands or falls on up-to-the-minute availability of information, this may well be a good example of false economy. *All* operating statistics are not needed daily. And for those actually required, extreme accuracy is not necessary." On the other hand, day-to-day figures sometimes only confuse; monthly, quarterly, or annual reports are more often meaningful to managerial planning and control.

Specificity. Variance reporting does well when it avoids generalities. Management, when taking action, must deal with facts and realities. While trends and forecasts frequently represent a generalization about a condition, reports of exceptions, in the main, ought to be specific. In effect, the report isolates a particular problem from a generalized assumption that "all's well." For instance, "Costs tended to rise again this month," is the kind of generalization that needs to be supported by specifics such as, "Costs rose an average of 3 per cent this month. They were stable for the first two weeks, but rose 4 per cent in the third week and 7 per cent at closing. Last month, costs rose 2 per cent over the previous month."

Uniformity. A control report is something like a road map. The user expects to find a standard, stabilized format in each document he examines. For instance, units of measure should remain the same from report to report. Methods of visual portrayal should guard against too much variation. If ratios are shown in tabular form this month, so should they next month. If trends are shown by MAT charts this week, so should they be next week. This axiom is also well to follow in the organization of the report. If sales figures always precede manufacturing figures, a change in order of their presentation will confuse some readers and raise questions in the minds of others.

Flexibility. The opportunity to include anything that's important in a report shouldn't be sacrificed at the altar of standardization. Having a proper place for everything in a report sometimes discourages the insertion of brand-new data simply because no one can figure where it ought to go. On the other hand, "miscellaneous" sections ought to be kept to the minimum. If an item is worthy of attention, it ought to be broken out clearly under its own heading and not be buried in what could appear to be a collection of nonessential odds and ends.

Readability. Readability begins with good organization of the material. It is aided by clear labeling of the report's sections, charts, tables, and graphs. It is abetted by simple language. Abstract verbiage and too many qualifications conceal the essential in a report, but, paradoxically, too much terseness can make it cryptic. Rudolph Flesch, author of *The Art of Readable Writing*, insists that clear writing for reports depends upon (1) fluency, (2) redundancy, (3) force, and (4) veracity.[6] Fluency can be improved by writing much as you speak, by not creating an artificial style for what you set down on paper. Contrary to what many of us learned from our high school English teachers, redundancy can be a valuable asset to clear writing. Repetition of important facts, said in various ways, emphasizes for the reader what it is you want him to remember. Force in exception reports should come not from the choice of words so much as from letting the facts speak loudly for themselves. Veracity (authenticity or reliability) makes a report persuasive. If the reasons offered for a variance are true, they will be easily understood. If they are spurious, they will be hard to comprehend.

Reliability. Exception reports should not "cry wolf." While it is not the charge of information handlers to make decisions, it *is* their responsibility to verify that exceptions they report truly exist. Double-checking, or cross-checking an observation that doesn't ring true will often avoid the possibility of getting management upset about a measurement that turns out to be in error. And where variances are attributable to obvious but often overlooked causes (such as holidays, supplier strikes, fire at a customer's plant, etc.) the report compiler should draw attention to these qualifying circumstances.

Exception Reports for Top Management

The great number of performance and variance reports will be prepared at the lowest echelons of management. Obviously these will cover all four business inputs: money, machinery, materials, and manpower. These detailed, first-line reports will be progressively eliminated, consolidated, or digested as the data flows up the organization to the top. What actually appears in a report to the chief executive officer will vary widely. It depends upon such factors as the size and nature of the business, its organization, personnel, and philosophy.

Rose and Farr divide the subjects for the management control reports into four categories:

1. *The business position,* which includes reports on orders received, production output, backlog, and invoices issued.

2. *The operating position,* which includes reports on production cost variances, status of industrial engineering and methods improvements, quality-control performance, industrial relations, employment, direct/indirect labor ratio, machine utilization, and status of research and product development projects.

3. *The profit and loss position,* which includes reports on profit and loss (current and cumulative), sales income, and expense details.

4. *The financial position,* which includes reports on the balance sheet, cash forecast, asset variations, funds movement, accounts receivable, liquid and current ratios, and a statement of legal matters.[7]

The late Carter C. Higgins, president of a relatively small company, Worcester Pressed Steel Company, divided his control reports into five essential categories:

1. *Volume:* invoices issued; orders booked (total according to product, and cancellations); moving annual totals of business (new business and profit margins); report of promising jobs; lost business report; percentage of new orders to estimates; backlog and current schedule; and break-even analysis.

2. *Production costs:* weekly summary of orders closed plus cost cards on each job.

3. *Operating Performance:* monthly budget report; daily report of jobs shipped on time and those delayed; employee attendance; force report; production machine report (ratio of hours spent on production, set-up hours, tool-repair hours, idle time, and maintenance time).

4. *Finance:* monthly balance sheet, balance sheet comparison, fund flow, and cash forecasts.

5. *Other elements of company strength:* merit reviews, grievance committee reports, safety reports, and reports on research and development projects.[8]

Which kind of variance reports to prepare, and the determination of which of these reports should go to the chief executive officer, is a matter of highly placed decision.

Chart Rooms

Even back in the days of Taylor, Gantt, and Gilbreth, management envisioned mammoth corporate control centers into which data would flow at high speeds and be translated automatically into tables, charts, and graphs. The concept was that the manager would sit at the center of a control console and make split-second decisions based upon what he could see on the screen. Today the *process* control center has materialized. In steel mills, giant bakeries, oil refineries, paper mills, and other process-oriented operations, information is collected automatically and relayed to a centralized control center. Overall management control on this basis has been slow to materialize. However, there are some notable exceptions that anticipate what will probably be common in another decade.

For Project Control. A three-man team headed by a critical-path analyst at Olin Mathieson Chemical Company, utilizing a computer and critical-path scheduling techniques to control construction of a new brass mill in 1962, exercised control from a large chart room. This group supervised the plotting of network type charts to (1) allocate the optimum number of construction workers on each job, by craft, (2) watch closely over equipment vendors' delivery dates, (3) keep up with changes in customer requirements that affected present mill's finished-goods inventories, and (4) adjust for last-minute design changes. This group, working out of the chart room, used three key devices to keep projects moving forward:

1. A color coding system to flag trouble (variance) spots. Narrow green, yellow, and red adhesive tapes indicated on the network chart the status of various activities. Green—work on schedule; yellow—work not started but float time unused; dotted red—work lagging but still expected to meet deadlines; solid red—work definitely behind schedule.

2. A weekly work-status report on which the analyst listed equipment and construction events that failed to meet deadline dates, with the reasons. It also itemized the events to be completed in the next two weeks. The report went to the project task force, construction personnel, engineers, and contractors. With this information, the task force planned moves to pull jobs up to schedules.

3. A computer update that corrected the critical path as the final stages of construction quickened. As soon as the staff processed new punched cards indicating status changes, the computer was able to reroute a new path, at the rate of about every other week.[9]

For Maintenance Control. In the same year, Air Force maintenance-control centers built around chart rooms at each of fourteen bases reduced the backlog of man-hours at each installation from

4,000 to 2,500, the backlog of service calls from 160 to 40, the work-order delay days due to lack of materials about 80 per cent, and the processing time for new work from a range of three to six months to two to six weeks.

A typical Air Force control room of 900 square feet featured two kinds of charts:

1. Work load (Gantt) charts and status boards that show current status of all work proposed and underway

2. Information charts that do not rely on progressive movements, such as listing of work orders on hand by number, a personnel regis-ter showing daily utilization of people by crafts in various shops, layout maps of facilities, and rosters of vehicles with their location and usage.[10]

For Production Control. A third, "Buck Rogers" kind of visual control is used by Hughes Aircraft Company's El Segundo, Cali-fornia, factory to observe and report production progress and ex-ceptions. A plant-wide closed-circuit television system links the works manager's office with purchasing, receiving, stores, machine-load scheduling, two assembly departments, and finished stores. Telecasts alert interested functions to parts shortages on scheduled projects, for instance. And machine-loading progress is marked on a continuous strip chart that is photographed as it rolls past the camera. The company had formerly used electronic data processing to check on small parts shortages, but it found that the half a day, or more, needed to feed data into the machine and process it was too slow. Now one TV camera and fifteen monitors provide information al-most instantaneously. Initial cost for installation was $8,000. Rental cost of cameras is $200 per month. In addition to providing manage-ment instantaneously with the variance data it needs, Hughes esti-mated its paperwork savings alone at $50,000 in sixteen months.[11]

For Purchasing Control. At Martin Company's Orlando Division the purchasing department built what *Purchasing Week* calls a "goldfish bowl" to display its purchasing performance charts. It en-ables staff, management, and government auditors to get a quick, graphical interpretation of purchasing trends. But most of all, the displays facilitate comparisons and provide purchasing managers with early warnings of problems developing in their departments.

There are fifteen division-performance charts, four of which show how Martin is doing in small-business contracting. This is shown in terms of dollars, in number of awards, in commitments versus gross sales, and in percentage of total disbursements. Other divisional charts measure the work being done by purchasing and the efficiency with which it is being accomplished. Among the charts are ones that show the division's operating budget, dollars committed, sale-source programs and targets, rejects and shortages, schedule requirements versus end-line delivery, and inventory versus production sales.

Another display shows how the number of requisitions issued per month stacks up against a previous forecast. The flow of requisitions is plotted against division expenditures for manpower, postage, travel, and freight. Each of the cost factors is represented by two lines, one for the forecast figure and one for the actual rate of expenditures. Other divisional charts show:

• Comparison of the average cost of issuing a requisition with costs in other months

• Labor costs per requisition compared with past performance

• Lead times in relation to a horizontal line representing what Martin considers to be normal

Still another key panel chart in the departmental section measures subcontractor performance. It includes graphs showing how planned expenditures stack up against actual contracts let and how contracts let match with deliveries of hardware. Rejection rates are broken down to show how much work was rejected while still in process at the sub's plant, number of rejections at Martin's receiving stations, and number of rejections on the Martin plant floor.[12]

For Executive Briefing. More and more companies are creating complex briefing centers in which all three forms of reporting are combined. A good example is that provided by United Air Lines. According to *Business Week*, each morning just before 10 A.M., a group of nineteen UAL executives gathers in what looks like a wartime general's command headquarters. For the next fifteen minutes they receive a briefing—right down to the last nickel of revenue—on the current state of operations. The UAL briefing is made as dramatic as possible to avoid boring executives with reams of statistics. But it adds up to a complete rundown of how well the company did during the preceding twenty-four hours and a forecast of the company's plan for the next twenty-four hours. The room itself, which cost $35,000 to equip, is designed around visual presentations that include color transparencies, several types of film projections, and multicolored wall displays.[13]

References

1. Charles E. Anderson, "EvE Charting: A Simple Way to Plot Effort vs. Event," *Factory*, April, 1964, p. 86.
2. *Time*, Dec. 28, 1962, p. 53.
3. Frank B. Gilbreth, "Graphical Control on the Exception Principle for Executives," Paper 1573a, American Society of Mechanical Engineers, New York, December, 1916.
4. "3-D Charts Stand Tall to Tell the Tale," *Factory*, December, 1960, p. 149.
5. Phil Carroll, *Profit Control*, McGraw-Hill Book Company, New York, 1962, p. 200.
6. Rudolph Flesch, *The Art of Readable Writing*, Harper & Row, Publishers, Incorporated, New York, 1949.
7. T. G. Rose and Donald E. Farr, *Higher Management Control*, McGraw-Hill Book Company, New York, 1957, p. 15.
8. Carter C. Higgins, "Management Controls for Small Business," H. B. Maynard (ed.), *Top Management Handbook*, McGraw-Hill Book Company, New York, 1960.
9. "Nerve Control Aids Modernization," *Factory*, October, 1962.
10. Carl G. Wyder, "Unique Control Center Keeps Tabs on Maintenance," *Factory*, September, 1962.
11. "Plant-wide TV System Keeps Eye on Production," *Factory*, June, 1962, p. 114.
12. "Martin-Orlando Puts Purchasing in a Goldfish Bowl," *Purchasing Week*, Sept. 23, 1963, pp. 14–15.
13. "Chart Room—New Style," *Business Week*, Nov. 2, 1963, p. 150.

Chapter 8

THE ACTION PHASE

*In Which You Complete Your Decisions and Take Action
to Either Control or Exploit the Exceptional Conditions*

"Good controls are not a substitute for good management. They are
a part of good management. The idea of a control system is to organize and present information so that managers of a company can
tell in a hurry what actions they should take." [1] Edmund J. McCormick, an especially perceptive accounting consultant, makes this distinction between controlling and managing. It's a good way of thinking about this final phase of management by exception, for it is at
the decision-action crux that a control system is vitalized.

Somehow or other, control has come to be regarded as the province of staff personnel rather than of line management. This is a
misconception. Staff people are important, even essential, to the
control function, of course. But their primary role is to set up the
measure-project-select-observe-compare-report system and to keep it
operational. Obviously, staff assistance is valuable in making forecasts and in drawing up optional courses of action. Staff is needed
to provide both leg work and advice, if requested. But the manager
accountable should—must—make the basic *control* decisions just
as he must make the vital *action* decisions. He must decide which
criteria to measure and compare, when to accept a projection and

146

when to reach out with a forecast, how far to tolerate a variation from expectations—and for how long. Finally, he must decide when to exert control actions. He must choose when to act, who should act, and, in many of the ultimate decisions, what the action will be.

Decision making is an art. Attempts to reduce it to a science are snares and delusions. What is possible, however, is to so illuminate the many variables affecting a business problem that the area of choice is clearly delineated. Such illumination is best attained by the systematic process of management by exception as outlined in the preceding chapters. The results of this process, and an attitude deriving from it, are exemplified by an international incident that occurred in 1962.

During the Cuban crisis in the fall of 1962, Robert McNamara, United States Secretary of Defense, became a key figure in President Kennedy's deliberations which led to a firm, and successful, stand against the introduction of missiles by the Russians into Cuba. *Life* magazine observed that what made Mr. McNamara's contribution so valuable was that he "leaned on the systematic gathering of hard facts and logical analysis, avoiding emotion and instinct. . . . Before attacking such problems for final decisions, the secretary demanded that they be reduced in every instance to a detailed, quantitative range of alternatives—with facts and figures for each option open to him." Mr. McNamara summed up his approach this way: "I never worry about making the decisions. As long as I can make them through analysis of the problem and thus base them on the greatest evidence on hand, the decisions are not difficult." [2]

The point is that decision making (contrary to Mr. McNamara's optimism) is never easy. But following the step-by-step management by exception process can remove much of the risk—and the pain—of decisions.

Decision Making

Inexorably, there comes the time when planning, policy making, and procedure outlining can carry neither the individual nor the company further. A decision must be made. It is the sanguine moment of truth to which each must face up, in very small matters as well as in large. Probably it could best be described not as the moment but as the hour or day—sometimes month, or even year—of truth, for few business decisions must be made in a spit second.

Consequently, even the decision-making process can be pulled apart into segments that march or mix through the brain. One executive has said that it falls into four steps: (1) spotting the variation, (2) determining the reason, (3) evaluating the causes, and (4) taking corrective action.[3] Certainly his second and third steps—determining reasons and evaluating causes—ought to precede any action. In philosopher John Dewey's terms, this would be called an "analysis" of the problem.

Analysis of Causes. When a deviation pops up, the basic question to ask is, "What caused it?" Is the deviation due to human error? Material deficiencies? Machine failure? Financial inadequacy? Market changes? Can the deviation be attributed to organizational weaknesses, functional shortcomings? Are the measurements correct? Is the basic plan sound?

Too much cannot be said about the need to localize the difficulty. It's a temptation to vaguely attribute the variation to, say, faulty material and feel that the problem has been identified. Further probing should pinpoint the specific nature of the faulty material: specifications that are too tight to be met, "price buying" that invites off-quality shipments, suppliers who are unqualified in the first place, poor inspection procedures in your own organization, or any of a dozen other reasons. Continual chipping away at the more general reasons to find the real cause for a variation will make final decision making easier and more effective.

Other important questions to be asked during the analysis phase include the following: What is the effect of the variation upon short-range operations? Upon long-range plans? Upon return on investment? Upon customer relations? Upon public and community relations? Upon employee and union relations? Upon legal and government influences?

You will also want to seek answers to these questions: How big is the exception? How frequently has it occurred? How delayed is its effect? How broad is its impact? Does it affect policy, planning, organization, staffing, marketing, finance, operations, research, purchasing?

Variance Meetings. Decision making, while it reverts to an individual in most cases, need not be a lonely affair. In fact, the best decisions will usually be made when based upon the diagnostic contributions of as many involved people as possible. Calling responsible managers together in a "variance meeting" to discuss causes and cures is a sound way for an executive to tap these resources.

Typically a well-run management by exception program holds four kinds of such "variance meetings":

1. Weekly meetings to review those short-term fluctuations that are deemed to be at critical variance from standard

2. Monthly departmental meetings to analyze specific variations from monthly objectives

3. Quarterly general meetings to discuss broad trends and to consider revision of either projections or action plans

4. Emergency meetings when an urgent need for unusual high-level action is detected

At any of these meetings, the presence of the budget director or control officer, chief accountant, and chief industrial engineer or their representatives is highly desirable. Where there is a cost reduction committee, or the like, representatives from this group should attend, as well as those operations managers who are charged with meeting performance standards. In any event, the makeup of variance meetings should reflect management's belief that corrective action on variances must be anticipated, or be taken, by all levels of supervision.

Edmund J. McCormick urges that variances should be considered in rank order according to the following priority:

1. Those that most immediately affect profits, with the sales quota receiving top billing in most instances, and control of operating costs next in priority

2. Those variances requiring new equipment to offset them

3. Deviation in material and supply costs

4. Factors outside of the business itself [4]

It is also wise to anticipate at variance meetings the pressure from subordinates to alter established standards. "Scapegoating" of the budget is a natural tendency on the part of those who fail to meet it. It is then that the "control" executive must show his mettle. He must be able to resist this pressure while still maintaining an open mind in reviewing the performance standards themselves.

Outline of Options. Only after the real cause of the deviation has been positively identified and its impact on the organization's operations estimated should you proceed to reassemble and reevaluate alternative plans of action. If you and your staff have done your homework well at the exception-indicator stage, you will have already at hand a number of choices. And in nine instances out of ten, the route to take is so obvious that the decision can be made without further ado.

But in the one or two cases out of ten where the impact is more severe or more lasting, you should seek other new options at the time the difficulty arises, and then reexamine all avenues that are open.

Actually, in any exceptional condition your final decision should be based upon a wide choice of action options. For example, you can:

1. Do nothing until you have checked for faults in your measurement-observation-reporting system.

2. Wait for a predetermined period of time to see if the condition is self-correcting.

3. Establish new performance standards.

4. Follow a series of preplanned corrective steps that are arranged in proportion to the degree of variations.

5. Seek expert, outside, and objective advice.

6. Move in an entirely new and unplanned direction—based upon a reassessment of the situation and followed by creative or intuitive thinking.

Exercising Control

Most of the texts, and the management language, emphasize decisions taken as the result of variances as "control" decisions. Actually, action options—in any kind of variance event—ought to embrace a spectrum which ranges from pure control of undesirable performance to outright exploitation of opportunity. Action at the control end of the spectrum is spoken of as "beating costs back into line." Variations at the sunny end of the spectrum, can be viewed as "profit-producing." Phil Carroll likes to cite G. Charter Harrison on this point. "The outstanding defect of the conventional profit and loss statement is that . . . it reports profits *made* but it does not show profits lost." [5] It follows, then, that management by exception should invite action that is positive as well as negative.

Donald E. Farr, president of H. B. Maynard & Co., internationally known management consultants, expresses the control problem this way:

When a man is driving an automobile, the control which he exercises over his vehicle will vary from the light guiding touch on the wheel while all goes well to slamming on the brakes in a sudden emergency. So in an industrial undertaking the indications may remain steadily favorable, and only vigilance is required—apart from the eternal quest for greater efficiency. This fact is sometimes responsible for a sense of disillusionment to chief executives who wish to install this method, and find when it is working that a sound and satisfactory condition is shown and they are not called upon to go out and make sweeping changes. They tend to overlook that they are also offered a wide range of minor recorded results all capable of improvement if they will take the trouble to study them. By paying attention to these, the efficiency of the business will slowly improve as well.[6]

What is to be avoided is the concept of slamming on the brakes at each minor deviation. What is to be encouraged is a continual search for minor deviations that offer an opportunity for improvement.

Clarence B. Randall, former president of the Inland Steel Company, warns of the danger of such overcontrolling or panic cost cutting:

> When a sudden fury of ill-considered cost slashing sweeps through a company, "We must cut overhead," becomes the slogan. Yet this mystic catch phrase seldom means the same thing to different men. To many, it is a simple command to cut off, overnight, every expense that does not pay off at once, here and now. Hack away at the intangibles. Forget the future. Have no thought for human values. Give up planning for the long term. Stop construction. Suspend plant maintenance. Permit no nonsensical talk about that overdue paint job. Forget equipment replacements. Cut inventory to the bone, even though it means shutting down the plant of a loyal supplier. Take care of yourself, and let the devil take the hindmost, through the whole dizzy descent down into the abyss.[7]

The accounting expert Herman Heiser also cautions that a manager "draw a sharp distinction between budget deviations arising from variations in the efficiency of the organization and those arising from the fact that the budget itself is unrealistic."[8] In its diagnosis, management must verify its measurements and also give some thought to the validity of its original projections.

Where Drastic Action Is Needed. Occasionally, just exercising control is not enough to correct a deteriorating condition. Sometimes the executive has to decide whether to keep on fishing or to cut bait. Abandonment of a project into which time, money, effort, and enthusiasm have been poured is the most difficult kind of a conclusion to reach. When William T. Taylor became chairman of ACF Industries in 1957, he was faced with this kind of a dilemma. He had to decide whether or not to divest the railroad car manufacturer of obsolete production facilities. But according to the *New York Times,* he did not leap for the scalpel. Moving with deliberation, he first took ACF out of the nuclear reactor field. Mr. Taylor in retrospect said, "Our volume in the reactor field was good, but we weren't making any profits out of it. We had built a reactor for a leading university but had lost our shirts on it." Next, Taylor sold the company's Berwick plant, its last facility for making passenger cars and heavy ordnance. ACF then shifted the focus of its remaining car building to freight car plants in the South and West, where Taylor felt the markets were more promising. The company's success has been outstanding ever since. Profits, for example, rose from $2 million in 1959 to $7 million in 1963.

Actually, while ACF exercised the ultimate in control, it also seized the initiative in a field that appeared to be drying up. It recognized the opportunity to satisfy a growing need for highly specialized, high-cost freight cars. Mr. Taylor points out that the railroad equipment industry had changed drastically. There had been a continuing drop in demand for mass-produced freight cars, and the railroads themselves were tending to build them in their own shops. "We didn't take it lying down," he said. "I'm proud that ACF became one of the leaders in this positive action." [9]

Counterattack. Another noted industrialist, J. Paul Getty, also emphasizes the need to convert control action to positive gains. He observes that there "are those businessmen who are the real leaders. These are the imaginative, aggressive individuals who base their business philosophies on the ancient military axiom that attack— or at least, energetic counterattack—is invariably, the best defense." Getty concludes that there are certain fundamental principles that, if followed, will greatly aid any businessman in meeting adverse situations and transforming setbacks into successes. He advises:

> 1. No matter what happens, do not panic. The panic-stricken individual cannot think or act effectively. A certain amount of trouble is inevitable in any business career—when it comes, it should be met with calm determination.

2. When things go wrong, it is always a wise idea to pull back temporarily—to withdraw just long enough and far enough to view and evaluate the situation objectively.

3. In the opening stages of any developing adverse situation, it may be necessary and advisable to give some ground, to sacrifice those things which are least important and most expendable.

4. Next, all factors in the situation must be examined with meticulous care. Every possible course of action must be weighed. All available resources—cerebral as well as financial, creative as well as practical—must be marshaled.

5. Countermoves must be planned with the greatest care and in the greatest of detail—yet with allowances for alternative courses in the even unforeseen obstacles are encountered. Counteraction must be planned on a scale consistent with the resources available—and the goals set must be conceivably attainable. It is well to bear in mind, however, that the impetus of a properly executed counterattack very often carries the counterattacking force far beyond the point from which it was driven in the first place.

6. Once everything is ready, actions should be taken confidently, purposefully, aggressively—and above all, enthusiastically. There can be no hesitation—and it is here that the determination, personality, and energy of the leader count the most.[10]

There are many other notable cases of management scoring on a counterattack. Henry Ford, when faced in 1927 with overwhelming competition from Chevrolet, gathered his resources and introduced his Model A that pulverized his competition. Similarly, American Motors under the leadership of George Romney staged a spectacular comeback by introducing compact cars while the rest of the industry was still producing oversized luxury cars.

Danger in Overoptimism. In the desire to take advantage of unexpected opportunities, there is always a danger in being overeager. Some above-standard variations, instead of implying opportunity, may mean trouble—or at least signal caution. For instance, an over-aggressive sales campaign in the fall might bring sales for that period far above what was projected. But this may not be cause for optimism. There is the greater possibility that the fall sales have been made at the expense of those for winter and spring.

Sears Roebuck, for example sets its profit goals between 4 and 5 cents on the sales dollar. This is almost 1 cent higher than most of its competitors. But in the early 1960s, this figure crept above 5 cents. Was this good? Not in the judgment of Sears' management, which decided that overly large profit taking would enable its competitors to make inroads into its markets with lower-priced, lower-profit goods. Consequently prices were adjusted to hold within the 4- to 5-cent return and to attract higher volumes for what Sears felt were better bargains for its customers.

Balance

What, then, is the key to management's ability to deal effectively with variances? How can it know when a situation cries out for control and when it suggests a chance to gain ground? The experts seem to conclude that the best manager for management by exception is the one who is poised, ready to move in *either* direction. Here are the observations of three students of the management process who arrive at this conclusion, although with different words and different labels.

Balance. Lyndall F. Urwick says, "The principle underlying all planning calculations should be balance." He cites Field Marshal Viscount Montgomery's use of balance as the principle of war. Montgomery felt that an army had achieved balance when it was so poised that it could react quickly and easily to the enemy's action —whether it be an attack or a retreat.

Optimology. Harry Arthur Hopf defined this concept:

Optimology has as its principal task the analysis and measurement, by scientific means, of all facts, experience, techniques, processes, and trends in any field of human effort and their classification and codification, with the objectives in view of defining for a given enterprise the level of optimum relations to which it should aspire, and of providing it constantly with reliable data through the use of which the progress made in realizing and adhering to the optimum may be determined. . . . Optimology seeks to associate with the concepts of changing size, cost, and human capacity that appertain to an enterprise, a philosophical acceptance of the likelihood that, through proper planning, organizing, coordinating, and controlling, a condition may be achieved that will represent the optimum.[11]

Situational Management. Dr. George S. Odiorne quotes Nicholas Murray Butler, former president of Columbia University, as saying there were three kinds of people: those who make things happen, those who watch what goes on, and those who don't know what happened. Odiorne says,

The manager of situations knows what is happening, and he's also making things happen. . . . He's more of an expert in analyzing situations, classifying causes, and identifying proper course of action for others. . . . He's got his eyes fixed squarely on results and responsibilities. He'll delegate more, but the vital point is that after delegating details he'll spend more time in studying and organizing the situation than if he attended to too many lesser facets of the job himself.[12]

William Blackie, the Scottish-born accountant who became Caterpillar's president in 1962, sometimes quotes Arnold Toynbee to illuminate the balanced course his company has steered in recent years. "It's like Toynbee's Yin and Yang," he remarks. "You swing, from time to time, from aggression to defense. As you attain a measure of success, you find compulsions that cause you to do things to preserve your success, alternating with further opportunities to expand it." [13]

Timing the Action

"Time has telescoped for people in industry," says Frank S. Capon, vice-president of Du Pont of Canada. "Technology and competition have put such a premium on time that it is not enough to make the right decisions. The right decision must be made quickly." [14]

Business history is full of pathetic examples of decisions deferred for "just a little more information." This attitude is typified by designers who are reluctant to finalize their designs, who are always making one more improvement before releasing it to production. A manager is almost always working against a deadline—five minutes from now or five months from now. There is *never* enough time to bring together *all* the information or to explore *all* the facts.

Now Mr. Capon's "time collapse" is forecast by many to have an impact on management equal to the impact of automation on labor. The time has come when management must be able to "get on and get off" minor projects without making Federal cases of them. Turnaround time from research to production must be tightened, for instance.

Take a dramatic case in point. In 1961 Procter & Gamble Company was completing market tests of a new medicated shampoo. A competitor, Alberto-Culver Company, caught wind of these area tests. Immediately, A-C decided to race P & G to the national market with a similar product. By midyear A-C had created a product name, a package, a marketing plan, and even a TV jingle. The only catch was that A-C researchers hadn't yet come up with a medicated shampoo.

"After many experiments," A-C's president, Leonard Lavin, said, "we finally hit upon a winning formula. And by January 1962 our product had achieved national distribution, while P & G was still selling only in its test area. Now P & G had to knock our product off the limb rather than vice versa."

Said Mr. Lavin, "Our only edge over P & G was our manufacturing flexibility. We were able to produce and bottle our product for national consumption without delay. P & G was unable to do the same for theirs in the short time allowed them." [15]

Mr. Cordiner stresses the importance of timing like this. "Time is an asset that all competitors share in common, but the management of time can be one of the decisive elements in success or failure. The chief executive needs to sense when the market is ready, when the technology is ready, and when the organization is ready for a major push into a new field." [16]

Committee Action

There are two principal ways for arriving at a final decision: committee vote of a majority of an individual's choice. While it has been increasingly popular to joke about committees, in many instances there is more than casual merit for it in democratic decision making. First of all, the integrated judgment of a qualified group of executives has a good chance of being superior to that of any one individual. But even more important is the feeling that action arrived at by a majority is more likely to win the needed cooperation of that majority than action directed independently by one of the group's members. However, to use a rough rule of thumb, for every decision that needs or benefits from group participation, there are ten that are best handled by a final, individual judgment.

Before Lowell E. Krieg headed up the Winchester-Western Division of Olin Mathieson Chemical Company, a committee was responsible for the decisions related to each of the company's major products. Today each product still has a committee, but decision by committee has been eliminated. Decision-making power rests solely with the responsible manager. Says Krieg, "Committees are now only advisory. Every staff member has to stand up and be counted at least once a month. Not only must he know whether his projects are on schedule, but if they aren't he's got to know why not —and offer a plan for getting back on schedule." [17]

Alfred P. Sloan, Jr., clarifies his position regarding committees in much the same way. "I have often been taxed, by people who don't know me, with being a committee man—and in a sense I most certainly am. But I have never believed that a group as such could manage anything. A group can make policy, but only individuals can administer policy." [18]

Personal Leadership

And it is at this point that management by exception differs little from any other system of management. All the measuring, planning, comparing, analyzing, and diagnosing are merely prologue to the step forward, sideward, or backward the leader must take.

David Lilienthal, former director of the TVA, describes management's overemphasis on planning and immobility in situations demanding action. "There is an unfortunate lack of distinction between a plan and accomplishment." Mr. Lilienthal calls for "an end to surveys and reports. Too many business people—and government administrators—believe 'We have a plan, therefore the job is done.' Most of the time what we need is not a new principle or a fresh philosophy but a simple answer to 'How do we get it done— now?'" [19]

It is true, however, that some situations solve themselves. That is, forces other than those the executive can understand or control somehow or other bring about desirable results. The director of industrial relations for a nationwide chemical company once told the author, "There is real danger in being too eager to correct problems in the personnel field. It's better to wait and see how a situation develops—if it develops at all—before becoming exercised about it."

Too many executives, however, adopt the "watch and wait" approach, not so much from belief in its reliability as for a rationale to justify their fear of decisions. The tragedy of General George B. McClellan, commander of the Union's Army of the Potomac during the Civil War, was that although he was a highly efficient administrator, he could not spur himself to conclusive action. Bruce Catton records this viewpoint:

McClellan was always going to make his big move in just two or three more days—as soon as the rain stopped, as soon as so-and-so's division joined him, as soon as this or that or the other thing was all ready. The two or three days would pass, the rains would stop, the other things would work out right, but nothing would happen. Never could he bring himself to the point of action.[20]

General Grant, on the other hand, was selected to command the Army of the Potomac not because he was a brilliant strategist but because he was willing to fight when the situation called for fighting. For executives, too, just "doing" may not be enough, but deciding *and* doing are absolutely necessary in executive leadership.

Caesar weighed all pros and cons before he crossed the Rubicon. But he made the move. It could be redundant for this text to digress into the field of leadership techniques as such, but some discussion seems pertinent—especially since so much up to this point has emphasized system and logic.

Intuition. The relationship between the will to decide and the action chosen is often indefinite. A noted scientist, Dr. Jerome B. Weisner, President Kennedy's Special Assistant for Science and Technology in 1963, said that in complex space matters, with their jumble of technical and political aspects, some problems can be decided only with a "flash of intuition." He observes, "Even if the wisest Nobel laureate in physics were president, he would have to fall back on intuition. Some problems are just too complicated for rational, logical solutions. They admit of insights, not answers." [21]

Character. Another great man, neither scientist nor industrialist, speaks of an even more important quality. Ernest Hemingway concluded, "In the affairs of life or business, it is not intellect that tells so much as character, not brains so much as heart, not genius so much as self-control, patience, and discipline, regulated by judgment." [22]

Confidence. Vance Packard, a journalist usually associated with criticism of business and businessmen, concluded in *The Pyramid Climbers* that a demonstration of self-confidence and the guts to go ahead is often enough to assure that the decision will be proved right. Packard says, "He must have a dependable vision of the future. From hindsight and wind-sniffing, he has discerned where the company can be or should be tomorrow. When it comes right down to it, what most managements and subordinates yearn for above all are leaders who seem to know where they are going—and clearly are going toward a goal which all would like to achieve." [23]

Responsibility. Still another nonbusinessman speaking to this point with great insight is Captain Blackburn, who was quoted earlier about the need for flying by the book. He says, "We don't earn our money on the easy trips. I think all honest pilots will admit that the easy trips—the ones where everything goes right and the weather is fine—are almost outings. . . . On the other hand, there's the old saying that flying is long hours of sheer boredom followed by moments of stark terror." Businessmen who have learned to cut the mustard agree with this notion. When the organization is rolling along, most decisions are routine. Success seems the easiest thing in the world. But when things turn sour and routine decisions no longer bring shining results, then the boys had better let the men take over.

But listen a little longer to Captain Blackburn:

I've always said that if anybody has to be killed in an airplane accident, I hope it's the captain. After all, he's the one who gets the most pay, the one who makes the decisions, and the one who can do the most about it. Then in descending order of rank, the first officer and on down to the fellow who can't get at the controls. This is our business. We accept the money. We accept the working conditions. We accept the fun of it. We should also accept the liabilities—the possibility that something will go wrong. I think it poor taste for anybody in this business to take any other attitude.[24]

Could a businessman state the case any clearer? Perhaps. Here's the harsh view of George M. Bunker, president of the billion-dollar a year Martin Marietta Corp.: "Real management must begin with a chief executive, good or bad, who is willing to take the rap for his acts." [25]

Competence. James Menzies Black, vice-president of the National Metal Trades Association, cautions:

The incompetent company is never respected, nor is the incompetent manager. A decision-maker must have the respect of his subordinates. Of course you want your employees to like you, too. But if you lose their respect you lose everything. Nobody likes a boss to whom they have given a vote of "no confidence." When Neville Chamberlain became Great Britain's prime minister he was very popular, but his reputation withered because he could not bring himself to make the hard decisions necessary for his country's survival. He lost the con-

fidence of his people, he lost his job, and he lost his reputation. The
popularity of a leader turns quickly to contempt if he does not measure
up to the task he has set himself.[26]

Perspective. It would appear that when faced with a decision,
perspective is what an executive needs badly. To get this perspective, he should try to develop:

• A responsible regard for the leverage his position can exert in
the particular situation

• Ambition for reliable, consistent performance, but not for perfection

• Respect for the contribution others can make to aid his judgment and support his actions

• Sense of proportion for his own role, relatively small, in the total
situation

Depth. Finally, every mature person can testify that the inner
fiber which a leader must demonstrate when put on his mettle is the
real difference between great decision makers and lesser ones. History provides the example of General Joe Hooker when he was pitted
against Robert E. Lee at Chancellorsville. Let historian Bruce
Catton tell it:

> What would matter most in all of this would be the result of a
> searching inquiry into the character of two men. . . . It would be a
> moral issue, finally—a test of inner integrity and manhood. In this
> test Hooker would be so badly overmatched that it would be no
> contest.
>
> Hooker's plans were excellent, and so was his execution of them
> . . . up to the moment of testing. . . . The Army of the Potomac
> was in perfect condition, stripped for action, wagon trains cut to a
> minimum; it would move fast, it would fight where all the chances
> would be in its favor, and fighting so, it ought to win.
>
> So went the plan. So went the execution, too, until the time came
> when everything depended upon Joe Hooker. Then the whole busi-
> ness fell apart like a sheet of soggy blotting paper, and the South won
> a spectacular victory.[27]

Such moral strength is essential to the business situation, too. The
trials which leaders in management face are subtler than those of a
military commander, but they are nonetheless demanding. In fact,
managers operate under greater handicaps. Few employees are
aware of the pressures that test their superiors. And only occasionally does the public extend either plaudits or sympathy to the thou-

sands of leaders who labor unnoticed in the arbors of business. Leadership, like virtue, most often is its own reward.

Closing the Loop

After decisions are made, actions directed, controls exercised, and results obtained, management must see that its most recent experiences are considered in the development of each of the six phases of management by exception. This process is commonly referred to as "feedback." But feedback implies a clear-cut beginning and ending of a process. And up until this point in this text, we have been implying a simple, step-by-step process that might occur in a straight line. Unfortunately, like most of life's activities (and especially human ones), the management by exception path is more nearly circular.

What is needed now is a closed-loop concept in which (1) any of the six phases of management by exception might be either a beginning or an ending and (2) the relationship between any two of its links might be either cause or effect. Consequently, while many of management's activities are toted up (like the profit and loss sheet) at the preestablished end of a period, there is value in thinking of the process as offering a chance to check results at *any* stage —and to feed these results back into the system.

Feeding Backward and Feeding Forward. Techniques for feeding back data that will help correct or adjust the system fall into two categories: automatic and human.

Automatic types of feedback need little discussion. These are the self-regulating physical devices (like speed governors) that transmit directly related results back to the originating source by means of hydraulic, mechanical, or electronic linkages. In the computer, especially, this feedback can be applied at any stage of a system and to any degree that has been predetermined by the programmers. Consequently, accumulating experiences can modify future output of the system (1) either cautiously or radically and (2) either at the end point or at any and all of the intermediate stages.

Human feedback, people-to-people feedback, can do everything the computer can do (except match its speed and accuracy). Human recycling or results can be achieved by:

- Routine and exception reports
- Interdepartmental conferences

• Personal exchanges
• Variance meetings
• Postoperations critiques
• Counseling sessions

Human beings in the organization, however, are not limited to the unreasoned assimilation of results data (as machines are). People have the unique ability to interpret results and to accept them, modify them, or reject them. Human beings can add not only fresh data from untapped sources, but also new insights and new judgments.

Hugh Estes suggests that an intensified emphasis on informal, personal information exchange will vastly improve the effectiveness of feedback. He says, "Each individual can be encouraged to *reach* for the information and help that others have; to telephone, write and talk directly; to *volunteer* information and help when he knows he has something others can use." [28]

Coordination. This human ability to feed back yesterday's results to today's plans for tomorrow's results calls upon one of managements most needed skills—coordinating ability. *Dun's Review,* in choosing Jersey Standard as one of the ten best-managed companies in the United States cited it for "coordination: For all its sprawl, policy is made by the parent company. At headquarters all the threads are woven into the most profitable pattern possible, with experts on producing and refining and the other operations keeping the strings from getting snarled."

Coordination of functions by management at each successive level is the true feedback that keeps an organization of people consistently on course. Oversystematizing this activity renders it inflexible and impairs its effectiveness. Ignore the need for continual coordination, and the organization will falter or fail.

It is at this coordinating stage—feedback, adjustment, and integration (closing the loop, if you will)—that characteristics of good management are tested. It is at this stage that management must reexamine its delegation practices and shuffle assignments upward and downward and laterally. It is here that managers and subordinates need coaching to see how they can better handle and prevent recurring situations. It is here that appraisals are made. Good results or good approaches (or both) are rewarded. Failures are counseled, remotivated, redirected, reassigned, or cut out of the organization altogether.

Almost all the classic management techniques stem from the concept of management by exception. Such systematic management helps to simplify the managerial process and to make as much of it as possible automatic. It irons out many of the recurring perturbances and furnishes consistent and desired direction. But when variations from desired results occur and cannot be corrected by preplanned routine actions, then management must apply judgment to produce new action. And then actions and reactions must be coordinated *after the fact* to prepare the organization for *before-the-fact* decisions, which will in turn affect future action.

References

1. Edmund J. McCormick, "Profit Leaks—How to Find Them and Plug Them," *Factory*, April, 1950.
2. *Life*, Nov. 26, 1963.
3. Norman E. Alexander, "Evaluating and Measuring Results," in H. B. Maynard (ed.), *Top Management Handbook*, McGraw-Hill Book Company, New York, 1960, pp. 374–396.
4. McCormick, *op. cit.*
5. Phil Carroll, *Profit Control*, McGraw-Hill Book Company, New York, 1962, p. 200.
6. T. G. Rose and Donald E. Farr, *Higher Management Control*, McGraw-Hill Book Company, New York, 1957, p. 217.
7. Clarence B. Randall, *The Folklore of Management*, Little, Brown and Company, Boston, 1962, p. 68.
8. Herman C. Heiser, *Budgeting*, The Ronald Press Company, New York, 1959, p. 111.
9. *The New York Times*, Oct. 6, 1963.
10. J. Paul Getty, "The Businessman at Bay," *Playboy*, September, 1963, p. 191.
11. Harry Arthur Hopf, paper presented at Sixth International Congress for Scientific Management, London, July, 1935.
12. George S. Odiorne, *Michigan Business Review*, University of Michigan, Ann Arbor, Mich., November, 1960.
13. "The Gentle Bulldozer of Peoria," *Fortune*, p. 171, July, 1963.
14. "The Information Revolution," *Plant Administration & Engineering*, December, 1962, p. 30.
15. Lester R. Bittel, "Better Be Nimble," *Factory*, April, 1963, p. 83.
16. Ralph J. Cordiner, "The Nature of the Work of the Chief Executive," paper presented to CIOS, New York, September, 1963.
17. "Gun Producer Aims for Bigger Profits," *International Management*, November, 1963, p. 29.
18. Alfred P. Sloan, Jr., "My Years with General Motors: Our Strategy Works Out to a T—and the Model T Goes Under," *Fortune*, November, 1963, p. 167.
19. Interview with the author, 1960.

20. Bruce Catton, *This Hallowed Ground*, Doubleday & Company, Inc., Garden City, New York, 1956, p. 168.
21. "A Scientist's Advice—Part II," *The New Yorker*, Jan. 26, 1963, p. 37.
22. Ernest Hemingway, "Man's Credo," *Playboy*, January, 1962, p. 120.
23. Vance Packard, *The Pyramid Climbers*, McGraw-Hill Book Company, New York, 1962, p. 171.
24. *The New Yorker*, Nov. 10, 1962, pp. 92–94.
25. Charles V. Murphy, "The Millions under Martin Marietta's Mattress," *Fortune*, November, 1963, p. 240.
26. James Menzies Black, *How to Grow in Management*, Prentice-Hall, Inc., Englewood Cliffs, N.J., 1957, pp. 107–108.
27. Catton, *op. cit.*, p. 293.
28. Mason Haire, *Organization Theory in Industrial Practice*, John Wiley & Sons, Inc., New York, 1962, p. 24.

PART 3

THE PRACTICE
of Management by Exception

How to recognize the strategies, tactics, insights, measurements, and compromises found in the application of the system to everyday business problems.

Chapter 9

UNIFYING THE SYSTEM

In management by exception, the transition from theory (or principle) to practice varies from the imperceptible to the abrupt. Management's "planning" function is often just one of a series of steps in a gradual transition from theory to practice. Management's "control" function most nearly activates the exception principle. Yet management's ways of making decisions and taking action often seem far removed from the exception principle.

When the concept of control springs from an orderly process of budget making, progressive recording of achievements, and reports to management highlighting variations between budgeted and actual performance, the exception principle is at work. But that is not enough. What is needed in most instances is to extend the practice of management by exception into all corners of the management operation. And these practices must be systemized in every phase of technique in order to get complete and effective utilization of the principle.

It would be misleading, however, to imply that management by exception is always carried to its ultimate fulfillment. In many cases, the concept does not carry deeply into the action-indicator phase. Too few companies have fully formalized progressive stages of exception intensity for which action responsibility moves progressively up the executive ladder. But this lack of perfection in practicing management by exception is not critically serious. In most cases, it

167

represents the result of a careful economic decision rather than disagreement with the principle. But best results will come when the practice is complete in every phase and feature.

Up to this point in this text most of our discussion of management by exception has focused upon a single function. To grasp the entire scope of its impact we must also study the interrelation of various functions within an enterprise. Knowledge and understanding of this interdependency are qualities a top executive must possess. Without this capacity for the integrated picture, he would be at the mercy of a myriad of independent decisions made by his functional subordinates. Each might act in the best interests of his particular function, yet find the effect of his decision is at odds with the welfare of the total organization. The top executive, therefore, must be able to foresee the interplay of cause and effect between functions and coordinate decisions between finance, operations, and marketing.

Fortune magazine, for instance, commented about the Hertz Corporation this way:

> The key to profits is to keep every car as busy as possible—thus achieving maximum utilization, as the trade puts it. This means, first of all, timing purchase and resale of cars throughout the country so that they aren't left lying around in garages. Second, it involves moving cars from city to city—and within a city from one rental station to another—in order to catch peak demands as they develop. And finally, it means thinking up merchandising schemes that will create new demand at normally slack times. In these three techniques, Hertz has no peer. On the average, its rental cars are on the road almost eleven hours of every day in the year.[1]

In other words, Hertz's top executives attain maximum utilization by coordinating (1) financial control of car inventories, (2) efficient operation of the system, and (3) maximum merchandising activity.

Maximum utilization of facilities is not limited to car rentals. It is, of course, the objective of every organization—even a nonprofit organization—to make maximum use of its facilities. And management by exception becomes an ideal tool for pointing out where utilization is below par and where it can be extended. A complete management by exception system builds a web of interconnecting measurements, projections, observations, comparisons, and reports. These interlock each minor functional area with each of the three major areas of finance, operations, and marketing so that top management can make key decisions in an informed manner.

Decisions and Profits

Donald Hoodes and *Factory* magazine have provided a rather elementary but illustrative example of how these interlocking actions and management reactions affect the final course of a company's affairs.[2] The chart, Fig. 9-1, demonstrates the interdependence of all business functions. The necessity for coordinating them becomes obvious as the chart tells its story.

The elements that make up the chart exist in any business. But the several segments of the management team know about them only piece by piece. The operations manager, for example, knows his capacity and production figures. The sales manager knows what his backlog and current sales are. The controller knows how much cash is on hand, net working capital, and available assets. But only one man has a grasp of the entire picture—the company president.

The chart is a simplified picture of what can happen to any business in periods of sales downtrends and uptrends. It tells the story of a typical small company under projected and actual operating conditions under the guidance of an average management (A). Then it tells what happens to the company under poor management (B) and good management (C) during a two-month sales downtrend. Finally, it tells of the company during a six-month sales uptrend in which its management (D) failed to take advantage of this opportunity.

Look at the top line on the chart (Fig. 9-1). It shows that management expects $150,000 in sales orders during the month. Its backlog of orders amounts to $225,000. And it is operating a three-shift operation at 100 per cent capacity.

The plant will issue $45,000 in purchase orders (using a ninety-day lead time) and receive $45,000 worth of direct material (material used in the product made for sale). Inventories will hold fairly constant at $135,000, $75,000, and $150,000. Fixed factory overhead is $10,000 (rent, taxes on property and equipment, and salaries for key employees who won't be let go regardless of production volume). Variable overhead includes maintenance (janitorial and production-supporting labor) and supplies that can vary with production volume. Gross profit here totals $60,000. "Net quick" is all assets that could be converted to cash quickly, less current liabilities. To get net quick, you add cash and accounts receivable, then subtract

Fig. 9-1. Effect of Management by Exception Decisions on Profits Illustrating (1) Average Management Results as Compared with Its Projected Performance, (2) Good and Poor Management in the Face of Falling Sales, and (3) a Weak Management in a Rising Sales Condition

How Management Can Make or Break a Company

Conditions		Sales			Production data					Manufacturing cost elements						Current financial factors		
		Sales orders ($1,000's)	Order backlog ($1,000's)	Shipments ($1,000's)	Production ($1,000's)	Capacity	Material purchase orders issued ($1,000's)	Direct material ($1,000's)	Direct labor ($1,000's)	Inventories: Raw material ($1,000's)	Work in process ($1,000's)	Finished product ($1,000's)	Mfg. overhead Fixed ($1,000's)	Variable	Gross profit ($1,000's)	Cash	Net quick assets ($1,000's)	Net working capital
Projected	Mgt. A	$150	$225	$150	$150	100%	$45	$45	$30	$135	$75	$150	$10	$4.5	$60.5	$150	$125	$383
Actual		100	150	100	100	66⅔%	30	30	20	Start 90 / End 90	50 / 50	100 / 100	10	3	37	100 / 100	40	205
Sales falling	Mgt. B Mo. 1	50	Start 150 / End 100	100	100	66⅔%	30	30	20	Start 90 / End 90	50 / 50	100 / 100	10	3	37	Start 100 / End 100	40	205
	Mgt. C Mo. 1	50	Start 150 / End 100	100	75	50%	22.5 (b)		15	Start 90 / End 67.5	50 / 50	100 / 75	10	2.25	37.75	Start 100 / End 135	105	235
	Mgt. B Mo. 2	50	Start 100 / End 100	50 (a)	75	50%		30 (c)	18 (d)	Start 90 / End 97.5 (e)	50 / 50	100 / 125 (f)	10	3 (g)	9	Start 100 / End 40 (h)	20	165
	Mgt. C Mo. 2	50	Start 100 / End 100	50	50	33⅓%			10	Start 67.5 / End 52.5	50 / 50	75 / 75	8	1.5	16.5	Start 135 / End 115	85	200
	Mgt. D Mo. 1	150	Start 150 / End 200	100	100 (i)	66⅔%	50 (j)	30	20	Start 90 / End 90	50 / 50	100 / 100	10	3	37	Start 100 / End 100	40	205
	Mgt. D Mo. 2	250	Start 200 / End 350 (k)	100	100	66⅔%	50	50 (l)	20	Start 90 / End 110	50 / 50	100 / 100	10	3	37	Start 100 / End 80	0	185
Sales rising	Mgt. D Mo. 3	100	Start 350 / End 325; 200M Cancelled (m)	125 (n)	125 (o)	83⅓%	50 (p)	50	25	Start 110 / End 122.5	50 / 50	100 / 100	10	3.75	48.75	Start 80 / End 67.5	125	210
	Mgt. D Mo. 4	50 (q)	Start 125 / End 75 (r)	100	150 (s)	100%	30 (t)	50 (w)	30	Start 122.5 / End 127.5 (v)	50 / 50	100 / 150 (w)	10	4.5	35.5	Start 67.5 / End 62.5	17.5	185
	Mgt. D Mo. 5	50	Start 75 / End 75	50	100	66⅔%		50	20	Start 127.5 / End 147.5	50 / 50	150 / 200	10	3	12	Start 62.5 / End 17.5	113.5	160
	Mgt. D Mo. 6	50	Start 75 / End 75	50	50	33⅓%		50	10	Start 147.5 / End 182.5	50 / 50	200 / 150	10	1.5	11.5	Start 17.5 / End 17.5	147.5	135

source: Donald Hoodes, "Pinpointing Soft Spots in Costs," Factory, April, 1959, copyright McGraw-Hill Publications, New York.

accounts payable and other current liabilities. Net working capital is net quick plus inventories (all current assets less all current liabilities).

Effects of Good and Bad Management. The second line of the chart shows results of a typical operation. Instead of operating at 100 per cent of capacity, it operates at 66⅔ per cent. Gross profit at this level of operation is $37,000.

The chief difference between poor management (B) and good management (C) is their speed and thoroughness in meeting changes in business conditions. The well-managed operation (C) gets accurate information on sales trends variations early enough to make manufacturing cutbacks. And the company cuts back its direct labor, material purchases, and other variable expenses as fast as it cuts production. The poorly managed operation (B) moves slowly, stalls off reductions in labor, purchases, and other expenses. The result for management (B) in just two months is a red net quick figure. The company doesn't have enough cash and receivables to meet its current payables and other liabilities. Management (C) uses foresight and doesn't get into this sort of trouble.

The following points are keyed to the small letters in the chart:

a. Sales shipments are shown as $50,000 for this month. Because of the declining market, some of the customers who had placed orders (for the $100,000 order backlog) postponed delivery. Therefore only $50,000 could be shipped during the month. The order backlog started at $100,000 and ended at $100,000. This company's customers were feeling the pinch of slack demand in their own markets.

b. Material purchase orders issued for the month total $22,500. No more should have been issued. Poor purchase control and coordination are the reason for the error. More detailed analysis of future raw material requirements and a better knowledge of suppliers would have helped. Normally, as the economy turns down, lead time can be cut.

c. Orders placed for this material should have been either canceled or postponed.

d. For direct labor, management (B) spent $18,000 in this period. If direct labor was variable with the amount of production, this figure should have been $15,000.

e. An ending inventory of $97,500 in raw material was caused by purchase of material in excess of needs during the month.

f. Low shipments plus overproduction increased the finished goods inventory to an ending value of $125,000.

g. Variable manufacturing overhead was not reduced in proportion to production.

h. Cash has dwindled to $40,000. The excess cash investment made in material and labor, the overinvestment in inventory, and slower accounts receivable collections were responsible. Here's where the controller gets nervous. And, in the last block, net quick is a red figure. The company's receivables and cash don't cover payables.

Missed Opportunity. Now see what happens to management (D) during a sales uptrend. Again, follow the letters on the chart:

i. As backlog goes up, current production cannot be increased fast enough to meet the change.

j. Material purchase orders are issued for $50,000 worth of supplies, based on the sales department's forecast. The purchasing department should have been informed of the limitations in production and should have used the information to reduce purchase orders.

k. Another increase in the order backlog occurs because of production and shipment problems.

l. Direct material costs for this period are $50,000, but only $30,-000 worth of raw material is used. This is because of purchase orders that were placed ninety days previously, plus other orders placed in anticipation of higher sales and production volumes.

m. Because the company cannot increase production and shipments, customers cancel a total $200,000 worth of orders.

n and *o.* Shipments and production are finally raised 25 per cent.

p. In spite of the above $200,000 sales cancellations, heavy purchase orders continue. Inventory control is not properly related to current sales.

q. The company cannot deliver goods on time, so its customers lose enthusiasm for it and its sales force becomes demoralized.

r. Sales backlog drops with reduced sales and increased shipments.

s. Production finally gets geared up to 100 per cent capacity after the need is past.

t. Months too late, the purchasing department reduces its raw material purchase orders.

u. Heavy shipments of direct material are still being received, in spite of the low sales, production, and shipment levels.

v and *w*. Ending inventories of this month are unbalanced. Considerable overinvestment in inventory is evident.

Control Actions

Since a good part of management by exception is geared defensively to protect projected profits, look now at another example of how one company uses the exception technique to find and check profit leaks.

The nine charts shown on these pages (Fig. 9-2) represent a minimum package of controls for a manufacturing company.[3] By watch-

Fig. 9-2. How a Manager uses Variance Charts to Stop Profit Leaks, Illustrating the Actions of Executive John Jones in Controlling Costs of a Manufacturing Operation.

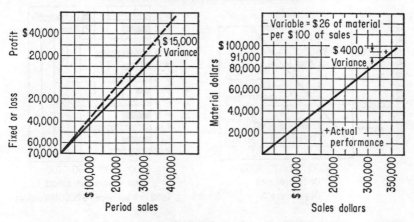

source: Edmund J. McCormick, "Profit-Leaks—How to Find them and Plug Them," *Factory*, April, 1950, copyright McGraw-Hill Publications, New York.

1. Profit path. When John Jones takes a look at the reports from his control department for the preceding month, the first chart tells him that his profits were $15,000 less than they should have been. Sales were $350,000; profits were $20,000 (lower line). But at that sales volume, the company's standard calls for profits of $35,000. This shows on the upper line, which gives the target profit for each level of sales. To find where the money leaked out, Jones goes to . . .

2. Material costs. The sloping line shows him how much he should be spending for materials at each level of sales. The cross, placed on the chart by the control department, shows how much was actually spent—$4,000 too much. The cost estimates used in setting up the line of allowable costs were made by Jones's supervisors at the beginning of the year. A certain amount of variance is permissible. But $4,000 is too much. Jones knows that he has found part of his trouble, but not all of it. So he goes to . . .

FIG. 9-2

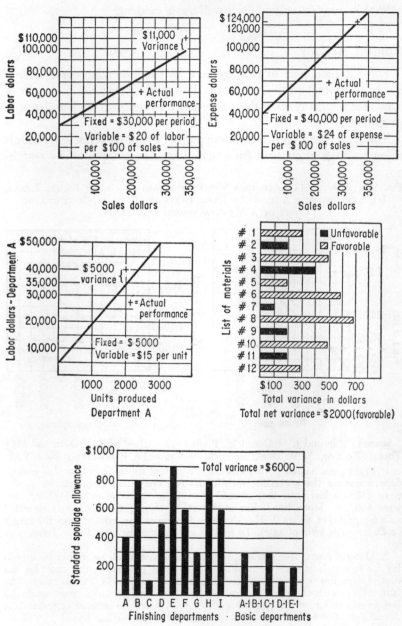

ing them, management can make sure that it is making the most out of its business. In other words, it can plan its profits in the same way that it plans its production.

To see just how this control system works, imagine that you are

---

3. Labor costs. Here is where the other $11,000 went. When he set up his profit targets, Jones assumed that he would have a fixed labor cost of $30,000 a month plus $20 variable labor cost per $100 of sales. At $350,000 sales, this would have meant $100,000 in labor costs. But the cross on the chart shows that total labor costs were actually $111,000 in the past month. Jones has now accounted for all of his $15,000 profit loss—$4,000 went into excess material costs, $11,000 into labor. To make sure, he checks . . .

4. Other expenses. Everything is all right here. Jones has planned on the assumption that his expenses other than labor and materials (supplies, services, purchased power, and the like) would run $40,000 plus $24 of expense per $100. The cross on the chart shows that he was right on the nose in the past month. He knows now where to look for his profit leaks, but he still has to find out the specific causes and decide what to do about them. The chart of total labor costs is no help to him here. It tells him that he paid too much for labor, but it doesn't tell him just where or how. He needs a more detailed breakdown to pin the excess down. In order to get specific information he needs, he turns to . . .

5. Departmental labor costs. There is one of these charts for each manufacturing department in the company. All of them are younger brothers of the main labor cost chart that Jones already has studied. They show allowable labor cost at various levels of production, but on their horizontal scale, output is figured in terms of physical units rather than sales dollars. In Department A, the standard calls for $5,000 fixed costs plus $15 a unit of production. The chart tells Jones that in the past month Department A accounted for $5,000 of his extra costs. Similar charts for the other departments will locate the other $6,000 of excess labor cost. Now he can trace the $4,000 in additional material costs. First he checks . . .

6. Material price variance. This chart shows how much the prices of materials used during the month varied from the prices assumed in setting the profit target. Solid bars are unfavorable variances (prices higher than expected). Shaded bars are favorable variances (prices lower than expected). Jones discovers that the favorable variances have been larger than the unfavorable by $2,000. In other words, profit should be $2,000 higher than the target set on the basis of the previous price forecasts. Obviously, his materials profit leak isn't an unexpected price change. In fact, he now has to find where the $2,000 favorable variance went, in addition to hunting up the missing $4,000. He turns to . . .

7. Departmental spoilage analysis. Here is his trouble. Spoilage has got out of hand. The bars show spoilage in each department in excess of the standard allowance (predicted by the supervisors at the beginning of the planning period). Total excess spoilage comes to $6,000. It has eaten up all the $2,000 gained through favorable purchases and, in addition, has pulled profits $4,000 below the target. Jones has now found his $15,000 and can take suitable measures to control expenses in the current month. But there are still two other things he wants to check. One is . . .

FIG. 9.2.

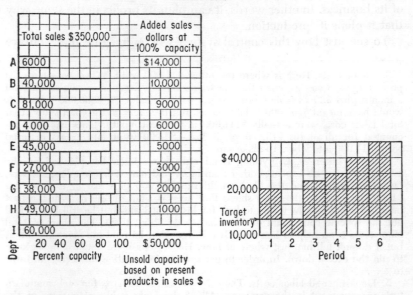

Percent capacity

Unsold capacity based on present products in sales $

Period

8. Unused capacity. Not all the manufacturing departments are going full blast. Jones wants to know how much additional production he could handle and what that would mean in terms of profits. The chart tells him that his unused capacity could add $50,000 a month to sales. Going back to his first chart, the profit path, he sees that this extra $50,000 sales would add $15,000 a month to profits. Knowing this, he can make recommendations to his sales department or plan expansions of capacity. As the last step, he looks at . . .

9. Change in inventory. The chart tells him at once that trouble is brewing. The company is getting too much money tied up in materials. And the excess is building up month after month. The base line of this chart shows the target inventory for each period. The bars show how far above or below the target actual inventories came. Four months earlier, Jones had cut his inventory $10,000 below target. Since then it has been creeping up. Now it is $50,000 too high. This means that Jones is taking an unnecessary risk.

looking over the shoulder of a company president—we'll call him Mr. Jones. Follow him through the charts, one by one.

Jones, as can be seen from the chart, was able to tell at once when his profits started running $15,000 below his targets. He also was able to find what was causing the trouble and plan steps to straighten it out.

Steps to Profit Control. But how did Jones attain this fortunate position? In other words, how did he set up his control system? And how did he figure out his target profit and costs?

Here is a brief sketch of the steps he took:

1. With the help of his functional managers, Jones framed standards of performance for labor, expense, and materials. These standards were not scientific documents but rather carefully considered practical statements by each supervisor reporting what he would require at various levels of volume in his department.

The accounting, purchasing, and personnel managers translated these statements into dollars of cost and standard crews for all levels of production.

2. As the standards were being built, Jones brought the managers together at significant intervals, explaining with blackboard talks what the standards meant and how they would be used. He was surprised and delighted with the enthusiasm and excellent ideas these meetings brought forth. Soon the controls became identified to each manager as *his* control rather than reports that were only for top management.

3. Jones integrated the standards so that they tied in logical sequence with the company profit picture.

4. He allowed a reasonable tolerance in judging results, say 5 per cent of an individual control, for he realized that actual behavior seldom falls along a straight line. This tolerance gives him a freedom of action and speed not obtainable when the last penny must be brought into balance.

5. He separated his accounting functions from his control functions and did not attempt to put his variances into the accounting books, although his control system balances with the accounting books.

6. He placed his standards on graphs so that he could quickly take a look at trends as well as current performance.

7. He designed his graphs so that few needed to be redone each period; thus he kept maintenance work to graph posting and a minimum of redrafting each period.

8. He used the graphs as the center of his presentation because they get the ideas across with clarity and encourage discussion.

9. He placed the responsibility for management by exception controls in a small control department, thus relieving his overworked accounting department of a timetaking extra burden. This department was Jones's time saver. It performed his footwork in measuring actual performance and organizing the meetings with his managers.

10. He selected the manager to head control with great care, for he realized that this post was the training ground for a future top

executive. For this job he sought knowledge of production and understanding of accounting, as well as an analytical mind and the ability to get along well with personnel. He allowed this man a clerical assistant. In addition, with the cooperation of his controller, another man from accounting was trained for the position as a standby, while continuing regular accounting duties.

11. Each month the control department conducted a preliminary investigation of the arithmetic of performance so that inventory adjustments, transfer of labor, and unclear definitions of productive machine- and man-hours did not cause a false impression of substandard performance.

12. Jones planned his meetings with managers for certain days each period. Thus Friday became labor and expense day; Thursday, material day. Managers could now plan meeting attendance with crack-train timing.

13. With the help of his control department Jones planned the design of each meeting in advance. He reviewed past promises and pitted them against current results to see if promises were now in action. He spotted new causes for substandard performance and at the meetings developed plans with his managers to investigate and correct the fall-downs.

14. With the plan of the meeting developed, Jones authorized the control department to circulate the graphic reports so that the managers knew in advance the problems they would be asked to solve.

15. Jones carefully planned the group which would see each control, and the groups might differ widely in composition. For example, the chief chemist might attend only the material control meetings, whereas the purchasing manager might attend both material control and labor and expense control.

16. Jones cleared away surplus paper work and reports in setting up his control system. His control department was designed to replace rather than supplement previous reporting and clerical personnel.

17. Finally, mindful that early reporting means clear memory of events reported and the bulk of the month for action, he worked out with his accounting department an early release of payroll, expense, and material figures.

Thanks to the cooperation of the controller, Jones saw the major control reports in the first week of the new period.

References

1. "It's Hertz Itself in the Driver's Seat," *Fortune*, October, 1963, p. 119.
2. Donald Hoodes, "Pinpointing Soft Spots in Costs," *Factory*, April, 1959.
3. Edmund J. McCormick, "Profit Leaks—How to Find Them and Plug Them," *Factory*, April, 1950.

Chapter 10

MANAGING FINANCIAL ACTIVITIES

Owen Robertson Cheatham is chairman of the board of the Georgia-Pacific Corporation. He has helped to guide that company to a $260 million annual sales figure. During the 1950s he directed the purchase of $300 million of timberland and nearly $80 million in new plants and equipment. In speaking of the essentials of financial management effectiveness, he recalls this incident. In the summer of 1954, Cheatham was riding from Dallas to Abilene in a car driven by a business acquaintance. In his pocket was a special-delivery letter just received from G-P's general offices. In it was the report of a firsthand exploration of forest property. The report urged the acquisition of 19,000 acres of old-growth Douglas fir. And it detailed year by year the cash return on this acreage. This information was essential since, if the company were to move on the project, it would have to supplement equity capital with borrowed funds.

Cheatham studied the report, then asked the driver to pull over to the next service station so that he could make a telephone call. He placed a call to the chairman of the finance committee of one of the nation's largest banks. "Georgia-Pacific needs $12 million," he said. "The situation is urgent enough so that I have to know right now whether you're interested and in a position to make the loan." The banker's reply was instantaneous: "I think we can do it. Come in and let's work it out."

Now what's the connection between this incident and manage-

180

ment by exception? It's a subtle but essential one. Cheatham had, for a number of years, kept the financial committees of a number of banks apprised of his company's financial position, its short- and long-term objectives, and its plans for carrying them out. "This bank chairman wasn't in the least surprised to hear from us about this deal," says Cheatham. "We had made it a point to keep him informed, and he was ready."

"Never surprise" is a dictum that Mr. Cheatham follows for both external financial operations and internal financial controls. Four times a year, G-P presents its financial status figures to the top officers of all its banks, large and small. Most of the time, this is a routine report. But when an exceptional condition arises, the bank people are better able to recognize its relationship to the total company picture and of course are more likely to respond to a request for funds.

Internally, Mr. Cheatham depends upon a "knowledgeable financial vice-president to whom full authority for execution can be delegated . . . a controller who is a courageously conservative judge of figures, budgets, and facts . . . and a wise treasurer who understands the productivity of money as well as its security." As chairman, Cheatham initiates plans and coordinates the management by exception tactics of the triumvirate.

Standards of performance at G-P are established and are compared by the twelfth of each month in a report to the president and other company officers. Following his "no surprise" dictum, Cheatham feels that in almost every instance he must be already aware of below-par conditions before the confirming figures are received. And looking to the future, he insists on solid financial planning for every project proposed. He advises, "You may have 10 plans in operation and 100 plans on the shelf for future reference, but you should have 110 budgets." [1]

We have dwelt at length on Mr. Cheatham's approach because it includes so many of the essentials of management by exception. Observe his procedures: (1) he builds all strategy on a solid foundation of accurate measurements; (2) he insists on thorough financial projections for all proposed projects; (3) he has set up a regular, prompt comparing and reporting system, but he feels it isn't functioning properly unless he gets wind of variations beforehand; (4) he has organized his staff and delegated responsibilities to support the system; and finally (5) his decisions are prompt and vigorous, but in the majority of instances they reflect preplanned courses of action for which he has laid adequate groundwork.

Financial Measurements

It is not the intent of this text, nor is it within the qualifications of the author, to provide a complete and weighted list of the many measurements of financial position that might be considered when instituting a system of management by exception. However, Table 10-1 proposes a fairly comprehensive list of measurements that could be made.

Probably the most common of all measurements of capital employment are the various measures of return on investment. These measures reflect the viewpoint that, regardless of all the contributing factors, the final measurement of managerial effectiveness (in business enterprise) is summed up in its ability to generate profits from the resources provided. When they are examined more closely one discovers, however, that measures of rate of return are rarely absolute. The most rough and ready gages (the accounting method and the payback method) are simply ratios (or reciprocals) of the first year's saving of a particular investment compared with the original investment. Other, more complex, but surer yardsticks of capital employment are (1) the annual cost method, (2) the MAPI system, and (3) the investor's method. Each of these incorporate several financial variables and is especially characterized by the inclusion of the cost and/or time-value of money in its computations.[2] The major drawback in using rates of return as measures in a management by exception system is that too often they can be computed only long after the fact. However, in making decisions and establishing alternative choices of investment action, they are an essential adjunct to systematic management.

Budgeting

Making other than straight-line projections of financial trends is usually a matter for economists. There are literally hundreds of indicators that can be used. One reliable source is the National Bureau of Economic Research, Inc. Each year it publishes a text called "Tested Knowledge of Business Cycles." This report includes a number of continuing studies of the relationship between many popular

Table 10-1. Some Possible Measures of Financial Position

Balance Sheet Items
  Current assets
    Cash on hand
    Cash in bank
    United States government bonds
    State and municipal securities
    Accounts receivable for sale of merchandise or services
    Notes receivable for sale of merchandise or services
    Trade acceptances for sale of merchandise or services
    Merchandise inventories, finished
    Merchandise inventories, in process
    Merchandise inventories, raw materials
    Advances on merchandise
    Marketable securities
  Fixed assets
    Land
    Buildings
    Machinery, tools, and equipment
    Furniture and fixtures
    Trucks and automobiles
    Leasehold improvements
  Miscellaneous assets
    Cash surrender value of life insurance
    Due from officers, directors, and employees
    Investments
    Investments in and advances to subsidiaries and affiliates
    Deferred charges and prepaid expenses
  Intangible assets
    Bond or debenture discounts
    Brands
    Catalogs
    Contracts
    Copyrights
    Designs
    Development expenses
    Drawings
    Formulas
    Franchises
    Goodwill
    Leaseholds
    Licenses
    Magazine titles
    Mailing lists
    Models
    Organization expenses
    Patents

Table 10-1. Some Possible Measures of Financial Position (Continued)

Patterns
Processes
Subscription lists
Tracings
Trademarks
Trade names
Current liabilities
  Notes payable to banks
  Notes payable for merchandise, machinery, or equipment
  Trade acceptances for merchandise, machinery, or equipment
  Accounts payable
  Loans payable
  Accruals
  Advance payments
  Reserves for taxes
  Dividends declared but not paid
  Reserves for contingencies against possible losses
  Current maturity of a funded debt
Deferred liabilities
  Long-term liabilities
  Valuation reserves
  Reserves for contingencies
  Unearned income
Net worth
  Preferred stock
  Common stock
  Capital surplus
  Retained earnings (surplus)
  Undivided profit
Periodic or profit statement items
  Gross sales
  Returns and allowances
  Net sales
  Selling expense
  Gross profits
  Operating expenses
  Administrative and general expense
  Materials expense
  Manufacturing expense
  Operating profit
  Depreciation expense
  Provision for doubtful accounts
  Net profit or loss

business indicators. One of these studies is shown in Fig. 10-1. From it you can get some idea of the relative timing of various indicators. This time relationship is essential when you try to find out whether financial factors in your own company and industry precede or follow those major indicators that guide trained economic forecasters.[3]

Besides the obvious value of economic projections in establishing sales forecasts, manpower forecasting, and operations forecasting, such economic projections are also helpful in determining:

Availability of money for loans or for equity financing

Whether to borrow on short or long terms

Estimates of collection performance

Extent to which accounts receivable will be discounted

Activity of installment buying

Inflation or deflation of inventory values

Price movements affecting purchase expense and sales income

Interest rates on deposits

Whether to lease equipment or to purchase outright

On the financial side of business, projections or forecasts are generally called "budgets." And budgeting is inseparable from the practice of management by exception. In financial budgeting, emphasis is placed essentially upon two factors: forecasting cash inflow and anticipating cash outflow.

Cash Inflow. This usually comes from five sources: (1) cash sales, (2) collection of receivables, (3) interest and dividends, (4) loans, and (5) miscellaneous items, such as sale of capital assets and tax refunds. However, collection of receivables often becomes the critical item in this list. And it in turn is affected by many variables which should be projected at budget time. These variables include volume of cash sales, sales on account (and the terms of these), sales returns, discounts for prompt payment, bad debts, and the time period in which payments are actually received. These factors can be projected from past experience and then adjusted on the basis of current observations and forecasts of change.

Cash Outflow. This will be affected by (1) anticipated accounts payable—and their rate of payment, (2) payrolls, (3) payroll taxes, (4) income taxes, (5) real estate taxes, (6) interest, and (7) other accruing liabilities.

As a consequence, the most astute typically make two kinds of budgets—on a weekly, monthly, quarterly, and annual basis. These are:

Fig. 10-1. Lead-lag Timing of 26 Business Cycle Indicators

(Average through 1958 and at 1960–61 Turning Points; Leads and Lags in Months)

Indicator	No. of timing comparisons through 1958 at business cycle		Median lead (−) or lag (+) through 1958 at business cycle		Lead (−) or lag (+) at	
	Peaks	Troughs	Peak	Trough	May 1960 Peak	Feb. 1961 Trough
Leading Group						
Sensitive Employment Indicators:						
1. Average workweek, mfg............	7	8	−5	−4.5	−12	−2
2. Gross accession rate, mfg...........	9	10	−10	−4	−14	−2
3. Layoff rate, mfg., inverted........	9	9	−9	−7	−12	0
New Investment Commitments:						
4. New orders, durable goods.........	7	8	−6	−2	−11	−1
5. Housing starts....................	8	8	−14	−5	−17	−2
6. Commercial and industrial building contracts.......................	7	8	−9	−1.5		
7. Net change in number of businesses	20	22	−3	−5	0	−3
Profits, Business Failures, and Stock Prices:						
8. Business failures, liabilities, inverted	17	18	−7	−7	−12	−8
9. Corp. profits after taxes	8	9	−4	−2	−12	0
10. Common stock price index........	19	19	−4	−5	−10	−4
Inventory Investment and Sensitive Commodity Prices:						
11. Change in bus. inventories	4	4	−17.5	−5.5	−12	0
12. Industrial materials spot market price index......................	8	9	−7.5	0	−6	−2
Roughly Coinciding Group						
Employment and Unemployment:						
13. Nonagricultural employment.......	16	16	0	0	−1	0
14. Unemployment rate, inverted.......	5	6	−4	+1.5	−3	+3
Production:						
15. Industrial production index........	17	17	0	−1	−4	0
16. Gross national product, current prices	6	7	+0.5	−1	0	0
17. Gross national product, constant prices	3	3	0	−3	0	0
Income and Trade:						
18. Bank debits outside N.Y.C........	16	17	+1.5	−3		
19. Personal income..................	8	9	+1	−2	+5	0
20. Sales by retail stores..............	6	6	+2.5	−0.5	−1	−1
Wholesale Prices:						
21. Wholesale prices, excl. farm products and foods...............	6	7	+1	+1	−10	+8
Lagging Group						
22. Plant and equipment expenditures	9	9	+1	+2	0	+3
23. Wage and salary cost per unit of output.....................	6	7	+6.5	+9	+10	+6
24. Manufacturers' inventories, book value, end of mo.................	7	7	+1.5	+3.5	+1.5	+1.5
25. Consumer instal. debt, end of mo....	4	4	+5.5	+3.5	+7.5	+5.5
26. Bank interest rates on business loans, last mo. of quarter..........	8	9	+5	+5	−5	+10

source: "Tested Knowledge of Business Cycles," June, 1962, pp. 66–67, copyright National Bureau of Economic Research, Inc., New York.

Balance sheet budgets, including
  Cash
  Capital investments
  Raw materials
  Finished goods inventories
  Receivables
  Payables
Sales dollar budgets
  Sales income
  Selling costs
  Production (in units)
  Cost of production
  Direct materials
  Administrative charges

Accounting and Auditing

Responsibility for financial observations are traditionally placed in the hands of accountants—and verified by auditors. If you were to ask your accountant, however, for a daily closing, he'd be dumbfounded. Yet essentially that is what you need. For management by exception purposes, generally speaking, it is false economy for management to wait a month or more for a precise report of the situation. Consequently, each organization must determine what (for it) are the key financial factors and then devise ways to get daily—or at the worst weekly—estimates of these key financial positions. If the limits of accuracy demanded are reasonable, say within 5 per cent, most accountants can report such observations economically. In any event, prompt financial observations are needed. Control, especially financial control, depends upon timing. It cannot work from postmortems.

The Financial Report

Many accountants have done themselves and their employers a disservice by erecting a protective jargon around their work. Instead of aiding management, they confuse and obstruct. The accountant who would be valuable in the management by exception system must be more than a clerk. He must consolidate and refine clerical reports. He must choose the important figures and discard the less significant ones. And he must also phrase his reports in terms meaningful to the management echelon which must act upon them. Top management will understand and interpret dollar values in their broadest profit implications—as percentages of sales income or capital invested. Lower levels of management, however, will find financial figures more useful when stated in terms of departmental objectives or measures—such as dollars per ton produced (or whatever is the local unit of measure).

Specifically, Rose and Farr have urged that a minimum set of items appear on a financial control report:

Sales income: current, cumulative, and moving annual total (M.A.T.)
Calendar days elapsed: current, cumulative, and M.A.T.
Dollars per sale day: current, cumulative, and M.A.T.
Circulating capital (current assets) in dollars
Circulating capital (M.A.T. sales days)
Circulating capital makeup (in dollars and M.A.T. sales days)
   Cash
   Accounts receivable
   Inventory, finished products
   Inventory, work in process
   Inventory, raw materials
Circulating capital flow speed in revolutions per year (365 divided by circulating capital in M.A.T. sales days)
Accounts receivable in dollars
   In current sales days
   In cumulative sales days
   In M.A.T. sales days
Accounts payable in dollars
   In current sales days
   In cumulative sales days
   In M.A.T. sales days
Liquid assets
Current liabilities
Ratios: Liquid assets/current assets
       Current assets/current liabilities
Working capital (current assets less current liabilities)
Investment (expressed in dollars and per cent of totals)
Accounts receivable
Inventory, finished products
Inventory, work in process
Inventory, raw materials
Total capital employed M.A.T.
Turnover (total capital employed M.A.T./sales income M.A.T.)
Operating profits expressed as per cent on total capital employed M.A.T. and as per cent on sales income M.A.T.

Rose and Farr's technique calls for comparative data to be gathered from the balance sheet ("point" figures) and the profit and loss sheet ("period" figures). The link between the two is the number of sales days. To each item on the report, Rose and Farr would attach a comment indicating analysis of performance with respect to anticipated, and a recommendation for corrective action.[4]

Financial Control

The comparison reports last mentioned form the basis for the determination of many of the action indicators pertaining to financial management by exception. Actual selection of indicator levels is aided by reference to published norms. For example, Dun & Bradstreet regularly publishes fourteen ratios based upon study of financial reports of hundreds of companies in a number of different lines of business.[5] These fourteen ratios include:

Current assets to current debts
Net profit on net sales
Net profits on tangible net worth
Net profits on net working capital
Net sales to tangible net worth
Net sales to net working capital
Collection period in days
Net sales to inventory
Fixed assets to tangible net worth
Current debt to tangible net worth
Total debt to tangible net worth
Inventory to net working capital
Current debt to inventory
Funded debts to net working capital

Rules of Thumb. In addition, many texts provide rules of thumb with reference to these and other ratios. For example, one Dun & Bradstreet official suggests:

1. That a typical ratio for current assets to current liabilities is 2 to 1

2. That current liabilities to tangible net worth ought to range between ⅔ and ¾

3. That total liabilities to tangible net worth is better if it is under 100 per cent

4. That, similarly, funded debt to net working capital should be under 100 per cent

5. That the ratio of depreciated fixed assets to tangible net worth is expected to range from ⅔ to ¾

6. That ratios of net sales to inventories vary widely according to industry and broad generalities are to be avoided

7. That inventories to net working capital are a measure of the ability of a concern to provide service, and for manufacture and wholesale business a check should be made if the ratio exceeds 100 per cent

8. That the average collection period reflects the worth of receivables and should not exceed one-third more than the net selling terms offered

9. That for net sales to net worth, exceptions should be noted if your figure exceeds twice the median ratio for your industry

10. That net sales to net working capital should not become top-heavy, although generalities here are hard to draw[6]

Similarly, data have been published showing as per cent of net sales (1) the cost of materials, (2) the cost of manufacturing labor, and (3) expenses and net profit for various manufacturing industries and retail and wholesale trades.[7]

However, Roy A. Foulke, a vice-president of Dun & Bradstreet, Inc., cautions in the use of ratios:

> A ratio or a series of ratios that are good in one year may become poor in succeeding years under business management. Managements are constantly changing in ability, ingenuity, aggressiveness, and power, and in the relationship of these attributes compared with competitive managements. A knowledge of the significance of important ratios will point out weaknesses and whether a financial condition is wholly or partly good, questionable, or poor. But the great unknown is always management, which has the power to improve the condition or hasten the ruin of any business. It is not the ratio or the ratios *ipso facto*, that mean a business concern is out of line. The ratio is the symptom, like the blood pressure, the pulse or the temperature of an individual. Some managements can overcome or mitigate the symptoms; other managements fail to recognize the symptoms or lack the ability, the aggressiveness, and the knowledge to overcome or mitigate them.[8]

Control Points. In applying the break-even-chart principle (see pages 129–133), there are labels that are commonly applied to financial action indicators. For instance, the "crisis" point is the point at which losses end and profit begins; the "danger" point is the point below which preferred dividends are not earned; the "unhealthy" point is the point at which common dividends are not earned; and the "deadline" is the point at which budgeted expectations are exceeded.

Alfred P. Sloan, Jr., recalls the early need for centralized cash controls at General Motors. Depositary accounts were established in 100 banks. All withdrawals were placed under corporate control. GM's financial staff then set fixed maximum and minimum balances for these accounts—according to the size of the account. Sloan then pins down the management by exception practice: "At this time, we begin calculating a month ahead what our cash would be each day of the month. Against this projected curve we compared each day the corporation's actual cash balances. A divergence of the actual curve from the projected curve would be the signal to find the reasons for such divergence and to take corrective action at the appropriate level of operations." [9]

Eventually, similar controls of cash and its withdrawal from the General Motors corporate system resulted in schedules of authorized expenditures (at the discretion of the individual and not requiring further approval) such as those cited for Westinghouse earlier in this text.

Auditing Performance. Finally, many companies require the preparation of "make-good" reports, which analyze the results of capital expenditures. These reports compare projected performance and savings with the actual attained. From the analysis, conclusions are drawn that are fed back into the management by exception system. New measurements may be added, or old ones dropped. Future projections may be modified. Observation techniques may be improved or speeded up. And action indicators may be tightened or liberalized.

In many ways, formal auditing procedures may be utilized in the same way. They need not be limited to mere verification. Observations secured during the financial audit may serve a positive purpose in making the management by exception of financial position more effective.

References

1. Owen R. Cheatham, "Top Management's Responsibility for Finance and Control," in H. B. Maynard (ed.), *Top Management Handbook*, McGraw-Hill Book Company, New York, 1960, pp. 633–648.
2. Lloyd G. Smiley, "Rate of Return—Toughest Measure of a Manager," *Factory*, November, 1958.
3. "Tested knowledge of Business Cycles," 42d Annual Report, National Bureau of Economic Research, Inc., New York, June, 1962, p. 66.
4. T. G. Rose and Donald E. Farr, *Higher Management Control*, McGraw-Hill Book Company, New York, 1957, p. 234.
5. "14 Important Ratios in 36 Manufacturing Lines," *Dun's Review and Modern Industry*, December, 1962, p. 43.
6. Roy A. Foulke, *Practical Financial Statement Analysis*, 5th ed., McGraw-Hill Book Company, New York, 1962.
7. *Ibid.*, p. 157.
8. *Ibid.*, p. 177.
9. Alfred P. Sloan, Jr., "My Years with General Motors: Our Strategy Works Out to a T—and the Model T Goes Under," *Fortune*, November, 1963, p. 167.

Chapter 11

MANAGING OPERATIONS AND
AUXILIARY SERVICES

Nowhere else is management by exception practiced so routinely—
or so well—as in manufacturing operations. And rightly so. Taylor,
Gantt, Gilbreth, and the rest were industrial engineers whose focus
was on production management. Their good pioneering work persists today. Take several recent examples:

 • At the McKinnon Industries, Ltd., of Saint Catharine's, Ontario,
a statistical maintenance control system enabled management to cut
its expenditures for breakdown repairs from 52 per cent to 40 per
cent of its total maintenance dollars. Obviously, machine utilization
increased proportionately at the same time. McKinnon's SMC plan
is a costing method that permits detailed segregation of maintenance
costs into 4,000 accounts. Accurate measurements of costs show
management where its money is spent, item by item, and why—for
breakdowns, preventive maintenance, construction, rearrangement,
or safety. From this base, management sets up monthly budgets for
each department and for each kind of equipment. Performance
against budget is reported at month's end. Variances that result in
savings are highlighted, and excessive charges are pinpointed in
final analyses.[1]

 • At International Business Machines Corporation, a superfast
production control system provides management with the kind of

193

up-to-the-minute shop information that closes 11 per cent more orders on schedule, reduces expediting 6 per cent, decreases dead orders by 50,000 hours, and raises machine loading potential by 20 per cent. Weekly reports furnish management with machine-load trends. These trends include changes in the total load level, variations in the relationship of past-due and behind-schedule loads to the total load level, and bulges and dips in the load forecast. The system itself cannot eliminate overload conditions, but it does identify them as they arise. In addition, the system is programmed to recognize exceptional conditions (attributed to errors) as they occur. For instance, it automatically flags for management's attention an order with an excess lead time, an order started ahead of schedule, an order released too late, etc.[2]

• At Westinghouse Electric Corporation, plant modernizations are guided by a set of goals selected to maximize investment returns while minimizing risk of too rapid process change. Such modernization goals include 20 per cent minimum return on investment, 40 per cent reduction in labor input, 15 per cent cut in indirect labor, 15 per cent drop in material costs, savings of a half day in manufacturing cycle time, 25 per cent reduction in setup time, and no increase in floorspace requirements. In 1962 one ten-year-old plant was able to meet each of these projected goals with the exception of setup times. But management could sacrifice this subgoal by reducing the overall manufacturing cycle, which in turn shortened delivery time.[3]

• At Hughes Aircraft Company, plant engineering made spectacular gains attributable to a labor-reporting system which provides management with a number of performance ratios for comparative analysis. Some of the results reported by Hughes include these: ratio of maintenance craftsmen to total plant personnel went from 1:28 to 1:41, monthly power consumption in kilowatt-hours rose from 125 per electrician to 200, average number of plumbing fixtures serviced by one plumber increased from 80 to 180, average tons of air conditioning per air-conditioning mechanic rose from 155 to 255, all while the average number of hourly personnel under one plant engineering supervisor increased from 7.6 to 9.6.[4]

• At the Massey-Ferguson tractor plant in Detroit, safety performance goals for departmental foremen helped cut workmen's compensation payments from $88 per employee per year to $7 in 1962. This management by exception technique uses past history to establish safety cost, housekeeping, and attitude targets. Detailed monthly reports show each foreman how he is doing and where his record needs improvement. Corrective action is up to him.[5]

• At Chrysler Corporation's highly automated Mound Road engine plant in Detroit, management by exception is highly visible. At a final test stand, engines are automatically tested for more than 100 quality items. An inspector plots each defect indicated by the test equipment on a master control board. When the frequency of defects warrants action, an inspector switches on a red danger light which alerts the production foreman upstream to take corrective measures. In addition, the inspection manager issues a "chronic quality defection memo" when (1) an abnormally high frequency of any single defect occurs, (2) the same defect occurs on two or more successive checks, regardless of frequency, or (3) the frequency of the defect is statistically erratic.

• At Olmstead Air Force Maintenance Base, quality control and inspection costs were slashed 30 per cent in one year by using a management by exception action-indicator-levels analysis and reporting sheet. Space vehicle parts are segregated into several categories according to the specified reliability required. In each category, frequency of inspection samples is preselected on the basis of past history. On some items with good quality history records, as many as nine days pass between sampling inspections. However, each category starts with a predetermined acceptance quality level (AQL). This may mean that for category 1, 3 per cent defective is normal. When this rate is exceeded, the exception moves into zone A, where an established sampling procedure is followed every five days. If the defect rate increases, the exception moves into zone B, where the sampling procedure is followed every three days. If this is exceeded, sampling procedure becomes daily. Responsibility for corrective action is up to the foreman while the conditions are in zones A, B, or C. When the defect rate exceeds this, the quality control supervisor may institute 100 per cent inspection at his own discretion—while simultaneously notifying the department head of the condition.

• At the AC Spark Plug division of General Motors Corporation, production control supervisors set and reset their own standards of performance—fourteen in all. They establish such goals as limiting overtime to 5 per cent of the hours worked and attaining a 90 per cent conformance to factory schedules. Failure to reach a monthly goal calls for discussion with the department manager. The goal may or may not be loosened as a result. AC management, however, observes that in most instances, supervisors meet the challenge and ask for increasingly tighter performance goals.[6]

Measuring Operating Conditions

The previous examples demonstrate the proliferation of measurement schemes which operations management has developed to aid in the practice of management by exception. To compile a complete list would be a subject for an expensive research project. As a compromise approach, Table 11-1 presents some of the many measurements that can be made at the measurement step.

Manufacturing measurement techniques are generally oriented toward some kind of measure of time utilization. This has been accomplished by (1) comparing labor input over a fairly long period—say a day, week, or month with the total output for that period in units; (2) directly measuring by stopwatch the time needed to accomplish a task—counting fractions of a minute or even of a second; (3) predetermining the time needed to make certain basic human movements and computing total times according to the number and kind of movements needed to accomplish a task; and (4) observing activities at random intervals (work sampling) to determine what part or how much of the labor input is gainfully employed at various tasks, and then relating these observations to labor employment over a substantial period of time—such as a day, week, or month.

Measurement in manufacturing usually begins with some sort of job analysis—in which a job or task is progressively fractionated into smaller and smaller elements. Gilbreth calculated that most human activities could be described by any one or a combination of eighteen movements, which he called "therbligs." [7] Later systems, such as MTM and work factor, are mainly modifications of this approach. However, the cost of measuring, especially for nonrepetitive work, is so great that emphasis today is on making faster and cheaper estimates. Consequently, precision has been sacrificed—even to the extent of using very broad-gage measurements such as breaking down a typical warehousing job into loading, unloading, order picking, etc., and using broad time measures of hours, weeks, and years. Surprisingly, the results in many instances seem still to be accurate enough to make the management by exception practice pay off.

Table 11-1. Some Possible Measures of Operations and Auxiliaries

---

PRODUCTION MEASUREMENT
From payroll sources
Direct labor:
Number of employees
Man-hours on day work
Man-hours on incentives
Man-hours on standards
Man-hours earned
Man-hours off standards
Man-hours of overtime
Man-hour distribution per cost center
Indirect labor:
Number of employees
Man-hours on day work
Man-hours on incentives
Man-hours on standards
Man-hours earned
Man-hours off standards
Man-hours of overtime
Indirect labor distribution (number of employees and/or man-hours)
Tool and fixtures making
Setup
Maintenance and repair
Salvage, rework, reprocess
Housekeeping, sanitation
Clerical
Inspection, quality control
Factory engineering
Receiving, shipping, warehousing
Material handling
From nonpayroll sources
Manufacturing occupancy (per cent of available square footage)
Machine capacity
Machine utilization
Waste, scrap, rejects in units and dollars
Manufacturing output in units and dollars
Manufacturing shipments in units and dollars
Breakdown report
Utility consumption
Equipment age, condition, upkeep cost
Shop supplies usage
Nondurable tools consumption
Material yields
    Raw material costs
    Raw material consumption
    Shrinkages
    Per hour of direct labor

Table 11-1. Some Possible Measures of Operations and Auxiliaries (Continued)

Manufacturing cycle time
Productivity
    Net output per unweighted man-hour
    Net output per weighted man-hour*
    Net output per unit of weighted tangible capital†
    Net output per weighted unit of labor and tangible capital
PRODUCTION AUXILIARIES
    Industrial engineering
        Total industrial-engineering personnel
        Number of industrial-engineering personnel/1,000 factory employees
        Number of industrial-engineering personnel on standards work/1,000 factory
            employees
        Percentage of direct employees on incentives
        Percentage of indirect employees on incentives
        Average earnings as percentage of base rate
    Production and inventory control
        No. of production and inventory-control employees/total plant employment
        Inventory performance
            Inventory turnover rate
            Dollars in inventory
            Surplus inventory
            Obsolete inventory
            Cost of holding inventories
            Estimated material cost versus actual
            Percentage of items for which no receipts or distribution was made
            Percentage of stock-outs
            Scheduled levels of inventory versus actual for raw materials, work in
                process, and finished goods
            Levels of protective stock
        Production control performance
            Machine utilization
            Percentage of orders shipped on time
            Overtime attributable to production control
            Number of setups
            Factory production schedules met
            Stockroom tooling and kitting schedules met
            Schedule performance in shipping spare parts
            Schedule performance in shipping major equipment
            Receipt from vendor schedule performance
            Processing time related to total production cycle time
    Quality control
        Inspection and quality control personnel/1,000 factory employees
        Inspection productivity (percentage of time inspecting)

---

   * Reflects differences in average hourly earnings for different occupational groups.
   † Land, plants, equipment, and inventory.

Table 11-1. Some Possible Measures of Operations and Auxiliaries (Continued)

Inspection cost/unit removed
Scrap totals and per cents
Rework totals and percentages
Material handling
Ratio material handling personnel/1,000 factory employees
Percentage of time lost by direct labor in material handling
Ratio total number of moves/total number of operations
Ratio of sum of production operation time/total manufacturing cycle time
Percentage of usable cubic footage usefully occupied
Percentage of available time material handling equipment is used
Percentage of floor space utilized
Material handling costs as percentage of manufacturing expense
Maintenance
Maintenance employees per 100 production workers
1,000 square feet of manufacturing area per maintenance employee
Horsepower of connected electrical load per maintenance worker
Horsepower of connected electrical load per 1,000 square feet of manufacturing area
Percentage of total man-hours of maintenance on work planned
Percentage of total man-hours of maintenance on emergency work
Percentage of total man-hours of maintenance on overtime
Crew weeks of current backlog
Crew weeks of total backlog
Percentage of total maintenance man-hours on preventive maintenance
Maintenance costs as percentage of plant investment
Maintenance costs as percentage of costs per unit of product produced
Percentage of operating time lost in downtime due to maintenance reasons
Number of units of product produced per maintenance dollar
Percentage of time maintenance force is gainfully employed
Purchasing
Percentage of dollar commitments to gross sales
Percentage of dollar commitments to disbursements
Percentage rejects in goods received
Percentage shortages in scheduled production material
Schedule requirements versus end-line delivery
Inventory versus production
Inventory versus sales
Number of requisitions per month and versus forecast
Number of requisitions versus purchasing manpower costs, postage, travel, and freight
Average total costs of issuing a requisition
Labor cost per requisition
Average lead time
Vendors' performance against promised time and quality
Subcontractor performance against time, quality, and cost
Flow-time from request to purchase to purchase-order issuance

Table 11-1. Some Possible Measures of Operations and Auxiliaries (Continued)

Transportation
   Total pounds hauled
   Miles traveled
   Pound-miles hauled
   Number of trailer trips (loaded and empty)
   Percentage of empty trips
   Pounds hauled per trailer trip
   Number of tractor trips (with trailer or light)
   Percentage of light trips
   Controllable cost per mile
   Controllable cost per trip
   Total line-haul cost per mile
   Total line-haul cost per trip
   Man-hours for drivers, straight time and overtime
   Man-hours for ship, straight time and overtime
   Number of distribution stops
   Cost per stop
   Man-hours per stop
   Man-hours per pound delivered
   Dock performance
      Pounds handled
      Total dock cost
      Man-hours, straight time and overtime
      Pounds handled per man-hour
      Cost per pound handled
   Controllable costs
      Line-haul labor: drivers, dispatchers, clerical, other supervision
      Shop labor: maintenance, refrigeration, other
      Repair parts
      Tires and tubes
      Shop supplies
      Fuel, oil, antifreeze, etc.
      Tire wear
   Standing costs
      Licenses and permits
      Insurance
      Depreciation
      Housing

Setting Operational Goals

Manufacturing projections today—especially in terms of production goals—are almost always dictated by sales/inventory projections and decisions. It is hard to believe that until the 1930s (in some instances the 1950s) the production forecast rather than the sales forecast was the most commonly used projection. In other words, a plant's capacity, and the ability of the production manager to utilize it, often determined how much goods would be made in any one period. It is probably for that reason that the economic laws of supply and demand worked so well prior to World War II. Surplus goods were almost always cleared from the warehouse for what the market would bear. However, today most of us concede that it makes more economic and business sense to base production forecasts upon sales forecasts, as opposed to letting the tail wag the dog.

Today, then, the emphasis is, and rightly so, on making operational projections not so much of output alone (which is often established by the financial and marketing people) as of output related to cost, quality, and delivery. Then, too, most projections mean little in the absolute. They become meaningful only when they are spoken of in terms of unit costs. For example, an expense budget of $1.5 million for a producing department conveys little to the manager unless it is connected to an output figure. It comes alive when it is stated in such terms as, "We expect to spend $1.5 million for 75,000 units or 750,000 tons of throughput." It becomes even more meaningful when it is also tied to product specifications and delivery schedules.

Manufacturing projections have also been characterized over the years by a conservative adherence to past experience. Projections for next year too often follow closely last year's performance. When cost cutting is forecast, for instance, it tends to be cautious rather than radical. A manager will readily agree to look for a reduction of 2 per cent here or 5 per cent there. But it takes bold vision, plus the promise of capital equipment to aid him, to make a production manager reach ahead in terms of a 20 per cent or more annual cost reduction.

In nonproduction areas, management tends to be even more cautious. And in these areas it is hampered by a frequent absence of concrete measures of its activities. An inspection department, for instance, may project a higher percentage of qualified goods reaching the shipping door (or the acceptance of tighter tolerances), but it is reluctant to also project savings in inspection costs per unit. In other words, the traditional "overhead" departments are reluctant to alter their thinking to include objective measures of the quality and quantity of their services—and then to relate these to the cost of their services on a per unit basis.

Fortunately, forcing this progressive kind of thinking also forces more daring projections—with attendant managerial ingenuity in devising and persevering to newer, higher goals. For example:

• A quality control department might forecast a 15 per cent reduction of in-line inspection labor costs, while at the same time forecasting a 5 per cent increase in statistical analysis costs, a drop of 7 per cent in rework at final assembly stages, and a net savings of quality control cost per unit of 8 per cent.

• A production control department might forecast an increase of 12 per cent in on-time deliveries, while at the same time projecting a 20 per cent reduction in the cost of controlling production.

And so on. The point being that it is desirable to aggressively strive for new goals in terms of service while at the same time striving for new goals in the reduction of the cost of providing the service.

Observing Costs

Manufacturing long ago solved the problem of obtaining daily counts (quantitative measurements) of production. It has done so with tally sheets, weighing scales, raw material issue tickets, warehouse receipts, and mechanical and electronic counting devices. And in-process quality control (qualitative measurements), temperature, pressure, acidity, and other indicators have been invented and hooked up to flash lights or ring bells when undesirable or exceptional conditions occur.

Observing, comparing, and reporting of cost have been less rapid in their progress toward perfection. In earlier days, management's fundamental cost check was the labor head-count—for both direct and indirect employees. For production managers, this was the quickest way to find out whether costs were adhering to expectations or not. The needs, and the techniques, today are far more complex and representative.

Root cause of the lags in cost reporting can probably be placed in the lap of accounting departments, which traditionally are more oriented toward auditing and verifying financial positions than toward providing segments of operating management with observations or comparisons of exceptions—or if they do, it has been far after the fact. Today, of course, with the introduction of the computer, this situation is rapidly changing. Higher management is increasingly able to attain both greater financial accuracy and faster reporting of operating conditions.

The key operations observers, comparers, and reporters in days gone by were the industrial engineer and the quality control manager. Their techniques, reported in more detail elsewhere in this text, provide the basis for the wide application of management by exception found in industry today. The industrial engineer's point of view is quantitative. He is volume- or output-oriented. The quality manager's perspective is obviously qualitative. His observations and reports are concerned with product and process variables. In some respects, these differing approaches illustrate what must be achieved in all areas—control of the "means" in order to attain the "results" desired. What management, especially in production, is now striving for is a more representative and faster measure and control of the means, rather than what in the past was often a postmortem measurement and reporting of results.

Reporting Operational Variances

Comparison and reporting of performance can take many forms. An outstanding example of versatility is a "wheel of progress" audit of purchasing performance prepared by the Autonetics Division of North American Aviation, Inc. This management by exception checking system is prepared by a staff of internal auditors who plot their observations on a wheel-like bar chart. Its thirty-five spokes represent quarterly performance against purchasing activity objectives. Results of the grading system go directly to Autonetics' director of material, C. R. Raftery. He says, "The system meets our demands for improved visibility and surveillance techniques. It has extended management's influence and provided assurance of a high degree of compliance with policies, procedures, and acceptable practices."

A special team of experts, called the "administrative surveillance section," carries out the details of Autonetics' program. It performs a continuous review of purchasing performance through the use of nineteen separate check sheets. Each of three product divisions, headed by three purchasing managers, is covered by two specialists. One expert reviews all current orders of $25,000 or more and makes a random sampling of smaller orders as they are mailed. The results are summarized to establish ratings for seventeen of the thirty-five functions. The second analyst checks "after the fact" activities through documents, personal observations, and interviews with operating personnel. This establishes ratings for the remaining eighteen functional areas. Says Autonetics' top management, "A major benefit from the system is to furnish a basis for implementing timely corrective action." [8]

An example of an unusually good variance report is shown in Fig. 11-1. It is typical of that used by Genesco, Inc., to rate performance of its various operating and auxiliary groups.

Rising Action Levels

The proliferation of exception indicators and action levels used by various operating departments makes it difficult to generalize about key measures. The unit cost—of any input or service—is, and probably will continue to be, the most significant measure. But some of the old reliables (like the ratio of indirect to direct labor) are losing their original meaning. New relationships (such as the ratio of labor to connected horsepower) are being used more often. Others, too, will come along. But since operations are charged with producing a product (or offering a service) of specified quality, in predetermined quantities, and at a prefixed time, key management tools for management by exception will focus around the three variables that almost always characterize industrial or commercial marketing objectives: cost of products, quality of products, and availability of products.

The manufacturing manager (plant manager, plant superintendent, etc.), once the superb coordinator of functional decisions within his bailiwick, seems to be diminishing in importance. Systems and integrated data-processing equipment now juggle facts and time with ease, which only a skilled manager previously could do. Management by exception places more emphasis on making vital decisions that affect long-range operations than on short-range decisions traditionally handled by middle managers.

Action on R & D Problems

Research and development becomes a special case in practicing management by exception—not in all aspects, of course. For in routine administration of costs, manpower, and machine and material

Fig. 11-1. Example of Monthly Objectives and Performance
Report for a Purchasing Group

	Actual	Objectives for January	Variation
1. Damaged shoes charged to purchasing as percentage of value of production................	0.001%	less than 0.01%	O.K.
2. Standard price index as percentage of weekly bulletin price index......................	96.4%	less than 100%	O.K.
3. (a) Substitution losses as a percentage of value of materials used......................	0.07%	less than 0.2%	O.K.
(b) Low-grade upper leather substitution—month.........	$420	$500	O.K.
4. Obsolescence loss as percentage of materials used—month......	0.38%	less than 1.0%	O.K.
5. Raw materials inventories as percentage of month's usage (83,000 units)...............	107.2%	less than 100.0%	+7.2%
6. Department expense as a percentage of budget—month.....	119.8%	less than 100%	+19.8%
period......	105.3%		
7. Material shortage by week as percentage of total weekly production Week	Per cent		
1-9	2.6		
1-16	2.5		
1-23	2.0		
1-30	2.0		
Weeks average	2.2	less than 2.0%	+0.2%
8. Purchase gain or loss 23347			
period 76382		NA	O.K.
9. Number of job descriptions and job standards prepared or improved....................	2	5 per month	−3
10. List of projects to develop group image in and outside company	2	at least 2 per mo.	O.K.

source: W. M. Jarman and B. H. Willingham, in Mason Haire (ed.), *Organization Theory in Practice*, John Wiley & Sons, Inc., New York, 1962, p. 66.

utilization, this function would follow the same path as other operational departments. However, the specific objectives of research are often unknown, or at best generalized, and much of the progress toward these goals is difficult to assess.

Bruce Payne suggests that R & D goals can be set at a happy medium between the general and the specific, as illustrated in Fig. 11-2.

Dr. W. Wai Chao, director of research and development at Vickers, Inc., poses the R & D problem this way: "There are three ways to improve research effectiveness: select the right program, communicate project goals to managers, and know how to cancel a program." [9] How can these seemingly simple decisions be carried out? Rockwell Manufacturing Co. seems to know how.

Rockwell attacks the R & D problem by assigning responsibility to a man steeped in the management by exception process—Gen. Joseph M. Colby (USA Ret.). Colby first organized a planning and control pyramid of committees, subcommittees, and task forces. At the top of the pyramid he placed a group consisting of Chairman

---

FIG. 11-2. EXAMPLE OF RESEARCH AND DEVELOPMENT OBJECTIVES

First-year goals:
1. To achieve a major improvement in the quality of Product A
2. To develop Product B until it is marketable
3. To introduce Product B as a companion product to large Product A customers
4. To develop Product C to the point where it can be produced and sold commercially
5. To refine and improve several raw materials used in Products A, B, and C to the point where acceptable laboratory materials have been developed
6. To carry out research in several related product ideas which have shown superior quality
7. To develop Product D to the model stage

Five-year goals:
1. To increase the effectiveness rating of Product A by 28 per cent
2. To develop methods for producing more precise, impurity-free materials in Product A
3. To improve the efficiency in the manufacture of Product C from present raw materials and find alternate sources for raw materials
4. To develop new products from process Z in order to spearhead the diversification of the Company in this new field

---

SOURCE: Bruce Payne, *Planning for Company Growth*, McGraw-Hill Book Company, New York, 1963, p. 167.

Rockwell and a dozen corporate vice-presidents. This group meets once a month and acts as a final review board to make all "go–no-go" decisions. The work of Rockwell's several hundred scientists and engineers is observed and reported upward through the planning hierarchy by periodic progress reports at all levels, by monthly written reports from engineers and technicians in outlying plants, by daily inspection of the headquarters research laboratory by Colby himself, and by periodic plant inspections to determine project progress.

Rockwell places special emphasis on timetable projections for each project. Five steps are planned, and deadlines set for each: (1) concept analysis, (2) feasibility study, (3) engineering prototype, (4) preproduction prototype, and (5) product improvement.[10]

How can management forecast a time, cost, and payout goal for an R & D project? A. J. Weinberger of the Central Research Division of American Cyanamid Company feels it can be done by making an economic assessment at each of four stages:

1. *Exploratory.* This would be appropriate before appreciable experimental work has been done. Processes may be based on textbook reactions, literature (including patent) references, or a few brief laboratory experiments.

2. *Preliminary range.* At this stage, laboratory work is well advanced. Process steps, yields, and process conditions are fairly well worked out, and raw material grades have been explored.

3. *Probable range.* An evaluation at this stage would be done after a considerable amount of pilot-plant work has been completed. Raw material grades, processing conditions, yields, and quality will be established. Materials of construction and treatment of recycle streams and wastes will have been considered even if not established definitely, and samples of product will have been subjected to the intended uses.

4. *Preproduction.* This would be the final evaluation after research and development has been completed. The project is now ready for a decision on commercialization.[11]

When should an R & D project be released from the research department and turned over to an operating group? Carborundum Company sets its action-indicator level at the point when the product starts to make money. Up until that point the product is under the authority of the new products branch, which is responsible not only for research and development but also for pilot production, market analysis, and sales development. When black ink occurs, the product is released to a new or existing operating division along with the research file, study of uses, market studies, manufacturing methods, and key personnel in production and sales.[12]

How much control should there be of the R & D activities? Jesse Werner, president of General Aniline Film Corp., observes, "Left to their own devices research and development people will experiment in many directions, each following his own particular bent. Once in a very great while, this leads to a commercially profitable scientific breakthrough, but in most cases it leads up blind alleys, and the company goes absolutely nowhere." As a result, he says, "Management is not offered the choice of planning or not planning. The only choice is whether the planning will be orderly and effective or whether it will be haphazard, fragmented, and practically useless." [13]

References

1. J. A. Watson, "Know Where Your Maintenance Dollar Is Going," *Factory*, December, 1962, p. 50.
2. T. J. Harris, "It Reschedules 500,000 Shop Hours Daily," *Factory*, December, 1962, p. 73.
3. H. A. Depree, "Are You Penny-wise, Automation-foolish?" *Factory*, January, 1963, p. 72.
4. B. R. Costales and R. L. Waller, "Data Processing Perks Maintenance," *Factory*, February, 1963, p. 94.
5. W. A. Cavanagh, "Safety Scorecard Keeps Line Foremen on the Ball," *Factory*, March, 1963, p. 110.
6. E. A. Blondin, "Method Helps Supervisors Set Production Control Standards," *Factory*, August, 1963, p. 86.
7. George W. Chane, *Motion and Time Study*, Harper & Row, Publishers, Incorporated, New York, 1942, p. 39.
8. "How Does Your Department Rate on This Autonetics 'Wheel of Progress' Audit Plan?" *Purchasing Week*, Nov. 18, 1963, p. 40.
9. *Steel*, Jan. 7, 1963, Penton Publishing Co., Cleveland.
10. "R & D by the Numbers," *Business Week*, Aug. 24, 1963, p. 59.
11. Arthur J. Weinberger, "Improving R & D's Batting Average," *Chemical Engineering*, Oct. 28, 1963, p. 123.
12. "Starting Product at a Profit," *Business Week*, Sept. 22, 1962, p. 62.
13. "Achieving Full Value from Your R & D Dollars," American Management Association, New York, 1962, p. 5.

Chapter 12

MANAGING SALES AND MARKETING

One of the most significant organizational shake-ups of this century took place on January 1, 1964. That was the day United States Steel Corporation dissolved its divisional setup and created a new organization with a single marketing staff and a single operations staff. The new marketing staff was organized on a regional basis, the new operations staff on a product basis. The previous organization consisted of seven self-sufficient major divisions, each with its own sales and production organization. The reason for this drastic change: the corporation's share of the market—a major exception indicator—had fallen below all tolerable limits. Management (Chairman Roger M. Blough and President Leslie B. Worthington) had to make the decision. It was one that reaffirmed an existing objective of selling to 33 per cent of the market. But it was also one that called for a major policy change—with resultant changes in organization and staff. Hundreds of high-level jobs were changed, consolidated, or eliminated.

For over two decades, U.S. Steel had held about one-third of the industry's total sales. Then in 1954, this percentage started to slip. It was checked at about 30 per cent in 1956 and in 1957, then began to slide again. It dropped to 26 per cent in 1959 and in 1960, then dropped in 1963 below a figure that Big Steel's board had decreed as an absolute minimum—one-fourth of the domestic market.

The new marketing organization called for an executive vice-president for sales, who would direct overall distribution. Reporting to him were two administrative vice-presidents for sales—one handling marketing, the other solicitation.

Chairman Blough stated the reason for the change: "A primary objective will be to give further impetus to our marketing, solicitation, and customer service, and thus increase the Corporation's market participation and sales of steel products." The net effect was to reduce the number of district sales offices by twenty-five and to consolidate many of the corporation's activities. Both in production and in customer service the net effect was to make Big Steel faster on its feet—whether the customer problem was that of supply or of application.[1]

Market Measurements

There can be little doubt that just as U.S. Steel has kept an accurate measure of large marketing factors (such as its share of market), it also has kept detailed measurements of small sales items. Few sales organizations can exist for long without them. As with other functions, the list of sales and/or marketing measures that can be made are endless. However, a National Industrial Conference Board study[2] demonstrated that sales effort could be measured in terms of three factors: quantity, quality, and difficulty. The three factors, implied the report, include the ten performance measures most often considered for evaluating sales performance:

1. Sales volume attained
2. Degree to which specific sales objectives are attained (as in the promotion of specific products or accounts)
3. New accounts developed
4. Degree to which more profitable products are sold
5. Selling expense
6. Knowledge of job (products, prices, advertising, promotion, etc.)
7. Effectiveness in handling affairs of a territory
8. Diligence and accuracy of sales reporting
9. Customer relations
10. Personal qualities of sales staff (appearance, intelligence, interest, diligence, etc.)

When sales performance is measured, certain other variable factors must also be measured. These include such items as competitive conditions in a territory, physical differences in a territory, differences in territory potential, differences in headquarters or supervisory support, time devoted to new-account development, volume of windfall or inherited accounts, and extent of nonrepeat business.

In addition, there is the matter of customer service, for which tangible measures are often hard to get. Included in this category are such factors as how many complaints that must be handled, promptness in handling telephone and mail requests, and servicing of a customer that does not result in immediate sales.

It soon becomes obvious to any researcher that the job of enumerating all the items reflecting upon sales or marketing management would be monumental. However, another NICB study[3] suggests measuring such elements as prices and their movement; distributor channels; small and custom orders; customer services and premiums; discounts; order processing; sales organization and staffing; sales force selection and training; dealer training and assistance; salesmen's compensation; territorial structures; travel and entertainment expenses; advertising budgets and schedules; media effectiveness in developing attention, inquiries, and sales; direct-mail activity; sales promotion; packaging; dealer inventories; transportation and distribution; warehouse location and operation; and market research activities. For each of these elements (and for the management of each by exception) the manager in charge of the function should be able to produce a long list of measures—of the service or element provided, of the cost, of the timeliness, and of the general effectiveness or usefulness of that service.

As an example of what a simple, but intensive, measurement of sales activities can reveal, consider the following comparison drawn from a study conducted by the University of Michigan in 1954 (Frank R. Bacon, Jr., under the direction of R. G. Cowan, professor of marketing):

	Salesman No. 1	Salesman No. 2
Average time per call	84 minutes	223 minutes
Time with buyer	43 minutes	37 minutes
Average waiting time	3.6 minutes	9 minutes
Travel time per call	19 minutes	68 minutes
Office work per call	9 minutes	21.5 minutes
Entertainment time per call	4.3 minutes	21.5 minutes
Miscellaneous time (buyer out, etc.)	5.1 minutes	55.7 minutes
Total time worked	85 hours	126 hours
Number of calls	62	35

It is from actual data like these that management can establish standards of individual performance—standards which facilitate comparisons and highlight exceptions for correction, discipline, training, encouragement, and promotion.

Projecting Sales

According to Warren K. Schoonmaker, a respected marketing consultant, all methods of sales projections and forecasting spring from two basic concepts:

> *The Trickle-down Philosophy.* The forecaster starts with the national economy and national trends. Within these parameters, an industry forecast is developed. Then within the new set of parameters, the company forecast is developed. This "shell-within-a-shell" approach expresses itself in the "share of industry" type of forecast, forecasts based on mathematical models built upon a set of indicators, etc.
>
> *The Mosaic Philosophy.* This starts from the opposite end. The forecaster goes to the marketplace for his information, even to his customer's customer, if need be. Then with enough bits in hand, he pieces together a complete picture. This construction approach expresses itself in demand function forecasting, surveys, censuses, etc.[4]

Mr. Schoonmaker's terse analysis is an oversimplification, of course. Sales forecasting methods range, of course, from the very naïve to the extremely sophisticated. And they range from the opinion-solicited method to complex statistical techniques. The method chosen depends in large part on the time and funds available and on how detailed the forecast must be. The McGraw-Hill Department of Economics evaluates the following popular techniques:

Opinion Methods

The sales force opinion method is still the most widely used in industry. The market research manager queries the sales force on how much each one expects to sell in the coming year. He gets all the reports in. But before he totals the results, he evaluates each salesman's estimate. If one salesman is chronically pessimistic, an upward adjustment is made in his figure. The estimate of the salesman who has been optimistic in the past is cut.

Why evaluate each salesman's estimate of future business? Obviously, the market research manager wants to do the very best job he can. He may know that it is to one salesman's advantage to under-estimate his sales goal, particularly if he works on a quota bonus plan. On the other hand, another salesman may be worried about holding his job so he sends in a high estimate in order to impress the vice president in charge of sales. But in either case salesmen generally are good judges of how business will shape up in their own territories.

Another version of this method is the executive opinion survey. Instead of querying individual salesmen, the sales vice president asks his regional or branch managers to estimate how much business will be done in their respective areas. Again the market research manager has to evaluate the individual estimates because past experience may indicate that some regional managers are poor forecasters while others are very good predictors. So some adjustments may be necessary here, too.

Panel Method

The panel method is another system for forecasting future sales. Members of various related industries are brought together by an outside research organization to discuss their needs for the next year. Firms selling to these industries can then estimate how much business will be available. For example, a manufacturer of textiles may get a research group to sponsor a meeting of this type. His customers—manufacturers of women's coats and suits, men's coats and suits, sportswear, etc.—estimate the increase or decrease in their business for the coming year. Based on these detailed reports from the panel meeting, the textile manager can prepare an estimate of future total demand for his products.

Expectation Surveys

The survey method is one way to forecast consumer product sales. A sample of consumers is queried on what they plan to buy, what price line or what brand. However, past experience shows that consumers' purchases fluctuate with the economic climate. They may be hot to buy today, but tomorrow they may have cooled off. Consumer surveys on a continuing basis catch these changes in mood.

The industrial survey is another method of estimating future sales. A sample of companies is queried by an outside research organization and asked how much of Company A's industrial products they expect to buy in the next year. This type of survey may be carried out by mail, telephone or personal interview. The results, based on the sample, may be expanded to represent the total business of the company. But company executives may change their minds about future purchases of capital goods just as housewives do when it comes to buying appliances. A company forecast based on a recent survey may go awry when, for example, a competitor decides to put on a big advertising campaign in order to achieve a bigger share of the market.

Share of the Market

The share of the market technique is an arithmetic method of forecasting future sales. The forecaster applies his company's percentage of the market to an estimate of industry sales for the year ahead usually provided by the industry trade association or the leading trade publication. If a company has maintained a fixed share of the market in the past, it is a simple exercise to multiply that percentage by the predicted level of industry sales in order to arrive at next year's sales volume.

But what if the company aims to gain a bigger share of the market pie during the year ahead or if one of its competitors decides to do the same? Some adjustments would have to be made in the first estimate of next year's sales volume.

Statistical Methods

There are three major statistical methods for sales forecasting: The lead-lag relationship, the correlation with time, and the correlation with a general economic indicator such as the gross national product or the index of industrial production.

Market researchers who can come up with a lead-lag relationship for their company believe it is a guarantee of personal success. The lead-lag relationship means that a company's sales follow by a specific time period the pattern of a particular economic indicator. For example, a market researcher for a company making switches for new homes finds that his company's sales follow by six months the trend of the number of housing permits issued. This means that if he knows what happened to housing permits last month, he can predict sales of his company's product several months ahead, and with a high degree of accuracy.

Usually, it is a time consuming task to find a series which leads a company's business. Even then mathematical relationships have to be computed. And sometimes to the dismay of the market researcher, the lead-lag relationship disappears completely after years of working with it.

When no lead-lag relationship can be discovered, the technique generally used today is the simple correlation between a company's sales and the gross national product or physical volume of sales and the Federal Reserve Board's index of Industrial production. For such relationships to be valid, sales must move along—up or down at the same time, with GNP or the industrial production gage for several years. There is no lead here. To forecast company sales, the market researcher must make or have available a good forecast of the general economic indicator.

Estimates of the future level of GNP or production for six months or a year ahead are available from leading business publications or from economic consulting services. It is far easier to get a reliable estimate of GNP for the year ahead than it is to make an independent sales estimate for a particular company or a particular product line.

However, sales forecasts based on correlations of sales with GNP or industrial production may turn out to be inaccurate for reasons beyond the particular forecast. First, a company may raise prices sufficiently to price itself out of the market. Second, a company may run ahead of its competitors in a year and so gets a bigger share of the national business than it ever did before. All the forecaster can do is make arbitrary allowances for these special circumstances.

When the forecaster can neither find a lead-lag relationship nor a relation between his company's sales and general economic indicators, he can always settle for a trend relationship. This merely relates past company sales to time, either monthly, quarterly, semi-annually or annually. In effect a mathematical trend line is fitted to the sales figures. Having established the equation between time and past sales data, it is a simple matter to extend the trend ahead by one time unit. But as in all mathematical relationships, this doesn't work perfectly every time.[5]

For an interesting example of how one company uses selected economic indicators to forecast turning points in the business cycle, especially as the cycle affects its line of business, see Fig. 12-1.

Observing Sales Performance

Call reports and sales billings provide the hard facts about sales effectiveness. The former are usually collated and analyzed by a central sales administrative staff. The latter may be analyzed independently or simultaneously with normal accounting procedures. Backing up these two methods is personal observation—on the part of sales management and, in vital matters, the highest echelons of executive management. For instance, *The Gallagher Report* (an advertising newsletter) reported: "When Beech-Nut Life Savers marketing department recommended changes of baby food labels from yellow to white, company chairman Al Chapman personally set up a supermarket test in Queens, New York. It proved housewives preferred yellow labels four to one." [6] While this may not be manage-

FIG. 12-1. SELECTED ECONOMIC INDICATORS USED BY ONE COMPANY
TO FORECAST MARKETS*

Indicator	Source
Lead series:	
National Bureau of Economic Research Lead Indicator Series	National Bureau of Economic Research
Average hours worked—manufacturing	U.S. Department of Labor, Bureau of Labor Statistics
Industrial building contracts awarded	F. W. Dodge—construction contracts awarded for commercial and industrial buildings
Willingness to consume	Changes in relationship of consumption expenditures to total personal income
Surveys—plans for future action[1]	
Consumer expenditures	The Federal Reserve Board and Survey Research Center, University of Michigan
Business expenditures for plant and equipment	NICB Capital Appropriations Survey; McGraw-Hill; Securities and Exchange Commission; and U.S. Department of Commerce
Government expenditures	January budget report of President of the United States
Manufacturing employment	U.S. Department of Labor—Area Labor Market Trends
Surveys—opinions and expectations[1]	
Business executives	Dun's Review and Modern Industry; Fortune; and Business Week
Bankers	American Bankers Association
Economists	NICB—Business Outlook; National Association of Business Economists; American Economic Association; and various forecasting conferences
Dominant influences[2]	
Profit prospects	Various business press surveys
Inventory demand	U.S. Department of Commerce
Business psychology	Subjective evaluation of business news and the stock market
Favorable and unfavorable factors[2]	
Federal Reserve policy	Newspaper evidence of Federal Reserve operations and policies
Retail sales—total	U.S. Department of Commerce
New orders and backlogs—manufacturing	U.S. Department of Commerce
Residential construction	U.S. Department of Commerce
Manufacturing employment	U.S. Department of Labor
Consumer durable sales	Federal Reserve Bulletin
⌐ Manufacturing capital expenditures	U.S. Department of Commerce
Recurrent cycles[3]	
Textile	Trade publications and the press
Capital goods	U.S. Department of Commerce
Consumer credit	Federal Reserve Bulletin
Critical levels	
Inventories vs. sales and backlogs[3]	U.S. Department of Commerce—Monthly Wholesale Trade Report, Monthly Industry Survey of Manufacturers, Sales, Inventories and New and Unfilled Orders
Capacity vs. production	Econometric Research Unit, Wharton School of Finance and Commerce; and U.S. Department of Commerce
Consumer credit vs. disposable income[3]	Federal Reserve Bulletin
Rate of change	
Production: durables, nondurables, and total	Federal Reserve Board
Disposable income	U.S. Department of Commerce

[1] Examples of important sources are listed; others usually are also examined.
[2] Other sources are also examined, as required.
[3] Sources listed provide data only; for cycle analysis, these require further plotting and evaluation.
* SKF Industries, Inc., Philadelphia, a manufacturer of roller and ball bearings, uses these indicators forecast to turning points.
SOURCE: "Forecasting Sales," Studies in Business Policies, no. 106, p. 59, 1963, copyright National Industrial Conference Board, Inc., New York.

ment by exception per se, it demonstrates the need for an executive
to occasionally verify for himself the reports that flow from routine
sources—and especially those which originate in sources presumed
to be nonobjective.

The Sales Report

A major manufacturer of heavy machinery furnishes a sound example of comparison and reporting of sales results. The nature of its business is such that the amount of inventory carried is necessarily high in relation to sales. Consequently, the sales forecast (and the processing of sales) becomes critical to inventory levels and to the company's cash position. Too high a sales forecast tends to tie up too much money in inventory and creates the risk of inventory losses due to obsolescence. Too low a forecast results in critical component shortages. To get the best possible forecast, this company relies upon the detailed market knowledge of its sales forces in its various districts. Once each quarter, the several zone managers consult their sales staffs on the future sales prospects for their territories. They submit their forecasts of total dollar sales to the company's headquarters. And these forecasts are then divided into two major product categories by quarters for twelve months in advance. These forecasts are then transferred to control charts which are divided into quarterly segments.

Chart A, Figure 12-2, shows the actual sales orders booked for this company as compared with the quarterly forecasts. This chart is prepared monthly and submitted to the sales manager, controller, and production control manager. Chart B compares the actual backlog of orders with those which were projected (on the basis of six times the weekly sales rate). Also on Chart B is a comparison of the projected and actual rate of processing sales orders. This latter is a ratio derived by dividing the current backlog by the current sales rate (both projected and actual). When sales deviate from forecast to the extent that factory production schedules must be adjusted, sales forecasts are reviewed and revised. Otherwise, sales forecasts will be reviewed quarterly, at which time an additional three months' period forecast is made.

In *Successful Managerial Control by Ratio-analysis*,[7] Spencer Tucker recommends regular analysis, comparison, and reporting based upon what he calls "primary sales data." This basic information includes:

Total number of contacts
    To existing customers
        new products sold
        existing products sold

FIG. 12-2. SALES EXCEPTION CONTROL CHARTS

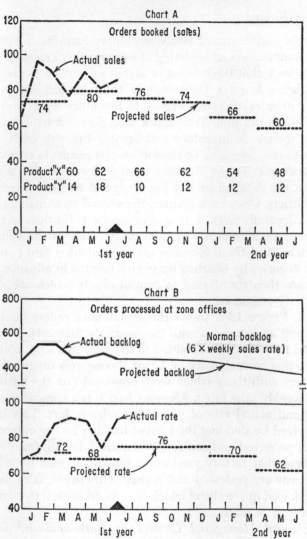

new products quoted
existing products quoted
To new customers
new products sold
existing products sold
new products quoted
existing products quoted

Tucker would also prepare the same analysis on a dollar basis and then add an expense summary including salaries paid, travel expenses, and entertainment expenses (for new and existing customers). Working with these basic data, Tucker derives twelve "productivity" measures of salesmen, territories, divisions, etc. These productivity measures provide such yardsticks as "dollar value per quotation," "quotations per contact," and "new-account entertainment expense related to total new accounts sold." There appears to be no end of useful ratios that can be developed from the basic data. These, in turn, can be followed on a comparative basis to derive normal and exceptional conditions to guide sales management.

Making Marketing Decisions

Generalized sales-guide norms for detecting exceptional conditions do not exist. In sales especially, the particular and specific are what are truly significant. And each company has its own ideas of what is important. For instance, one metal-fabricating company draws individual comparisons for carload customers on a monthly basis, but for ton buyers on a quarterly basis. One paper company calls for an annual analysis of shipments by customer and by grade of merchandise. One food company reviews its entire customer list twice a year in terms of estimated potential sales and actual sales to determine the rate of sales-call activity for the next six months. Another company in the same business maintains a daily chart for each of its salesmen. The charts help management keep track of each salesman's planning, travel, and number of contacts. A railroad equipment company establishes for each salesman ten target accounts, for which weekly comparison of activity and production are reported to the sales manager for action.

At Ford Motor Co., the marketing research manager of the Ford Division (according to *Business Week*) tries to relate advertising activity numerically to car sales. He looks for the percentage of

Ford's advertising audience that has changed its attitude toward the company's product during a campaign period. If results are below a point that Ford considers favorable, the campaign is restructured or abandoned.[8]

At Divco-Wayne Corp. (an auto-parts manufacturer that bills over $50 million a year), pricing policy is centralized, but the company president still permits divisional managers to handle exceptional problems on their own. For example, headquarters sets a rigid policy on discount allowances, but divisional managers can increase an allowance in making a deal to move damaged merchandise.[9]

The founder of Yale Express System, Inc., second largest trucker in the East, noted that retailers who open early or close late or who operate on Saturdays and holidays could not ship or receive merchandise during those hours. He initiated late receiving, late pickups, early-morning and Saturday and holiday deliveries, or whenever retailers are open for selling. By taking advantage of an obvious condition, Yale's exceptional service has enabled the company to become the principal carrier for many national department and chain stores.[10] The point, again, is that to manage by exception—especially in sales—the system need not always be formalized.

As an example of the philosophy of exploiting opportunity even when sales fall below expectations, there is the case of Hunt Foods and Industries, Inc. In late 1963 a stockholder asked Hunt's president, Norton Simon, "Since our earnings are down, is this the time to spend money on more marketing?" Simon replied,

> You can't always pick the best time from a corporate earnings standpoint. Often we have found that the time to expend our greatest efforts is when everybody else is most concerned. This is how we gained our position. If you look at our growth over the last 15 years —and the growth has been fantastic—you'll see this pattern. This isn't the other fellow's style of doing business. It's ours. And it's been tremendously successful. We're confident that *now* is the time to do our brand building.[11]

Obviously, Mr. Simon was relying more upon his experience and his intuition than upon routine controller-type philosophy to determine his course of action in the face of an exceptional condition. But here are an executive and a company which are noteworthy for their gathering of extensive marketing information followed by intense, rapid analysis of its movements. They manage their marketing very well. They manage creatively and forcefully. But their executive decisions are soundly based upon a management by exception measurement, projection, selection, observation, comparison, and reporting system.

References

1. "U.S. Steel Strips for a Fight," *Business Week*, Sept. 28, 1963, p. 114, and "U.S. Steel Adopts New Corporate Look," *Business Week*, Sept. 21, 1963, p. 29.
2. "Measuring Salesmen's Performance," Studies in Business Policies, no. 79, National Industrial Conference Board, New York, 1956.
3. "Keys to Effective Selling and Lower Marketing Costs," Studies in Business Policies, no. 71, National Industrial Conference Board, New York, 1954.
4. Warren K. Schoonmaker, "What You Should Know about Sales Forecasting," *Industrial Marketing*, October, 1963, p. 108.
5. McGraw-Hill Department of Economics, Publications Division, special report to editors, July 3, 1963.
6. *The Gallagher Report*, vol. 11, no. 48, Dec. 2, 1963.
7. Spencer A. Tucker, *Successful Managerial Control by Ratio-analysis*, McGraw-Hill Book Company, New York, 1961, p. 126.
8. "Ad Roles Shift for Agencies and Clients," *Business Week*, Dec. 8, 1962, p. 53.
9. "Turning Red into Black," *Business Week*, Dec. 1, 1962, p. 126.
10. *The New York Times*, Nov. 4, 1962, p. 3.
11. "Interim Report to Stockholders," 1st quarter, 1964, Hunt Foods and Industries, Inc., New York.

Chapter 13

MANAGING ORGANIZATIONAL MANPOWER

Manpower is at once a most costly ingredient in service or product mix and without doubt the most critical means by which business or organizational results are attained. Measures of manpower, it follows, fall into two classifications: quantitative and qualitative.

Measuring Manpower

Quantitative measures of manpower are those which tell us how many people are employed and how costly their services are, either in total dollars or in terms of cost per unit of product or service.

Qualitative measures of manpower are those which tell us what kind of people are employed (in terms of the jobs they perform or can perform) and how good they are now at this work (or can be trained to be in the future).

Quantitative Measures. Management collects quantitative data from pay sheets, labor reports, manning tables, cost-accounting records, and reports filed for conformance to the Wages and Hours Law. These data are collected in most firms by the payroll department and/or by the personnel and industrial engineering departments. Each functional activity or department may also accumulate or be furnished the same data in more detailed form. (For example, a plant manager knows he has 875 people on his payroll as of 5 P.M. Friday, a processing superintendent knows he has 360, and the heat-

222

treat foreman knows his total is 36. Qualitatively, the breakdown might continue: The plant manager has a head count of 500 blue-shirt direct labor, 100 blue-shirt indirect labor, 200 white-collar clerical indirect, and 75 managerial and engineering indirect.) And most manning tables at day's end would also show the number of people employed in every job classification that exists in the organization.

Qualitative Measures. Qualitative data of the simpler order are derived from the same sources as the quantitative data. But qualitative measures of the "how good" category come from personnel inventories, merit rating, and management appraisal forms. These data are gathered in most sophisticated organizations today. However, there are many, many firms that still do not systematically make these measurements.

Typically, qualitative "how good" measures include the following techniques.

Achievement Tests. These are merely skill tests that determine whether a mechanic can read a vernier, a stenographer can take dictation at a certain speed, a laborer can handle the arithmetic needed to complete a tally sheet, etc. It is surprising how few companies make such tests a criterion for classification of employees to regularly perfomed jobs. Without such measures, management typically assumes—often wrongly—that its organization is staffed in a certain way when in fact it is not.

Psychological Tests. These are more subtle, less dependable, and harder to interpret than the achievement tests. They are nonetheless valuable in appraising aptitudes and assessing potentials. These tests range from many standard ones for which hundreds of thousands of test scores have been accumulated to provide standards of comparison (such as the Psychological Corporation General Clerical Test, Science Research Associates Clerical Aptitudes Test, Minnesota Rate of Manipulation Test, Bernreuter Inventory, and How Supervise Test) to the Rorschach test (ink blot), which in the hands of a clinically trained technician may measure changes in personal, social, and job adjustment, and to depth interviews conducted by a trained psychologist to probe deeply into attitudes as well as aptitudes.

Job Evaluation. There are at least four ways to measure systematically the relative worth of jobs rather than people. In one way or another, each system weighs such factors as responsibilities, job knowledge needed, mental application, dexterity and accuracy, and tools used. Most frequently used techniques for job evaluation are the *point system* (in which point values are assigned to various job factors according to their degree of importance), *ranking* (in which a committee sorts job-description cards, arranging them in order from highest to lowest according to their relative worth), *classification* (in which jobs most nearly alike are grouped together for comparison), and *factor comparison* (which enables the analyst to compare unlike jobs—such as a manual skills job to a creative thinking job).

Accident Records. Careful reporting and analysis of job accidents enable an organization to measure the safety (and perhaps the morale) of its work force. Injury *frequency rate* is the number of accidents per total man-hours worked per year, multiplied by 1 million. Injury *severity rate* is the number of days lost due to accidents per total man-hours worked per year, multiplied by 1 million.

Merit Rating. This is the application of systematic judgment by a superior who tries objectively to assess various qualities of skill, achievement, and personality attributes of his subordinates. An example of a merit rating form for hospital employees is shown in Fig. 13-1. Note that it includes measures of both personal attributes and performance.

Attitude Surveys. Each of the previous techniques provides a measure of an individual's qualities. The attitude survey, while it is applied person by person, is useful mainly as an integrated measure of groups rather than of individuals. The survey is based upon a technique in which employees either complete a questionnaire or respond to personal questions by trained interviewers. Questions cover attitudes toward pay, the company, organization, working conditions, supervision, etc.

Integrated Measures. Several attempts have been made to collect personnel statistics within an organization and to integrate them mathematically into a single measure of how employees feel. The General Electric Company, for instance, has done much work on what it calls an "employee relations index" (E.R.I.).[1] It is composed of eight indicators: absences, separations, initial visits to the dispensary, suggestions made through the suggestion system, disciplinary suspensions, formal grievances, work stoppages, and participation in the company's insurance plan. The resultant index is used as a basis of comparison in gaging employee relations improvements in a single work group or comparing effectiveness of management in that regard between two different work groups.

Other manpower items (either quantitative or qualitative, or both) that warrant measurement and follow-up in a management by exception system include requests for transfer, voluntary quits, involuntary layoffs, numbers of openings filled by the personnel department on a crash basis, productivity, scrap losses, adequacy of talent reservoir, community wage rates, grievances about compensation, incentive earnings (both number of employees covered and amount of earnings), absenteeism, tardiness, turnover, insurance premiums for accidents, and employee participation in service programs.

Projecting Manpower Needs

Manpower forecasting is an activity in which every managerial person should participate. Thinking through the needs for staffing his organization to meet the objectives ahead inspires keener observation and assessment of the labor and management staffs. Personnel departments can be of great assistance in these matters—especially in supplying detailed data and in integrating manpower forecasts on an organization-wide basis. But the projections should ideally stem from the grass roots.

Projections are typically both short-range and long-term. Short-range projections affect acquisitions and layoffs most directly from a numerical basis. Long-term projections influence the qualitative character of the organization and should determine selection and training objectives. Short-term objectives can be met by juggling personnel. Long-term objectives can only be met by well-thought-out organization and staffing plans.

The simpler kind of manpower forecasting begins with a commitment about production (output) and productivity (cost) objectives. From these starting points, the manager backs into his projections of manpower need. His first calculation is of man-days or man-hours needed to meet his objectives. Then he must increase his estimate by allowing for retirements, illness, and turnover. In any well-run organization, historical data on these three variables are readily available. In addition, the manager will want to take into account learning rates, both of individuals and of organizations. The principle involved is that newly hired people will take time to achieve

FIG. 13-1. EXAMPLE OF A MERIT RATING FORM

CHILTON MEMORIAL HOSPITAL

PERSONNEL PERFORMANCE EVALUATION

NAME OF EMPLOYEE _____

DEPARTMENT _____ POSITION TITLE _____

EVALUATION MADE BY: _____ DATE OF APPRAISAL _____

REASON FOR EVALUATION: WAGE ADJUSTMENT _____ REVIEWED BY _____

PROMOTION _____ TRANSFER _____

Check (X) in Appropriate Place

	10	9	8	7	6	5	4	3	2	1
1. Attendance and Punctuality	Reports on duty promptly. Notifies hospital if going to be off duty. Rarely absent or late for work.		Tardy for work 1 or 2 times per month. Is absent 4 to 6 times per year.		Is absent 1 day per month. Tardy once per week.		Tardy 5 to 7 times per month. Absent 2 to 3 days per month.		Tardy 8 to 10 times per month. Absent 4 to 5 days per month.	
2. Quality and Accuracy of Work	Takes pride in job. Very accurate and neat. Work can be relied upon. Exceptionally high quality.		Occasionally makes errors. Superior quality of work.		Does well in routine tasks. Satisfactory quality of work.		Careless. Is inclined to make mistakes. Not up to standards.		Work frequently in error. Requires constant inspection. Doubtful value.	
3. Quantity of Work	Handles assignments with ease. Works rapidly and consistently. Not disturbed by sudden increases in work load. Very high output.		Accomplishes more work than most workers. High output.		Satisfactory output.		Slow worker. Limited output. Must improve.		Seriously below standard. Rarely meets standard production levels.	

4. Attitude toward others (cooperativeness, etc.)	Is tactful, considerate of others and very cooperative. Very easy to work with	Above average in tact, consideration, and cooperation most of the time. Gets along well with others.	Cooperative. Sometimes is lacking in tact and consideration. Generally exhibits normal relations.	Occasionally difficult but not antagonistic. Shows reluctance to cooperate.	Quarrelsome, antagonistic. No consideration of others.
5. Initiative	Gets assignments done without being told every detail. Is alert to needs of patients, public or other employees. Seeks tasks to do.	Frequently alert and resourceful. Has a high degree of initiative and is constructive.	Does assigned work well. Makes occasional suggestions.	Needs occasional prodding. Does assigned work in a satisfactory manner.	Always waits to be told. Needs constant guidance.
6. Knowledge of Work	Complete understanding. Handles most complex problems without aid. Exceptionally well informed.	Knows most tasks well. Is well informed. Handles many complex problems without aid.	Requires some assistance in solving job problems. Satisfactory knowledge.	Needs more direct help. Has some understanding.	Fails to comprehend. Gives up easily. Displays lack of job knowledge.
7. Work Attitude	Very energetic. Exceptional enthusiasm.	Eager worker. Interest evidenced by fullest participation.	Interested in work to be done. Generally desirable attitude.	Needs constant urging. Sometimes indifferent.	Lazy. Extremely indifferent. Not interested.
8. Supervisory Ability (To be used only if individual is in supervisory capacity)	Gets maximum efficiency without friction. Very efficient in leading, directing and training subordinates.	Efficient in leading, directing and training subordinates.	Nothing outstanding. Fair in direction, training, leading subordinates.	Below average as a supervisor. Should be taught supervisory techniques.	Lacks qualities necessary to be successful supervisor.

full production on an existing job, and even trained employees will take time to reach optimum output on a new assignment or product. In a typical situation, where the learning time has been judged to be six days, management might expect 60 per cent performance on the first day, 70 per cent the second, 75 per cent the third, 80 per cent the fourth, 87 per cent the fifth, and 100 per cent the sixth.[2] Regardless of the length of the learning cycle, for both individuals and groups, the shape of the learning curves tends to be similar.

Just as an allowance for learning will increase the estimate of the size of the labor force needed, planned organizational and methods improvements will decrease it. Management's projections of manpower needs, then, result (1) from projecting historical measures of labor productivity and attendance and by modifying these projections by (2) forecasts of learning situations and (3) improvements in labor effectiveness.

In making projections of manpower requirements, there is an increasing availability of standards upon which to base your estimates. One of the best sources is the U.S. Bureau of Labor Statistics. This Federal agency assembles all kinds of measures of employment levels according to broadly general job classifications for almost every kind of industry. It also accumulates wage data for them and makes accurate forecasts of the shape of the work force in the future. The National Industrial Conference Board also publishes manpower forecasts based upon BLS figures and those obtained from other sources.

Many business magazines have surveyed their industry segment to provide data on how many people are employed in what kinds of jobs. *Factory* magazine, for instance, has provided survey data on manpower distribution in manufacturing operations.[3] The American Management Association, in its "Group Ten" research project under the auspices of nearly 100 firms, has made one of the most intense and accurate studies of the way in which manpower is distributed throughout industrial organizations.[4] Unfortunately, the breadth of the AMA study is limited in scope and is confidential; however, a very valuable schedule of standard function descriptions (valuable in comparing measurements) is available to the general business public.

Manpower Inventory and Assessment. Apart from having some basis for predicting labor distribution according to function classification, there is also a great need for up-to-date personnel inventories, which detail existing employee skills. Such inventories, which can be kept on a current basis or compiled from personnel records periodically, aid in a company's plans for organizing and staffing to meet future objectives. At the management level, this activity is performed to its greatest extent. The techniques for doing so vary from simple file-card systems to elaborate codings on punch card or computer tapes, but a discussion of these techniques is beyond the scope of this book. However, there is an inventory analysis technique that is especially valuable in assessing organizational requirements for projected goals. It is known variously as "linear responsibility charting" (see Fig. 13-2) and "management activity analysis." The technique works like this. First an analyst lists every conceivable corporate objective or function (general management, marketing, operations, auxiliaries, etc.). Then for every managerial position he indicates the kind of responsibility assigned for each objective or function. Consultant Bruce Payne classifies these managerial actions and responsibilities as "initiate or recommend," "decide on for final approval," "participate in or advise," "activate or carry out," "be accountable for results," and "control." [5]

The value in such an exercise is that it helps management to guard against continuing an organizational setup that contains duplication of effort or conflicts in its assignment of authorities and responsibilities. Management by exception cannot be allowed to become routine or to be taken for granted, especially in handling the manpower ingredient. It is at the projection stage that much of the corrective action (initiated because of results noted at "compare-report" time) can most effectively be taken.

Observing Manpower in Action

A man's boss ought to be the one who is responsible for observing his performance. The increase in the number of formal management-development systems seems to have obscured this fact. No personnel specialist, no psychological counselor, no training director can do this for you. They may assist you and help you to be objective. But you can rarely delegate this task effectively.

Observing a person's performance means that occasionally we have to stand aside from our own involvement with him so that we can see him as an unbiased stranger might. And we should find time to do this often enough and in enough different situations so

FIG. 13-2. LINEAR RESPONSIBILITY ORGANIZATION CHART, SHOWING EXTENT AND DEGREE OF DELEGATION, AND ALSO INTERRELATIONSHIP OF RESPONSIBILITIES

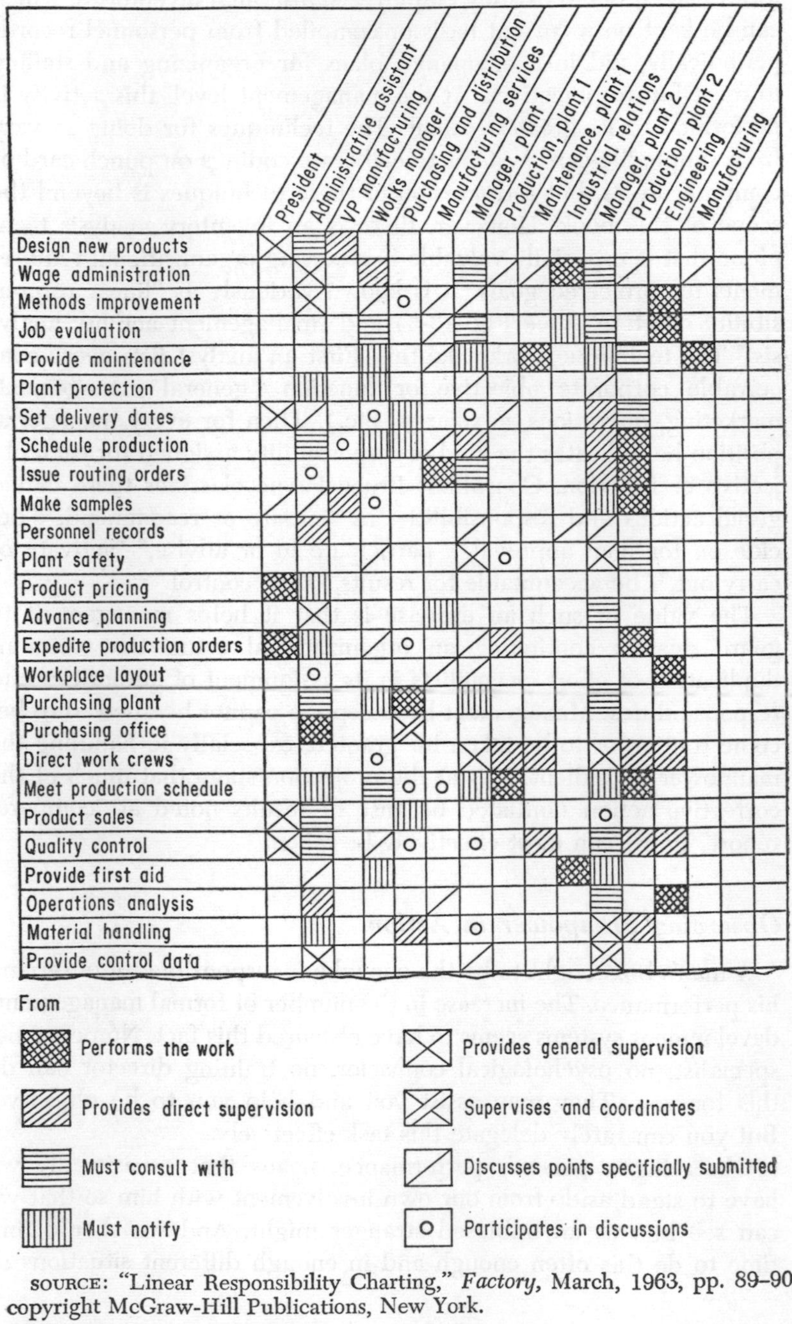
President
Administrative assistant
VP manufacturing
Works manager
Purchasing and distribution
Manufacturing services
Manager, plant 1
Production, plant 1
Maintenance, plant 1
Industrial relations
Manager, plant 2
Production, plant 2
Engineering
Manufacturing
Design new products
Wage administration
Methods improvement
Job evaluation
Provide maintenance
Plant protection
Set delivery dates
Schedule production
Issue routing orders
Make samples
Personnel records
Plant safety
Product pricing
Advance planning
Expedite production orders
Workplace layout
Purchasing plant
Purchasing office
Direct work crews
Meet production schedule
Product sales
Quality control
Provide first aid
Operations analysis
Material handling
Provide control data
From
Performs the work
Provides direct supervision
Must consult with
Must notify
Provides general supervision
Supervises and coordinates
Discusses points specifically submitted
Participates in discussions

SOURCE: "Linear Responsibility Charting," *Factory*, March, 1963, pp. 89–90, copyright McGraw-Hill Publications, New York.

that our estimate is based upon a meaningful number of occurrences.

One popular appraisal technique is called the "critical-incident method." It requires of the observer that he back up his general opinions about a subordinate's performance and capabilities with specific incidents which support it. For example, a vice-president of a photocopying company had the general impression that his sales manager was sloppy about verifying expense-account claims. The vice-president's judgment was accepted by the sales manager only after the V.P. cited a half dozen instances in which the auditor had challenged salesmen's expense vouchers.

But even when using the critical-incident method, a manager must guard against his prejudices. He has to try to separate his reactions to a man's personality or behavior from the results an individual is able to achieve. An R & D manager in a medium-sized electronics firm, for example, rated his senior engineer as being technically unreliable. He believed him to be so because his investigatory technique was not as painstaking as the manager would like to have seen it. Yet the R & D manager conceded that in no instance were the senior engineer's results found to be inaccurate. The manager's observation had been clouded by the fact that the man did not do the job the way the chief would have done it, even though the methods used had no deleterious effects upon the results attained.

Psychologists call this prejudice the "halo effect." It implies that if a manager is favorably disposed toward a person, he may see everything that person does as being exceptionally good. Conversely, if the manager's temperament is not in harmony with his subordinate's, or if a single unpleasant incident has permanently marred their relationship, the manager may always downgrade the subordinate's performance—no matter how good it might appear to an outsider.

To guard against this halo effect, many companies resort to group appraisals, in which two or more managers participate in the rating. And some unique plans call for ratings not only by superiors but also by associates, and even by employees subordinate to the man being rated.

Applying Manpower Yardsticks

In comparing observed performance, behavior, and attitudes with those anticipated, great care is needed. While comparisons of numbers, cost, and productivity of manpower are generally cut and dried, there is always danger in comparing manning tables of organization with those of other companies, even with those which appear very similar. Organizational factors are so varied and complex that rarely can valid intercompany comparisons be made of the number and distribution of employees. However, there are some norms against which manpower measurements can be compared. These norms provide rough guides, but that is about all. For example:

• The Bureau of Labor Statistics provides average figures on employee turnover, earnings, overtime, productivity, and accident frequency for many industries.

• The National Safety Council provides average figures on accident frequency and security.

• The University of Chicago's Industrial Research Center has also published yardsticks for average attitudes based upon a survey of over 500,000 workers. On page 233 is one of their "morale" yardsticks for hourly workers in all industries.[6]

Such average figures should also be used with caution. They are more helpful in making projections and forecasts than in finding exceptions in your organization. After all, industry averages represent neither good nor bad practice. It is better to confine your current comparisons to your own past measures and to your own projected expectations. Interpretation of the meanings of variances should also be approached gingerly. Rather than precipitate corrective action on a single exception, it is better to await the development of long-term trends before plotting a new course. As one industrial relations manager puts it, "Employee relations is one area where eagerness to act is not always a virtue. It's usually better to wait and see rather than to rush right out and do something." The reason for this advice is that we simply don't know enough about cause and effect in human relations to be very certain about what to do when an exception occurs.

Reporting Personnel Conditions

When it comes to reporting personnel activities, the late Seward H. French, vice-president of Crucible Steel Co. of America, developed one of the most comprehensive, yet practical, reports we've seen. Figure 13-3 shows it. In addition, Mr. French supplied

Category	Questions asked	Favorable answers, per cent
Job demands............	Work pressure, fatigue, boredom, work load, hours of work	72
Working conditions......	Annoyances, management's concern for conditions, equipment adequacy, safety measures, effect of these on efficiency	70
Pay..................	Adequacy, comparison with pay of others in the company and in other local companies, administration of pay system	44
Employee benefits.......	All benefits, comparison with benefits in other companies, knowledge of program, administration of benefits	74
Friendliness, cooperation of employees	Bossiness, friction	77
Supervisory-employee relations	Friendliness, fairness, treatment of suggestions, credit for good work, concern for welfare, follow-through on promises	71
Confidence in management	Belief in management's integrity and its concern for employee welfare, adequacy of personnel policies, friendliness	67
Technical competence of supervision	Administrative skill, knowledge of job, ability to train employees, decision making, work organization	73
Effectiveness of administration	Competence of higher levels of management, efficiency of company operations, cooperation among departments	65
Adequacy of communication	Freedom to express opinion and suggest improvements, complaint handling, information about operations and plans	64
Status and recognition...	Standing with the company, fair appraisal of work done, respect for judgment	71
Security of job and work relations	Security from arbitrary discharge and layoff, recognition of length of service handling of job changes	59
Identification with the company	Pride in the company, interest in its future, sense of belonging and participation with the company	80
Chances for growth and advancement	Opportunities to use one's skills, to grow and develop on the job, to get ahead in the organization	65

FIG. 13-3. EXAMPLE OF REPORT OF INDUSTRIAL RELATIONS PERFORMANCE

| | Monthly cumulative average | | Midland |
	Year to date	Previous year	Month
Employees, wages, and hours:			
No. of wage employees................	4,782		6,612
Total employees......................	7,618		7,470
Total man-hours (1,000)..............	1,334		1,595
Average weekly wage.................	$ 85.34		$ 78.05
Average hourly rate (including overtime)	$ 2.16		$ 2.15
Premium overtime cost per hour........	$ 0.07		$ 0.03
Premium overtime cost...............	$81,728		$36,565
Employment:			
* Applicants.........................	42.8		8.4
* Accessions........................	25.5		6.7
* Separations.......................	30.6		53.0
Per cent turnover rate per month.......	2.7%		2.1%
Labor relations:			
* Grievances pending first of month.....	4.4		5.6
* Grievances filed during month........	1.0		1.5
* Total grievances settled during month	0.7		0.4
* At second step....................	0.1		0.0
* At third step.....................	0.3		0.1
* At fourth step....................	0.3		0.3
* Arbitration......................	0.0		0.0
* Grievances pending end of month.....	4.7		6.7
Work stoppages: man-hours lost........	8.9		0.0
Safety:			
Frequency rate......................	1.54		1.69
Severity rate.......................	0.56		0.09
Compensation cost per 1,000 man-hours	$ 3.76		$ 8.06
Supervisory training:			
Average hours in training..............	1.7		2.1
Suggestions:			
* Received..........................	2.0		1.3
* Adopted..........................	0.6		0.9
* Declined..........................	2.0		0.9
Tangible savings....................	$ 5,561		$ 6,723

* Per 1,000 employees (total).

Report of one plant for October, 1953.

SOURCE: Seward H. French, "Measuring Progress toward Industrial-relations Objectives," *Personnel*, vol. 30, no. 5, p. 342, 1954, copyright American Management Association, New York.

FIG. 13-4. EXAMPLE OF ACCIDENT FREQUENCY CONTROL CHART

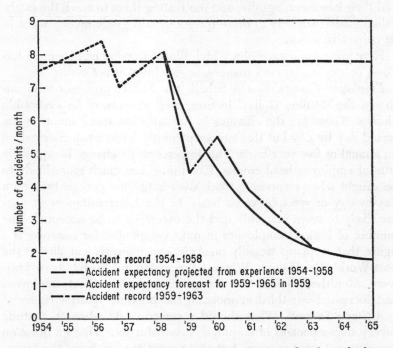

SOURCE: Seward H. French, "Measuring Progress toward Industrial-relations Objectives," *Personnel*, vol. 30, no. 54, p. 343, 1954, copyright American Management Association, Inc., New York.

us with an excellent example of a graphical exception report in the case of accident prevention (see Fig. 13-4).

How to Act on Variances

People are a principal means toward an organizational end. But it is a mistake to conclude that there is necessarily a direct relationship between a manpower measure and a tangible measure of corporate results—such as profits. Consequently, a manager must try to interpret exceptions in terms of the means only as a contributing factor rather than an end in itself. Specifically, you should ask: What does the exception mean in terms of hiring and firing, selecting employees, training them, placing them on their jobs, organizing them and their jobs meaningfully, and motivating them to reach the established goals? Answers to these questions will guide management in its corrective action.

Here are several examples which illustrate what management has done, or can do, when a manpower exception is noticed.

Employee Counts. Erwin Schell, the M.I.T. professor who authored the "Million Dollar" lecture, used to warn of imperceptible change. Those are the changes in organization that cannot be detected day by day but that are surprisingly large when checked on an annual or five-year basis. This imperceptible change is especially true of employee head counts. Exceptions are much more likely to be caught when comparing totals over long time periods than on a day-by-day or week-by-week basis. In the latter instances excuses are likely to seem plausible and the exception to be accepted. The number of indirect employees in most companies, for instance, is a figure that crept up steadily on American management during the post-World War II years. When the recession in 1957 hit, many firms were astonished to find that the percentage of indirect employees had increased one-third or more in the previous quarter century.[7]

Attitude Surveys. What should a company do when an attitude survey shows pockets of employee dissatisfaction? That's a question management must answer. A starting point is to seek out the exceptions from (1) past surveys in its own company or (2) national standards. The former provides the soundest basis for judging that an exception is occurring. The Garrett Corporation believes that once an exception is noted, there is only one reply that means much to employees—action. Most talk will be regarded as double-talk. As a result of its continuing attitude-survey program Garrett has overhauled a ventilating system, liberalized smoking regulations, made its payday more convenient for swing-shift workers, and improved rest-room facilities. Examination of one such exception will demonstrate the Garrett approach. For a number of years, the company had a group insurance program that it—and its employees—thought was superior. But in three successive surveys, employees who had a favorable opinion of it dropped from 66 per cent of total, to 49 per cent, to 29 per cent. Management revised the program and surveyed again. Acceptance jumped back to 65 per cent. Similarly, its retirement and severance plan dropped from an 86 per cent favorable evaluation to 66 per cent. A revision in the plan checked the downward trend at 66 per cent.[8]

Incentives. In 1959, Dayco Corporation was struggling with an incentive plan that had gotten completely out of line. At two of its plants examples like this were found: a laborer earning $4.50 per hour, another earning 400 per cent bonus, most of the employees pegging their output at 156 per cent of standard. For Dayco, this brought the action-indicator level right into the sphere of top management. Their decision: incentives must be revised, regardless of union opposition, strike or no. The union, faced with management determination, yielded. A sensible, up-to-date incentive system was installed.[9]

Manpower and Management Inventories. The principle behind most employee and management inventory and appraisal systems is the detection of gaps in the manpower backlogs and in the management chain of command. Some gaps are simply those that exist where an incumbent is not backstopped by a qualified, or potentially qualified, replacement. Other gaps occur where an incumbent is wholly unqualified for his present assignment. Still other gaps are those involving significant individual deficiencies which can be removed or blunted by training and experience. In this area, long-range evaluations are the most revealing, and long-range planning the most desirable. Joe, for instance, may be capable of doing the job as it exists today, but if the division expands in three years, he won't have had the necessary marketing experience to direct overall activities. Or Pete may be a world beater, but he's fifty-eight and has no one on his staff capable of filling his job in the future. The kind of action needed in these situations is not so much of a decisive, tactical nature as it is thoughtful, analytical, and strategic.

Job Analysis. An alert industrial relations department can be expected to make periodic checks of the work performed by rank and file employees and by technicians, engineers, and management personnel. Here again, changes that can be expected to be gradual are often surprisingly severe in retrospect. Some jobs will have shrunk in content and importance, while others have grown in scope and value. Managers rarely find time to conduct such an analysis. But management should insist that these be made. Such audits uncover significant differences and can lead to more effective distribution of labor and to a more realistic organization.

Wage Surveys. Many a management has long deceived itself by believing that a company's wages and salaries were adequate to attract and retain the kind of people needed to meet organizational objectives. A manager is unlikely to get a true feel of the relative level of his company's salary schedules by exchanging locker-room confidences with other executives at the country club. A systematic survey of wages paid by other companies in your community and in your industry must be conducted by trained personnel people to determine this. Comparison between internal and external structures will spot the exceptions—overpayment as well as underpayment. Based on these findings, top management must decide what its pay policy will be: to remain slightly below, coincide with, or be slightly above its neighbors. And then it must also determine how far a specific or general level of variation can range again before the company must either adjust individual rates or revise its entire schedule. Surprisingly, some companies do not find these wage and salary discrepancies until an attitude survey points them up or until a consistent thread of complaint becomes evident in exit interviews.

References

1. Edwin B. Flippo, *Principles of Personnel Management,* McGraw-Hill Book Company, New York, 1961, p. 101.
2. H. B. Maynard (ed.), *Industrial Engineering Handbook,* 2d ed., McGraw-Hill Book Company, New York, 1963, pp. 4-8, 4-9.
3. "Manpower Yardsticks," *Factory,* September, 1957.
4. *Management News,* vol. 32, no. 19, American Management Association, New York, September, 1957.
5. Bruce Payne, *Planning for Company Growth,* McGraw-Hill Book Company, New York, 1963, pp. 209–247.
6. David G. Moore and Robert K. Burns, "How Good Is Good Morale?" *Factory,* February, 1956.
7. "The Attack on Indirect Costs," *Factory,* November, 1961.
8. "Opinion Poll Gets Action—Not Double Talk," *Factory,* December, 1954, p. 108.
9. T. J. Wieczorek, "Your Incentives Can Be Revised," *Factory,* September, 1960.

PART 4

THE VARIABLES
In Management by Exception

*How to develop the versatile managerial skills
needed to use new technologies and to handle
the human variables.*

Chapter 14

OPERATIONS RESEARCH, COMPUTERS, AND INFORMATION SYSTEMS

The 1950s saw the introduction of two techniques that many managers thought would revolutionize decision making in business. The two techniques were operations research (OR) and electronic data processing (EDP). After nearly two decades of experience with them, one concludes that while both OR and EDP tools possess unlimited potential, their impact on management practices has been more evolutionary than revolutionary. Nevertheless, their increasing value to management by exception is certain.

Operations Research Defined

"Operations research" is a term applied to the use of advanced mathematical theories for solving management problems.* Four features generally characterize the OR approach:

1. It requires the construction of a set of mathematical equations which express the relationship between a number of variables (such as relating product characteristics, machine capabilities, labor effectiveness, and seasonal demands).

2. It requires the choosing of a standard of performance with

* Purists define OR as "the science devoted to describing, understanding, and predicting the behavior of man-machine systems."

241

which to measure the reliability of the formulas (such as specifying that the best solution for a production control problem will be one in which a particular schedule can be maintained with minimum manufacturing costs).

3. It requires that the algebraic symbols representing variable factors can be replaced in the formula by numbers. (Sources of the numbers are measurements, observations, and judgments based upon experience.)

4. It requires that the formulas can be solved algebraically. (The solutions represent a decision that best measures up to the standard of performance criteria decided in the second requirement.)

What OR does, then, is to design a rule for making a decision in a certain situation. In computer language, this is called a "program." The weakness in programmed decisions is that in assigning numbers to the variables, too many figures are based not upon measurement or historical knowledge but upon assumptions, hunches, bad judgment, and guesses.

Some of the more popular OR techniques that have been found useful in solving management problems are:[1]

• *Linear Programming.* In linear programming, mathematical formulas are used to obtain the theoretically best solution for the allocation of resources among competing uses. *Typical application:* Developing a schedule of which products to produce at each of three plants in order to reduce freight costs to a practical minimum.

• *Game Theory.* This is a science based upon probability rules, in which you determine ways to play against a business opponent so as to minimize your chance of losing. *Typical application:* Determining sales prices in the event of competitive price changes in order to gain a larger share of a market while maintaining optimum profit.

• *Waiting-line Theory.* Sometimes labeled "queueing," this theory makes use of probability laws to relate the capacity of your equipment to the number of parts you may have waiting to use that equipment. *Typical applications:* Minimizing finished products waiting for inspection, number of maintenance men waiting at a tool crib, or component parts bottlenecking through assembly operations.

• *Monte Carlo Method.* This technique depends upon making random calculations or taking random samples over and over again in order to find the probability of an optimum solution. *Typical ap-*

plication: Finding optimum tolerance of parts (such as ball bearings) that must fit into other parts (such as a raceway).

• *Network Theory.* Also called "PERT" (Program Evaluation Review Technique), the "critical path method," etc., this theory improves upon the Gantt chart by expressing relationships mathematically as well as visually. *Typical application:* Shortening total elapsed time in bringing to completion a number of interconnected contracts.

• *Industrial Dynamics.* Also called dynamic programming, this is an application to business problems of a technique borrowed from systems engineering and dependent upon finding continuous, interrelated processes. *Typical application:* Finding optimum production schedules that make on-time deliveries possible with minimum fluctuations in employment levels.

Scope of OR Approach

Another way of looking at operations research, according to expert Melville C. Branch, is to see it in context with all three highly technical management approaches to the solution of business problems.

Information Theory. This requires a mathematical quantification of the way in which two or more persons in a joint effort gather information from their surroundings and exchange this knowledge to advance their common purpose. The information theory for a specific organization will determine the way in which an information network will be established and the manner in which data will be studied and disseminated.

Mathematical Programming. This is the fundamental OR technique for translating business situations into numbers and formulas —mathematical models. The primary technique is linear programming (using linear mathematical models), and the characteristic of these models, and many other mathematical ones, is that there are *many* solutions rather than only *one* to the model. Consequently, hundreds of solutions can be made and examined before finding an optimum one.

Systems Engineering. This is the attempt to bring together—and to integrate—the many components that make up a complicated, productive organization. In so doing, systems engineering may include physical elements (engineering and finance) as well as nonphysical elements (social, psychological aspects), limited of course by our inability to quantify the latter. A system attempts to express the interactions of the various elements into a whole by means of mathematics and statistics.[2]

Simple Arithmetic

At the more readily understandable end of the mathematical programming spectrum, simple mathematics can be—and are—employed to clarify business problems and make resultant decisions easier to come by. Take these three examples cited by Dorian Shanin, director of statistical engineering for Rath & Strong, Inc.:

• A machinery manufacturer made a statistical analysis of all components going into its products and found that some 500 parts out of 25,000 accounted for over 60 per cent of its manufacturing cost. He was able to concentrate industrial engineering on the costly 500. Real economies were reached by changes in methods, fixtures, and tolerance evaluations.

• An iron foundry made a breakdown of its total scrap by types of defect. It unexpectedly found an almost equal contribution to scrap by each type. Some saving could be achieved by reducing any or all types of defect by some percentage. But this was a job shop using several hundred patterns, with runs of about 100 patterns in each week. With such a number it was possible to make analyses by pattern. A breakdown showed that 15 per cent of the patterns accounted for more than two-thirds of the total scrap. The solution was to concentrate on the pattern that produced most scrap rather than on type of defect. Emphasizing the fifteen big scrap-producing patterns and keeping new patterns out of this category reduced average monthly scrap loss from $20,000 to about $13,000 in four months, to less than $10,000 in eight months.

• Management wanted to drive down all avoidable costs—all costs not directly incurred in producing acceptable products efficiently. They included scrap, reoperation, inspection, replacement of product under warranty, processes out of control, too tight or too loose tolerances, engineering changes, and unequal efficiencies for similar manufacturing operations.

The question: How were these avoidable costs distributed? About equally? Or was a major portion from just a few of the possible causes—and from a few centers?

Obviously such costs could not be avoided entirely. But an almost equal distribution could well be the result of years of effective work by methods men and supervisors, with further gains difficult to achieve. On the other hand, if a serious difference showed up, concentration on these few areas might easily bring in large returns.

By sampling current activity records for only a few months with detailed temporary record forms, departments were able to secure data breakdowns. The data gathering was spread over many company personnel, reducing the chore of getting the raw information. The accounting department could in most cases translate this data gathering into cost per production hour. These day-to-day figures provided a good-sized sample that revealed the predominant influence of a few factors in a few areas—in the plating department, in three machining operations, and in the methods of packing for shipping. With the problem narrowed in this way, the plant was able to reduce its "unavoidable" costs by 12 per cent.

Shanin's mathematical techniques include (1) a variation on Dickie's ABC analysis to find the "vital few" controlling factors (pages 93–98); (2) trial-and-error searches for underlying causes; (3) use of "Multi-Vari" chart to isolate groups of causes of variations—such as variations within a component or operation, variations piece-to-piece, and variations time-to-time; (4) application of quality-control-type histograms to find the new pattern of variations within control limits; (5) "randomization" and "replication"—probability determinations that minimize pure chance and guard against the unsuspected effects of time; (6) "factorial design," in which all but one variable is controlled in order to observe the effect of an uncontrolled factory; and (7) random balance, a technique for handling a great many factors simultaneously.[3]

Complicated Mathematics

At the other end of the OR spectrum are the complex mathematical models that can be designed to simulate almost any kind of business condition. Lukens Steel Company, for instance, uses the Monte Carlo simulation technique to:[4]

• Estimate the effect of unpredictable variables in fabrication of steel plate, thus indicate size allowances for lowest total costs

• Tell whether Lukens gains or loses by stocking larger plates from which to make unpredictable custom fabrications

• Help reduce the "bunching" of furnace rebuilds

• Guide in sequencing weekly work loads and absentee man-hours

• Choose between a two-man, two-machine operation on the one hand, and a one-man, two-machine operation on the other, with the chance of waiting time figured in

Other problems suited to the simulation technique are:

Waiting-line and congestion problems, answering such questions as:

• What would be the effect on subsequent operations of a speed-up of some branch of the materials-handling system, e.g., a conveyor?

• How many cranes should be used in a work area where demand for crane service is intermittent?

• What is the proper staffing level for tool cribs, maintenance labor, and the like, in which demand for service is variable?

Production scheduling problems, answering such questions as:

• What is the best sequence of orders to minimize time in process through a job-shop operation?

• How much excess capacity to handle peak loads should be built into a production process?

• How much buffer space for storage should be provided between production operations?

Repair and preventive maintenance problems, answering such questions as:

• What is the optimum period between maintenance checks for selected classifications of production equipment?

• How many spare parts should be stocked as insurance items?

• How should maintenance crews be assigned by plant area?

Forecasts of the impact of operations research upon management decision making vary. One school believes that ultimately the entire planning process will be shifted upward in the organization. With this movement would be a reduction in the number and quality of middle management people and a return to greater centralization of authority. An opposing school believes that there will continue to be a long gap between introduction of statistical theory and its practical and successful application in business. This group also feels that the cost of applying these techniques, which almost always depend upon computer usage, is prohibitive.

Electronic Data Processing

"Electronic data processing" is the term applied to the use of electronic computers to "handle" information—business as well as scientific—of extreme complexity, at extremely high rates of speed, and with great accuracy.

Computers are distinguished by several outstanding advantages, including:

• *Speed*. A computer can accomplish in a few minutes calculations that would take a human a lifetime to perform. And the computer's accuracy is far higher than can be expected from humans.

• *Instantaneous Feedback*. Results of one set of calculations can be fed back to the input side instantaneously to modify the next series of computations.

• *Memory*. Computers can store enormous quantities of information, which can be classified and retrieved in the solution of future problems.

• *Automatic Data Collection*. A big advantage of computers is that they can receive input information directly from mechanical or electronic sensing devices that respond to light, sound, movement, etc. Production counters, pressure meters, etc., can transmit their data directly to the computer without the need of an intermediate collection and reporting system.

• *Data Integration*. The ability to combine sets of data to develop a universal is one of the computer's big assets. It can, for instance, make a sales projection by integrating ten or more elements whose relationship with sales and sales forecasts has been established in the past, and it can weight these elements in any way desired—such as placing greatest importance on most recent history.

• *Business Simulation*. Computers can easily handle a statistical model of a business situation, such as an assembly line or a financial statement. For instance, a model can be constructed to resemble the way in which various elements of a balance sheet flow into it in the course of a year. By varying hypothetical changes in cash flow, or any other critical items, during the year, its effect upon the year-end statement can be predetermined.

OR and EDP in Action. "Linear programming via computer is the greatest management aid to come down the pike in many a year."

That's the proclamation of Harlow Reed, vice-president of engineering at Olin Mathieson Chemical Corp. His firm uses computers—and OR—as other firms use management consultants. With their aid, Olin regularly determines which combination of products brings the greatest profits. For example, when specifying a new aluminum rolling mill, Olin determined ahead of time which group of products if sold in what quantity would bring the greatest dollar return. And conversely, Olin also looks ahead with computers to find out which products might become the biggest bottlenecks.[5]

Mr. Reed and others who are sold on the OR-EDP approach point out that another of their advantages is the way in which they drastically reduce the time needed to introduce new products. Profitable life cycles are contracting so rapidly, it is becoming essential to cut down the "concept-to-delivery" time. OR-EDP techniques are especially effective tools for accomplishing that end.

Small companies, too, find increasing value in their usage. "Don't think such methods are just for big companies," cautions L. F. Lewis, manager of advanced planning and projects, General Electric Company. He cites the case of a small commercial airline that applies operations research (via computer) to get quick, up-to-the-minute costs on fuel, oil, replacement parts, etc.[6] Unfortunately, small companies seem to be the slowest in utilizing these techniques. *Steel* magazine reports James Madigan, manager of systems development and data processing at B. F. Goodrich Chemical Company, as attributing this to "a complex. Have-not companies (erroneously) believe that applications of digital computers to production process control have been failures." He cites his conclusion based upon his own company's experience: (1) Computer reliability is not a problem. Computers function well 99.8 per cent of the time. (2) A relatively modest group of staff people can handle closed-loop computer control. "You don't need an army of mercenaries speaking a foreign language," he says. (3) You can count on an increasingly large body of process-control knowledge from which to draw solutions to your problems.[7]

Computer Programs. At Abbott Laboratories management has designed a formula that asks a computer, "What level of capital invested in research is required to maintain desired return on investment?"[8] Translating this basic question into a mathematical sentence is a skill practiced by a growing group of specialists. These specialists—"programmers" they are called—design computer programs.

Stated in mathematical terms, a computer program seems like black magic and the computer like an oracle in a black box. Actually, the computer may be likened to a highly sophisticated player piano; the program is the punched paper roll that works it. Management can make music without knowing where and how to punch the holes.

Management simply states the problem and then turns it over to a specially trained group of mathematicians and engineers to write the program. Management may never see the actual program; but it must "listen" and decide whether the "music" is on key.

Programs are expensive. The cost of a computer system is generally split equally between hardware (the computer) and software (mainly programming). Management must either hire its own programming experts or rent outside know-how. Computer makers themselves maintain either internal or independent-subsidiary operations to provide—for a fee—all the program-writing help a customer needs.

Computer makers also stock thousands of "canned" programs, available at no cost—but normally these must be modified to meet specific needs, and savings are slight. Other sources of rentable programming expertise are computer "service bureaus," which not only rent time on their own machines but also rent know-how.

Outside Services. Because of the cost and apparent mystery that surrounds computer operation, many smaller companies find the best approach is to use outside EDP centers. These service organizations sell computer operation—and other related functions such as tape preparation—on a time basis. The Research Institute of America[9] tells of a paint manufacturer who sends his invoices, cash receipts, and other credits to an EDP service center every ten days. Within twenty-four hours he gets back a list of transactions on each account, with the starting and ending balances. At month's end he gets a trial balance for each account showing amounts due. His collections have improved. But most important are the quarterly sales analyses that the manufacturer gets as a by-product.

According to RIA, an advertising agency with a soft drink account sends data on consumption patterns plus the audience makeup of newspapers, magazines, and TV and radio stations to its EDP center. Within a few hours the agency gets back a report showing the most efficient combination of media for promoting the beverages.

And a St. Louis automobile dealer uses a service to increase parts sales and to reduce inventory investments. A bakery headquartered in a small Georgia town analyzes route sales for eighty salesmen daily with the aid of a computer center.

Many service centers have enough experience to offer standardized programs for certain industries and for certain common clerical jobs. IBM Service Bureau Corporation offers ARM (management of route operations for laundries, dairies, and bakeries); RAMPS (resource-allocation and multiproject scheduling; a variation of PERT, it helps allocate men, material, and money among several projects; it's been very successful with shipbuilders, highway construction firms, and industrial firms in developing sales territories and in budget preparation); and TSA (time series analysis—a program for analyzing sales, production, and inventory figures to detect changes in demand trends; machine-tool companies and consumer-product manufacturers have found this helpful).

The danger in using package OR-EDP programs is similar to the risk in using any prefab idea: the system may not fit your operation, and the cost of adjusting it to your peculiarities may make it more expensive than a custom-tailored one. And there is always the danger of losing control of confidential data.

A Millennium for Decision Makers?

That's a question *Business Week* magazine posed about OR and EDP. It was answered in the affirmative by Lockheed Aircraft Corp.: "The great day—when all the information for solving a management problem is only a pushbutton away is closer than you think." The brave new world Lockheed sees in its future will have as its nucleus a control center out of a Buck Rogers dream. While the center was not a reality in 1963, the company could already boast of 383 remote-control input stations feeding operating information into a central computer brain. This network linked together two plants 300 miles apart. And Lockheed also had a full-fledged ADA (automatic data acquisition) system working in two corporate divisions. Its forecast was for 850 input stations and complete data integration of all five divisions by the end of 1964. Immediate benefits are an estimated savings of $4 million annually in clerical and administrative expense. But the real payoff will be in the speed with which today's data, perhaps last minute's data, is collected, analyzed, and visualized for its management.

Business Week described the system this way:

Input devices pick up information at the source of operations and feed it to central computers that process it and serve it up to decision makers. For example, the status and location of any part for any job is continually pinpointed. A plant manager can follow the flow of work from warehouse inventory right up to the shipping gate.

Soon the system will be able to supply even more sophisticated information. A plant manager, faced with a sudden critical labor shortage in one department, will only have to push a couple of buttons on an inquiry station. Within seconds, the machine will disgorge a complete rundown on all the workers in the plant, so that he can redeploy his workers most effectively.

In the not too distant future, minutes after top managers sit down in the control room, charts displayed on video screens will update them on all the company's operations. Computers, programmed with company policies, will take up-to-the-minute information, organize it into chart form, run it through a slide-making machine, and flash it to the waiting managers. Furthermore, if a project is in trouble, the computer can offer and pretest solutions before manpower and materials are committed.[10]

Obviously this projection seems farfetched. But Lockheed's director of systems, Norman J. Ream, has set a target date for this management millennium: 1966. The basis for this forecast? Says Ream, "The theory and the equipment are ready now."

Another seer in the information assimilation field, noted automation consultant John Diebold, has also envisioned an integrated information gathering, analysis, visualizing, and processing system for newspapers. Editors will sit at huge consoles where they will review incoming copy projected on a screen, selecting items and makeup by means of pushbuttons that transmit copy and layout directly to photocopying machines that will set type. And Mr. Diebold is already able to demonstrate actual installations of various phases of this conception.

Most larger companies by the early 1960s had concluded that computers were absolutely essential to meet the problems of (1) our accelerating and complex technology and organizational system and (2) the general shrinking of the time allowed management to mull over a problem and make a decision. While the computers improve in their skill at a much faster rate than management's knowledge of how to use the computers to the best advantage, there is little doubt of their becoming the ultimate tool for management decision making.

Fred C. Foy, chairman of Koppers Co., Inc., sums up the situation: "The new generation of executives need not have the scientific ability to use a computer, but they will need to know how it's used and—more important—what its limitations are."

What Men Do Best. So much has been predicted, so much sense and nonsense has been published about the role that computers will play in business, that a very important weakness is often overlooked. Obviously, the computer is not a brain. It *can* appear to think, in some selected instances, but more often than not, it can only attempt to imitate human mental processes. Its attempts, while imposing, are still far, far removed from what the human mind can do. For instance, the mind can remember—and manipulate—thousands of elements of information, such as sounds, tastes, odors, memories, imaginations, numbers, words, visual impressions, etc. The human nervous system also has a very fast reaction time, and it is highly selective. Human perception is more comprehensive than mechanical observation methods. And most important of all, man has a unique analytical ability. His mind need not follow logical progressions, sequences, or programs. His mind can literally jump across mathematical and logical barriers. He can synthesize abstractions from a specific instance—and reverse the process.

Viewed from a "systems" approach, computers and OR vary only in degree and intensity from the techniques and tools management has used and taken for granted for over fifty years. The basic process is one of collecting, analyzing, and utilizing information. Older and smaller businesses do it with telephone and typewriter. The difference is in the relative employment of men and machines. In the simpler business operation, people accumulate data, do simple arithmetic, file, and remember; the manager accomplishes the necessary analysis in his head or with pencil and paper. As mechanical devices are incorporated into the process, people operate the machines and perform progressively higher-level analytical and managerial functions. In every case, the most effective system and best employment of men and machines represents a balance between the informational needs of the company, its organizational capabilities, and the "net worth" or profit value of the analytical activity.

People Are the Biggest Problem

Despite its complexities and costs, the success or failure of an OR-EDP installation, however, depends not so much on the hardware and the system design as it does upon the people who must work with it. These human failures could be categorized this way.

Inadequate Planning. A computer will change the old organization. There is a great deal of meticulous preparation that must be done. The men responsible for the computer must manage by objectives and set achievable goals and benchmarks within those objectives. There must be careful job definition and training. Dual systems may be necessary during the shakedown period as a check on the computer. If a tabulating system is in use, it must be carefully phased out.

Somebody will have to follow up, too, and this must be planned for and scheduled. For example, payroll is often the first routine to be put on a computer. It's simple to convert and is a good teething ring. But it's usually uneconomical, so you must plan when it will be taken off the computer and replaced with machine loading or inventory control. Otherwise, you will exhaust your capacity on little ornamental jobs and will have to work more shifts or buy more hardware to do what's really important.

Distrust and Misunderstanding. People have read too many geewhiz articles about computers, and they've heard some computer jargon, loaded with science fiction terms: complicated expressions like "biquinary coding." They've heard that the new machines read, write, and make decisions. On the other side, you have the scoffer who will tell you, "I'm not going to turn my business over to that jukebox!"

Overcoming this kind of misunderstanding is a matter of education. The first thing to do is to get rid of the hocus-pocus ideas. If a computer reads and writes, so does a teletype machine or a tabulator. A computer can make certain decisions of a semiclerical nature, but it's always on the basis of a mechanical or electrical condition, not on the basis of judgment. Does water decide not to run through a pipe when the valve is shut?

The Skilled Labor Shortage. Two forces are at work—the supply is growing as more schools and manufacturers train specialists, and the demand is being slowed by new machines and coding systems that permit nonspecialists to do the programming. But it's still a problem to provide for hiring or training the computer specialists you need.

Empire Building and Politics. There may be jurisdictional disputes, with the controller suddenly finding himself in charge of—or performing—tasks like production scheduling, sales analysis, purchasing, and inventory control. It isn't easy to head off these high-priest situations, but it's well worth the effort.

But most of the political problems stem from the fact that the computer addicts are usually eager young Turks who chaff at the company's sacred cows. The controller, chief accountant, and others opposing radical change are generally older and more realistic—and may have a certain pride of authorship in the present system. Both can contribute a great deal, of course, but unless somebody arbitrates, the entire program may be scuttled.

Ill-defined Objectives. Things are not going to somehow get "better" as soon as you plug in a computer. It must be agreed upon well in advance just what "better" is—what's expected, what will be achieved, in what order of priority, and by approximately what date. Pin down exactly what improvements you want and where. Don't be vague or all-inclusive.

A timetable of some kind is important. Otherwise, people may expect instant results (even though they don't know what these hoped-for results should be). Tempers may flare over delays in getting reports and statements—especially if communications with customers are involved.

Not everything can be done at once, and every new application or report preparation has to go through its own period of debugging and growing pains. The people affected must be kept informed of what's being done at this time, so they'll have confidence in the machine, in its staff, and in the outcome.

Resistance to Change. Inertia, self-satisfaction, fear, and insecurity show up whenever a comfortable routine is disrupted.

A computer is a pretty severe creature to work with. It not only exposes mistakes no matter who made them, but can often hang a dollar sign on the mistake for everybody to see. And it wants everything just so. It puts out information in some fixed form and format. No longer can a department head decide these things arbitrarily. Once the form of a report is agreed upon, that's it.

If the computer is used properly, it will take over a certain routine—but sometimes important—decision. If a manager has misgivings about this, or doesn't trust the accuracy of the machine, he's going to grumble. Moreover, these are often the kind of decisions some managers enjoy making. But the computer takes over the easy decisions and leaves management with just the tough ones.

Since the computer can outremember and outsort a human, it will edit a lot of detail and circulate only those exceptional items which need attention or which are required for operating the plant. Everything else will stay stored in the machine—available, but not regularly distributed. Most managers will cheer over this—they'll be getting all the information they need without any time-consuming chaff.

Lack of Performance Standards. Management seems to have been hypnotized by the plush computer showrooms, the fancy job titles, the phenomenal accomplishments of computers. Perhaps some have felt too poorly informed to interfere with the operation. No doubt part of the difficulty is the traditional indifference of management to data processing. It is this indifference that led to the common situation of the data-processing group setting its own methods, standards, and objectives—and judging itself—before computers came upon the scene.

Whatever the reason, management has often not been in control of the computer function. With nobody riding herd, and without management interest and support, it's not surprising that a number of promising computer projects run out of gas. The obvious solution is for management to take an interest: to control the data processing and computer function as it does any other function. All that's needed is normal management by exception business sense:

1. Decide precisely what is needed or wanted.
2. Delegate responsibility for achieving it.
3. Demand progressive reports—and results.

This is a short answer to the problem of performance standards, but it's neither simplified nor simple.

Information Handling

The heart of any information system—good, bad, or indifferent, mechanized or hand-operated—is data processing. But don't make the mistake that some managers make in believing that data processing is the exclusive province of clerks, accountants, statisticians, controllers, and the like. Actually, everybody processes data each day. Right now, as you read, you're data processing. When your sales manager calls up to ask for a faster delivery to a key customer and you search your memory to see if you can move the order ahead of a less critical one, that's data processing. Or you write a personal check and adjust the balance in your book—that's data processing. Or Joe Jones calls in from Kansas City and says he can't cover a certain request and you check the schedule to see who can—again that's data processing.

Data are statistics, facts, specifications. Processing organizes, relates, and summarizes data into meaningful arrangements. It makes *information* out of data; information that tells you something.

A good information handling system incorporates three functions:

1. Gathering data from basic documents such as sales orders, work orders, and purchase orders.

2. Processing data—sorting, computation, and organization of data; establishing relationships; and preparing reports. (Processing turns data into information. This is the function that involves most of the repetitive activity, the one that lends itself best to automation.)

3. Distributing information on the basis of which decisions are to be made. These decisions bring about action, and the action results in the generation of new source data and then the cycle starts all over again.

Mr. Blackstone (see page 116) sets as the requirements of such an information system that it be only *adequate* enough to cover the decisions to be made and *accurate* enough to be reliable.[11] In some organizations, *security* of the system is also an essential requirement in order to protect information from competitors.

How Information Is Handled. The tools of information handling range from pencils and paper clips, display boards and Verifax machines, to punched cards and computers. The glamor, of course, and much of the unknown, lies with the last mentioned. Since 35 per cent of all clerical effort is used to check the work of other clerks, the potential cost savings for highly accurate equipment is a major factor when designing a system.

Even in the smallest companies, a sale generates about half a dozen documents. In most cases, the information problem begins right there because of the chronic rewriting of the same information for different purposes. First a sales order is typed. Then a requisition, followed by a multipage purchase order and confirmation. Then everything is retyped into a production order. It's typed again for billing purposes, redone for the shipping department, again for sales analysis, again for general accounting, and so on. Anywhere along the line, errors creep in. Time, money, and effort are wasted.

A simple, relatively cheap solution is the use of paper tape. As the original document is prepared, a paper tape containing the same information is automatically produced. From there on, machines prepare the necessary paper work from the tape.

A faster solution is the use of punched cards, or punched cards used in combination with paper tape. Cards can be rapidly sorted and collated, easily cross-indexed, and quickly reproduced and searched. They are durable and even can be used as invoices, checks, etc. (There are two kinds of punched cards—edge-notched, for hand manipulation, and those designed for machine handling.)

The ultimate solution to the information handling problem appears to be the computer.

Pitfalls in Mechanization. There are inherent dangers for management in mechanizing an information processing system. For instance, nothing can be mechanized unless it can be precisely defined. Many systems fail before they are launched because not enough attention has been paid to this fundamental. Secondly, information must be conserved in order to conserve the time of the people who use it. At successively lower levels of management, each echelon needs more detailed information about a narrower subject than the level above it. The trick is to send to each desk as little information as possible *without* shortchanging anyone. Thirdly, a useful system must be based upon information flow; paper flow should conform to this requirement rather than the reverse. Lastly, mechanization will always mean standardization. Everything—procedures, terminology, even the location of information on documents—must stay constant. Every time someone wants to do something the least bit different, he'll have to check with the data-processing people. This can be irritating, to say the least, to men who have become used to doing things in the way most expedient to them. But you can't manage such a system efficiently if each department insists on doing things its own way.

Another danger is in believing that an updated system is as good as a freshly designed one. In many progressive companies, information handling hasn't improved in years. As new data-processing methods and machines were developed, these companies simply hooked them onto their old systems. As new information needs arose, these, too, were added to the patchwork system. Outmoded reports were seldom culled out. The paper burden just grows—undirected, uncontrolled, and often ignored.

Still another self-deception by a newly aroused management is the "step-by-step" approach to automating information systems. The trouble with the step-by-step approach is that it is often a new disguise for plugging a hydraulic transmission into a Model T system without really having a hard look at the system being perpetuated.

What is needed to truly, and economically, serve the management by exception principle is a system designed in these three steps:

1. Information handling must be recognized as an important company function, decidedly worthy of top-level attention and control.

2. Present systems must be analyzed and a completely integrated company-wide information system be set up.

3. The new system must have top-level support, be put into force, and be kept up to date.

Who Should Be Responsible. It's wishful thinking to believe that a company-wide information handling system involving observing, comparing, and reporting can be handled on a part-time basis as a secondary assignment by anyone. Nor should it be, for instance, a left-handed adjunct of the accounting department. It should be a clearly defined activity supervised by a vigorous, intelligent individual with time enough to do the job right.

Ernest Dale and Lyndall Urwick like the idea of a staff assistant who would collect and disseminate information; bring various parties together to clarify misunderstandings; write up top management policies, plans, and procedures; control internal reporting systems and forms; and design managerial control reports.[12]

Rose and Farr favor the appointment of a control assistant. He would be responsible for collecting figures, performing calculations, and charting results.[13]

Edward Schleh warns only that the man who keeps the records should not do the controlling. He cautions top management to resist the temptation to accept the machine as a complete substitute for the information-processing manager.[14]

The Koppers Company, under the late General Somervell, was one of the first companies to perfect the "control" concept of information handling. General Somervell believed that information handling was a chief responsibility of the president. To fulfill this obligation, he delegated the task to a control section at an organizational par with staff assistants for legal work, public relations, industrial relations, etc. At the close of each month, the manager of the control section would obtain operating reports from control managers of the company's six divisions and from the General's staff. The control manager would then (1) analyze results, (2) compare results against the budgeted program for each unit, (3) assess the results and isolate the exceptions, (4) obtain reasons for the variations, and (5) prepare a fifty-page report of the data in tabular, chart, and text form. This report, published within a few days after the monthly closings, would be studied immediately by the president, his staff, and the managers of the line units.

In his penetrating article "Who Should Control Information Systems?" [15] Philip H. Thurston analyzes the strengths and weaknesses of specialists and operating managers with regard to their desirability for managing the information system:

Staff Specialists

ADVANTAGES. It is clear from corporate experience that there are advantages to using staff men in systems work:

• They are the principal source of new ideas. They develop these ideas because (1) their positions and time allow them to observe and study current operations and the implications of change, (2) they are not limited by the need to show a profit in a given operating period but can take a long-range point of view, and (3) underlying these other reasons, the principal significance of their job lies in examining and changing systems.

• Specialists are trained in new methods and new data-handling equipment and tend to take a broad view of systems problems. Whereas operating managers, with their emphasis on expense responsibility in the current period, tend to take a narrower point of view and regard systems problems as separated by department lines. Specialists depart in their planning from existing organization structures and look at business in terms of over-all flow of information.

• The appointment of a specialist to carry out systems work represents a commitment by management to improve systems. This commitment is translated into action not only by the direct work of the specialists but also through the suggestions and pressures in system matters that they exert on operating people and through the influence that they exert on the executives above.

LIMITATIONS. The systems work of specialists also has limitations. The following stand out from the industrial experience that I have observed:

• Operating people resist planning in which they have no part; they resist the efforts of specialists to seek information or to install systems changes; and they delay accepting responsibility for new operating systems installed by specialists.

• The flow of operating information to specialists is blocked not only by the resistance of operating people but also by the specialists' limitations. Few men can, in a matter of months or years, move between such diverse areas as manufacturing, engineering, and marketing, and in each assimilate not only the principal flows of information and the major exception routines but also every lesser requirement which must be met. Within one company studied, two quite similar manufacturing operations had dissimilar information needs. The specialists' failure to recognize these differences led to waste of raw material and misuse of productive capacity—both costly mistakes. Operating people have a distinct advantage in their understanding of the process with which they work.

• There is some reason to believe that specialists are limited also by their own overemphasis on systems change. That is, some specialists perceive the successful performance of their jobs in terms of achieving change to the extent of disregarding the practical needs of some operating situations and of underestimating the importance of cost and timing considerations.

Operating Managers

ADVANTAGES. Experience shows that this association leads to important "pluses" in favor of systems work by line people:

• They possess detailed knowledge of the jobs to be changed. This helps them in assembling information necessary for systems decisions and in recognizing what changes will improve the immediate work situation.

• Once the supervisor in control of an operation is convinced of the desirability of making a systems change, his position enables him to effect the change with greater ease than can the specialist.

• Operating managers make another contribution to systems changes through their strengths in manpower, which enable them to give substantial support to systems projects in many areas at the same time.

LIMITATIONS. Operating men have demonstrated shortcomings, too, in their systems work:

• They are limited in their knowledge of methods for handling information. As indicated earlier, they tend to think in terms of existing areas of responsibility, whereas the specialist has a broader outlook.

• Operating people also tend to emphasize current operations, showing a reluctance to change existing work patterns.

References

1. Morley G. Melden, "Operations Research," *Factory*, October, 1953.
2. Melville C. Branch, *The Corporate Planning Process*, American Management Association, New York, 1962.
3. Dorian Shanin, "Problem-solving Math Made Easy," *Factory*, June, 1959.
4. Paul Green, S. Reed Calhoun, and I. Landis Haines, "Solving Your Plant Problems by Simulation," *Factory*, February, 1959.
5. "How to Join the Profit Makers," *Steel*, Jan. 7, 1963.
6. *Ibid.*
7. *Ibid.*
8. "Computers Are Coming of Age," *Chemical Week*, Feb. 16, 1963, pp. 33–35.
9. "How to Choose and Use an Outside EDP Center," Management Report File 32, Research Institute of America, Inc., New York, Sept. 4, 1963.
10. "Millennium for Decision Makers?" *Business Week*, Aug. 10, 1963, p. 54.
11. Henry Blackstone, "Gathering Information," in H. B. Maynard (ed.), *Top Management Handbook*, McGraw-Hill Book Company, New York, 1960, p. 201.
12. Ernest Dale and Lyndall F. Urwick, *Staff in Organization*, McGraw-Hill Book Company, New York, 1960, pp. 51–52.
13. T. G. Rose and Donald E. Farr, *Higher Management Control*, McGraw-Hill Book Company, New York, 1957, p. 16.
14. Edward C. Schleh, "The Results Approach to Organization," Society for Advancement of Management, New York, p. 15.
15. Philip H. Thurston, "Who Should Control Information Systems?" *Harvard Business Review*, November–December, 1962, pp. 117–138.

Chapter 15

DEALING WITH THE HUMAN PROBLEM

When the first secretary of the Norton Company, Charles L. Allen, instituted in 1890 a system calling for itemized expense accounts, two of the company's officers were incensed by the idea and quit.[1]

When Peter Grace took over the family's business (W. R. Grace & Co.) in 1945, he was dismayed at the continual turnover among choice headquarters personnel, despite an attractive compensation policy.[2]

When Gillette bought Paper Mate Pen Company, it also got its president, Patrick Frawley, Jr., the man whose intuitive judgments had made that company a huge success in a highly competitive field. Within a year Frawley was out.[3]

When P. S. du Pont hired Charles F. Kettering in the early 1920s, he promised the inventive genius $100 million to produce for General Motors a better auto engine than Henry Ford's. Kettering's idea was the copper-cooled engine. GM's engineers did not like it. When Kettering tried to force the project on them, many had nervous breakdowns. P. S. du Pont got nervous too and cut the backing to $10 million. Although no one was able to disprove the basic soundness of Kettering's concept, GM produced only a few prototype engines and then abandoned the project.[4]

When British mining engineers after World War II attempted to change traditional mining practices from the "short face" to the "long wall," results were disappointing. The traditional two-man teams were replaced, for technically sound reasons, by forty-man groups in which sharp divisions of labor were prescribed. Surprisingly, coal production was only slightly raised while absenteeism, psychosomatic illnesses, and tensions became disturbingly high.

The Reason Why. In every company, in every organization, in every department, examples like these abound. Each is characterized by the introduction of well-laid, systematic, logical plans followed by failure. Why? In each instance, failure can be traced to the inability of management to cope with human variables.

Examine each of the preceding failure incidents one by one:

The executives who quit the Norton Company reacted as many of us do when challenged by sudden change, or when our prerogatives are threatened, or still worse, when an insult to our integrity is implied. Put on the defensive, we react outwardly by becoming aggressive or by running away from the problem.

The reason so many executives left Peter Grace, many of his associates said, was due to Grace's love of full reports, exhaustive financial analysis, and an inordinately large controller's staff. Many competent executives feel that rigid controls restrict their initiative and they cannot, or will not, adjust their personal habits to conform. Gillette's centralized control of its divisions had this effect upon Mr. Frawley, who proved his mettle by leaving Gillette and taking over as chief executive officer of a competitor, Eversharp.

Kettering's experience illustrates the frailty of logic as a persuasive technique—even among men trained to think logically as were the GM engineers. The copper-cooled engine was not judged on its merits or weaknesses. Instead it became a symbol for emotional outburst, and the emotional pressure thus built up proved to be stronger than the autocratic force with which Kettering's employers tried to gain acceptance.

The experience of the British mining engineers is an example of more of the same. Since people view change as a threat to their security, they rarely react to changes rationally. And so great does this fear of change become that we often call upon our primitive, emotional reserves to throw aside the logic and common sense others use to persuade us. Businessmen who practice any kind of systematic management are forever invoking change, followed by pressures to conform. Is it any wonder then that businessmen continually deal with human beings who are not rational just when they should be? The result is a discouragingly high occurrence of nonsuccesses attributable to our inept handling of human relations. Unfortunately, business executives win little sympathy for misfires attributable to their ineptness in human relations. While an executive may like to think of himself as a manipulator of plans, finances, or markets, in the long run he's human and he faces the same problem that all of us must. He must win the support and cooperation of others in order to achieve his goals and the goals of his organization.

In a 1963 editorial *Life* magazine was critical of what it called "McNamara's Human Problem." Although the editorial acknowledged that, "In most respects, McNamara is the best Secretary of Defense the U.S. has had," it deplored his coldly analytical efficiency, which in *Life*'s view destroys the support of military leaders "to whom strategy and tactics are arts, not sciences, and who need operating flexibility as well as the clear management line imposed by the Secretary." *Life* concluded, "We need not choose between efficiency and leadership; the nation needs both. It also wants the civilian Secretary to have the last word. But he has evidently been having it in too abrupt, rigid, and even contemptuous fashion. In short, he has a management problem of the most important kind—human management. When he surmounts that one, he will be a great Defense Secretary." [5]

Mr. McNamara, as are indeed most executives, was not unaware of the human problem. His difficulty was in solving it. He, like the rest, was trying to establish and hold that delicate balance between decisive, logical action on the one hand and intelligent permissiveness on the other. For without the latter, experience tells most managers, they will not gain the support and cooperation needed to move an organization forward in unity.

Ralph J. Cordiner, former chairman of General Electric, observes that the top executive "has the responsibility to organize all the resources of the company in order to make his program a profitable reality." But, he laments, "it also involves winning understanding and cooperation of associates at all levels, so that they will do their parts voluntarily and creatively." [6]

Fortunately, successful executives like Cordiner and thousands of others, are able to achieve this dual objective a majority of the time, if not always. Just how they are able to do so is difficult to reduce to copybook maxims. On inspection, the secret seems to be more an attitude than a definitive program. Louis Neumiller, who as president of Caterpillar inspired that company to its great surge forward in the 1940s says of Caterpillar's approach, "It's been a studied object to build a 'we' organization and not an 'I' organization. . . . Instead of talking profit, profit, profit all the time we talked about the atmosphere of the company, and the advantages of that kind of atmosphere. It isn't that I'm ashamed to talk about profits—oh no! But I know that profits flow from able people working wholeheartedly together." [7]

Historical Management Patterns

The ability or inability to handle the human affairs of business is the touchstone or stumbling block to the successful practice of management by exception. And it is the realization of this harsh fact that has led management through a maze of different management patterns during the last half century. The great social scientist Dr. Fritz J. Roethlisberger identifies five such patterns evidenced since industry began to recognize management by exception principles: [8]

• *Pattern No. 1.* Roethlisberger demonstrates that once a manager's control reports show a variance from standard, the manager has to get up from his desk and ask, "How come?" There are only two possible replies to this question, says Roethlisberger: either (1) the standard is not good or (2) someone is not doing what he is supposed to. In either case, the executive must criticize, discipline, or correct.

• *Pattern No. 2.* Because these actions of pattern No. 1 created just the kind of problems cited in this chapter's opening, another pattern of management came into vogue in the postwar era. Management now shifted its base from "How come?" to a more permissive "Why is it happening?" This pattern still left management perplexed, says Roethlisberger, because it didn't point out what specific action should ultimately take place.

• *Pattern No. 3.* Next, we tried to conceive of the manager as a motivator, relator, interactor, communicator, and leader. In this more completely openhanded approach, the manager simply asks, "What is going on here?" But this pattern, too, begged the answer of what to do next.

• *Pattern No. 4.* This rather late development begins to look surprisingly like plain old management by exception. It, however, was called "management by objectives." "Now, the manager," says Roethlisberger, "was supposed to manage not by *exception*, nor through *people*, but by *objectives*." It now became popular to ask, "What business am I in?" "What kind of people do I want to sell my products to?" etc. Roethlisberger feels that we were now closer to a compromise pattern most useful to all managers "because we were acknowledging that man has attitudes, values and goals to be satisfied." However, the pattern still tended to ignore the fact that the manager is an active decision maker and problem solver.

• *Pattern No. 5.* Roethlisberger conceives of this as "the manager as a self-actualizing person." Said more simply, this is the pattern that calls for management to integrate *all* the previous patterns into a single whole rather than to reduce one version to an established priority.

> The manager who managed [only] by exception never became a popular public image. . . . Although it is consistent with the corporate mission of running a good business that makes a profit, it does not reflect well the manager's place in the new economic society and the important part he plays in its development. . . . No matter how you slice up an organization, there are certain primary activities that have to be performed if the purposes of the organization are to be achieved. No new version of management or organization can deny or overlook these realities.

But he adds:

> Let's face it: (1) Organizations have purpose. (2) To carry out purposes, structure is needed and roles have to be assigned. Also (3) Organizations are peopled, and (4) People have needs.

Emerging Management Problems. Dr. Ernest Dale, an outstanding student of management techniques, sees other related problems of human and public affairs affecting management by exception today. He enumerates along this line:[9]

• Business concerns are becoming less private and more public. One has to look no further than the frightening example of the United States Steel Company when it tried to raise its prices in 1962. While the decisions were technically sound, Roger Blough, Big Steel's president, simply had not become aware of how critical the people at large—and their political leaders—would be of the way in which a private company would try to reach its reasonable goals.

• Internal political forces are becoming more powerful. Dale shows how hard it is to keep a sensitive balance between these forces. He feels that power struggles cannot be avoided simply by understanding them because "those who engage in them understand very well what they are about and have no intention of changing their ways."

• There is more emphasis on trading or bargaining ability. "A manager spends much of his time in making deals, in negotiating and presenting and persuading," says Dale. This is supported by a study of 241 managers performed by scientists at the Management Development Laboratory of the University of Minnesota's Industrial Relations Research Center. It found that all managers spent about 10 per cent of their time "negotiating" as differentiated from supervising (25 per cent) and coordinating (15 per cent). The most highly placed, highest-paid executives, however, spent the largest chunk (22 per cent) of their time negotiating.

• Techniques of group dynamics and participation are becoming more practical. While the concept of inviting advice from employees and subordinates with respect not only to their work but to their objectives and performance standards was considered heretical not so long ago, their real value in gaining cooperation has been demonstrated by many firms.

• Freedom to discuss and disagree is becoming more essential. Increasing complexity and number of difficult problems reduce the chances of simple, one-best solutions. Creative managers need the opportunity to think through the decision-making process along with their superiors and to test the soundness of their own judgment by challenging those laid down from above.

Organizational Patterns. An organizational adviser to General Electric's headquarters management, Hugh Estes, feels that the best human relationships in business derive from carefully designed organizational structures. While an iconoclastic social scientist, Chrys Agyris, has blamed the classic organizational structure for many of management's human failures, Estes counsels that this result can be minimized if you think of work as a "responsibility for results." He says:

> By doing so you avoid organizational emphasis on a certain kind of effort or activity. The organizational emphasis should properly be based on getting individuals to *want* to act more on their own; to *want* to make more of their own decisions; to *want* to grow as a result of their

own educational efforts; to *want* the added personal freedom that comes with the demonstrated ability to discipline themselves; to *want* to increase their own competence—their very ability to get needed work done and on time.[10]

In other words, Estes advises that an organization should aim to help individuals to *want* to do the kinds of things that make management by exception function.

Motivational Patterns. Glenn Gilman, special programs administrator of the Missile and Space Division of Lockheed Aircraft Corp., observes that exercise of control typically involves one of the following:[11]

• Coercion—the use of status-centered or security-oriented force to obtain action without the willing consent of the observer. Far too many managers rely exclusively—albeit unconsciously—on this technique when dealing with subordinates.

• Manipulation—a form of subtle chicanery in which persons are influenced without realizing it (at the time at any rate). As with any kind of essentially dishonest behavior, managers who believe that manipulation is the practice of good human relations are sure to be disappointed with results in the long run.

• Persuasion—in which an individual has the opportunity to become aware of the potential value of accepting someone else's will in place of his own. This is the most difficult, but also the most effective, kind of human relations to practice.

Of course, all three of these means are motivational techniques. While we shall speak more of motivation later on, it might be well to consider a clarifying statement by Prof. Keith Davis:

> *Motives* are expressions of a person's needs. They are his inner drives; hence they are personal and internal. *Incentives,* on the other hand, are external to the person. They are something he perceives in his environment as helpful toward accomplishing his goals. For example, management offers salesmen a bonus as an incentive to channel in a productive way their drives for recognition and status.

The testimony of Roethlisberger, Dale, Estes, Gilman, and Davis only serves to reinforce our conviction that the achievement of good human relationships is difficult—especially if it is linked to the negative control actions of management by exception. In actual fact, the outlook, while cloudy, is not without some hope. We *do* have a storehouse of reliable knowledge upon which to build an effective human relations platform. Let's take a look at it in detail.

The Enigma of Human Relations

Human relations in industry is neither psychology, sociology, nor anthropology. Most of all, it is not psychiatry. While these four sciences aid in our understanding of what happens to people when they come to work, labels such as these are more misleading than enlightening.

When a job applicant fills out an interview form, the science of psychology is being applied. When a manager asks a foreman what the boys in the shop think about the new rates, the manager is acknowledging the presence of sociological forces. When a plant in Michigan shuts down on the first day of the hunting season because it knows from past experience that most of the men will take off anyway, anthropologists may identify this action as a concession to group cultures. And when an office manager listens to a near-hysterical secretary without interrupting, he may be borrowing a technique from the psychiatrist.

All the above actions involve the behavior of people at work. It has become common—and convenient—practice to call this behavior "human relations." The operative words are *people, behavior,* and *work.*

Human relations is something that takes place between *people.* It takes place between a man and his boss, between one worker and another, between a staff specialist and a line supervisor, and between a manager and his superior. It takes place between a man and the other men he works with—between an individual and a group. The human interactions may be between an executive and his department, between a manager and his associates, or inversely, between a workman and "management" in general. It takes place between two or more groups also. It may be between the sales department and the accounting office, or between the production department and the maintenance department, or between two factions in the same group. As you can readily see from a purely statistical viewpoint, the *people* side of human relations offers dozens of situational possibilities for the average leader to cope with.

Apparently obvious, but more often than not overlooked, is the fact that human relations is something that takes place between *people* and *work.* It takes place between people and working conditions—the physical things, such as illumination, heat, and washrooms. It takes place between a workman and the tools he uses —and is influenced by their age and condition. It takes place between an employee and company practices—such as wage incentives, safety rules, seniority provisions, job instructions, and the like. It takes place, too, between people and intangibles—such as a company's reputation as an employer and as a product or service vendor.

Management is irresistibly concerned with the third operative word in the definition of human relations—*behavior*. For instance, how will an employee react to the introduction of a new machine? What will the union do if the company revises its wage incentive plan? Where will resistance develop when two sales territories are consolidated? Who will provide active support for a decentralization move? Answers to these, and to thousands of other questions vital to the running of a business, lie in employees' reactions to other employees and to their work.

Management's Responsibility. Management's task in this regard is threefold. Ideally, it must be able to *predict* employee behavior. (The term "employee" is used in its broad sense to indicate anyone working for a company, regardless of function or title.) Knowing how employees might act in a given situation, management must be able to *influence, control,* or *alter* employee behavior in order that the resulting behavior aid in reaching the corporation's goal. Finally, management must learn to *accept* employee behavior as a natural result of cause and effect and not as expressions of willfulness, obstinacy, or stupidity—even though it may often reflect any or all of these shortcomings.

Social scientists, who are usually under less pressure for immediate results than are business leaders, list these management objectives for human relations in order of their attainability by managers: (1) acceptance of human behavior in the work situation as rational rather than frivolous; (2) prediction of employee behavior for better or worse in terms of profit objectives; and (3) influence on employee actions, either short term or long range, to bring about management goals.

Managing situations that involve people at work is a major portion of an executive's job. There can be no denial of this fact. The anthologies are full of statements made by famous business leaders testifying to this fact. Dozens of scientific studies purport to demonstrate that human problems are by far the most time-consuming.

But how important, how critical to the attainment of profit objectives, is the management of human relations? And which aspects of the problems of human beings at work are the ones that must be mastered?

One answer can be found by a cursory examination of the top-management structure of a number of corporations. How often the examiner finds a key profit contributor, or profit retainer, present in the role of tax adviser, national warehouse-inventory manager, purchasing agent, treasurer, legal counsel, traffic manager, or the like! The profit contribution of these executives is considerable, while the human relations demands of their jobs are often slight. This line of reasoning could be pursued successfully in many sectors of business organizations. Its purpose is not to deflate the need for human relations management, but to broaden our concept of the management picture into which the human relations assessment must be cast.

An opposite viewpoint is that human relations consideration smothers all other management tasks like a blanket. And, truly, of later years there have been managers who have permitted their concern for people to pervade their every thought. No decision is made by such men without first and last worrying about how Pete will react to this, whether the boys will not resist that, or Mary retire to the girls' room to cry.

When kept in bounds, concern for human relations is simply good management. Managers are not paid to be surprised either by the turn of the market or by the apparent foibles of people. What is unfortunate is that so many managers cannot keep in balance their estimate of the human factor and those of the many other factors they are paid to handle.

A Human Relations Rationale. A proper way for keeping the place of people in business in focus is to avoid looking at them through either the near or the far end of the glass. A well-integrated person in a leadership role will ask of himself four questions in every decisive situation:

First: What is it that I want done?
Second: Which people are inclined to help or hinder this accomplishment?
Third: To what extent are they likely to be influential in this situation?

Fourth: Should I plan for their aid or at the least to minimize their interference?

Such a catechism should become less of a procedure than a frame of mind. It should be developed through experience and intimate knowledge of the people involved. Some managers acquire this frame of mind naturally and quickly. This is so because the value of an experience lies not so much in repetition as in variety, and especially in analysis and generalization upon the part of the manager who is intent upon learning. For those who do not have this natural inclination, the learning process is slow, puzzling, and often uncertain.

The process may be speeded up by developing an intimate knowledge of the people with whom the manager must "interact"—to borrow a term from the psychologist. Intimate knowledge must go further than mere statistical interests in marital status, children, home, car, hobbies, education, experience, etc. These data provide a good foundation but fall far short of what is really needed. The kind of intimate knowledge the manager needs in order to improve his frame of mind for more successful human relations is that acquired from keen observation, done with both eyes and ears. For instance, do you know what kind of assignments your associates welcome, and why? Do you know who likes whom in your group and whose hackles rise when Joe takes charge? Do you know who is fast in which kinds of assignments or who is slow in certain situations? Are the men whom your employees listen to most the ones whose advice they act upon?

Intimate information of this sort does not come from the personnel department on 3 by 5 cards. It does not come from assessments relayed to a manager by his first assistant, although this, too, is helpful. Neither does it come from an occasional friendly chat at the water cooler or a well-structured appraisal interview twice a year; although these kinds of contacts must be maintained, too. The kind of intimate information the successful leader needs is that which comes either from shoulder-to-shoulder association (which is possible in only a few situations) or from hard, objective, calculating study of what goes on among people in the work organization every day.

There are times, of course, when human relations activities demand a very high proportion of a manager's time. When a reorganization is under way, when radical changes are planned, when union negotiations are pressing, when key appointments are being made—these are all situations which warrant high priority. But continual devotion to this side of the executive curriculum ultimately spells bad management.

Urgency, then, is a variable which must occasionally be allowed to call the human relations tune. But Rensis Likert, a social scientist of note, warns that management planning in this sensitive area needs to recognize that human relations results are both immediate and deferred. Insensitive, self-serving, expedient personnel practices sometimes produce surprisingly good short-term results. No research is needed to prove this. The experience of most mature people in business is full of examples of "impossible" managers who achieved their aims over the backs of the people with whom they worked and who then moved on to important positions. Likert's point of view is that human relations is like a reservoir of good will. It does not dry up in a short hot spell. It will, he says, do so if the drought is prolonged. The company, rather than the hard-riding executive, is usually the one to suffer (or the luckless manager who succeeds the expedient fellow who has moved on). Conversely, Likert observes, the reservoir of goodwill and identification with corporate goals can be built up so that it will maintain itself through difficult periods of adjustment—periods in which the manager of proved human consideration may make mistakes or act unwisely.

Sugar-coated "Cookbooks." Obviously, the weight of the evidence shows that many factors affect job satisfaction and that, in turn, job satisfaction affects the behavior of people at work. In terms of productivity, low turnover, and good attendance (all goals which management strives for) the attainment of good morale seems to be desirable. None of these findings can be interpreted, however, to mean that there is a simple formula that equates job satisfaction to anything—neither measurable human characteristics nor observable human performance. The researchers do not say this. They have never implied it. But somewhere out of management's impatience for results and the demand for usable motivational tools, this belief—or ones like it—has crept into the literature, the folklore, and the behavior of management men in business.

Unfortunately, much "cookbook" advice on how to handle people oversimplifies and overgeneralizes without due regard to the limited scope of the studies upon which the conclusions are based, the varying definitions of characteristics measured, or the dependence upon a "test" individual's subjective opinion of what he likes or how he acts. Such books are useful in that they condense information that the average manager would never have time to study in detail, and present existing knowledge in readable and understandable form. But too often these books do a disservice; managers soon find out that the techniques suggested are not reliable, with the result that what we really do know about human behavior is often discounted or ignored.

Most of the books that management men read about human relations and leadership fall into this category. Most of the in-company training of management people is of the same ilk. Labels for these books and for these training courses should bear the warning: *Use with caution. If difficulty with people persists, consult a professional.*

A better approach is suggested by the writings of Prof. Keith Davis of Arizona State University. He says:

> The field of study of human relations is based upon four fundamental concepts: (1) Motivation, (2) Individual differences, (3) Mutual interest, (4) Human dignity.
>
> Motivation is the means by which the manager creates and maintains the desire of his people to achieve the planned goals. . . . Principles of motivation in business are derived from psychology. . . . It is assumed that all human behavior is caused. These causes act upon the individual, who acts in a way to satisfy his needs *as he sees them.*
>
> Each person is different physically, mentally, and emotionally. . . . Individual differences mean that management can get the greatest motivation and job satisfaction among employees by treating them differently. . . . If it were not for individual differences, some standard, across-the-board way of dealing with employees could be adopted, and a minimum of managerial judgment would be required thereafter.
>
> All studies of personal wants show that people desire to be treated with respect and dignity—to be treated as human beings. This recognizes that each person is a separate personality, free to pursue happiness within bounds of responsibility. It is the moral basis for human relations and came originally from religious concepts.[12]

Significant Landmarks. By far the greatest landmark in human relations research was set in 1927 under the direction of George Elton Mayo at Western Electric Company's huge Hawthorne Works on the outskirts of Chicago. Mayo, head of Harvard University's Department of Industrial Research, had previously demonstrated that workers, when given a feeling of responsibility, turned in remarkable production records. He came to view worker output almost as an index of well-being. Through the cooperation of Western Electric Company, Mayo found a measure of experimental proof for his thesis.[13]

The Hawthorne study started out as a simple experiment to determine the effect of illumination on work output. The researchers, using a laboratory-isolation technique, set up two production rooms, one as a control. First the lighting was increased in the experimental room. Production went up. But perplexingly, production also went up in the control room. Then lighting was decreased sharply in the experimental room. Production went up again. And production also rose in the control room. The researchers soon discovered that production kept rising regardless of their changes.

How did Mayo and his colleagues explain this? In the attempts to hold the experiments under steady conditions, the researchers had sought the cooperation of the two groups. This, in itself, Mayo concluded, was the major experimental change, not the changes in environment. Mayo realized that he had been confronted with the *total* situation. The "obvious" variables had not been as important in this instance as the variables of "group interaction" and "participation."

Mayo wrote, "What actually happened was that six individuals became a team, and the team gave itself whole-heartedly . . . to cooperation." The study blazed a guidemark in that for the first time the glimmerings of what many call "group dynamics" was scientifically demonstrated. The works of Mayo and his findings still represent the core of human relations theory and practice today.

What Mayo demonstrated by experiment was observed over ten years earlier by a pioneering management consultant by the name of Whiting Williams. In the time between World War I and 1920, Williams disguised himself as a workman and spent many months in a steel mill. What he found out was that "the workers' point of view was determined less by logic than by their emotional reactions" and that "final joy of his work was settled not by him nor his employers but by the social standing awarded him by his fellow citizens," and "the further a worker's skill took him away from a hunger minimum, the more his paycheck's ability to buy material things was overshadowed by its ability to purchase an immaterial thing of equal importance and vastly greater intricacy—social standing among fellow workers."

Mayo's Hawthorne research bore out Whiting Williams's first-hand observations. It documented the fact that while men may work for money, they work for many other important reasons. Mayo crystallized the inferences many had drawn about "teamwork" in industry. His work demonstrated that the effect of teamwork can be negative as well as positive. It lifted the curtain for all time on the amazing influence individuals have on groups, groups have on groups, and groups have on individuals.

In terms of readily applied management techniques, Mayo's greatest contribution was the discovery of the power of "participation." By enabling employees to have a say about their goals and to discuss their role in achieving them, management—almost unwittingly— won employee cooperation and productivity. What is most astounding—and discouraging—is that in the 1960s, management generally does not widely use or accept this technique. This rejection seems especially stubborn and shortsighted in view of the volume of supporting research which has followed the path of Elton Mayo.

Under the direction of Rensis Likert, the Survey Research Center at the Institute for Social Research of the University of Michigan undertook in 1947 a ten-year study of the "interpersonal" factors that affect organization effectiveness and employee satisfaction. These studies have been widely cited to support Mayo, and, in fact, offer new guides for management action. Specifically, the Survey Research Center work is best known for its identification of supervisory behavioral characteristics which encourage high employee productivity. These desirable characteristics of effective supervisors include the following:[14]

· More attention to look-ahead (versus day-to-day) planning
· More attention to problems of motivation than to performing routine institutional tasks
· Less direct supervision, permitting greater freedom among employees for minor decision making

These studies also shed light on the often-suggested need for a manager to devote more of his interest to his employees. While such interests are somewhat salutary, the Michigan group found that other things were more important, like whether a supervisor developed his people for better jobs, backed them up for these positions, and kept them informed about how well they were doing and what was going on around them.

Another Mayo conclusion was supported by the Survey Research Center studies—that of the value of participation. Especially in a study of railroad workers, there was good evidence that participation practices on the part of the supervisor made for higher productivity. In departments where the supervisor called his men in to discuss problems with them, morale and output were high. In departments where the supervisor, rather than the union steward, discussed work goals, the men tended to identify themselves with management objectives. In departments where both supervisor and steward invited employee participation, job satisfaction was very high.

However, Daniel Katz, one of the Michigan researchers, cautioned that "foremen who made decisions on the basis of superior knowhow could affect productivity, even though the lack of involvement of their groups may have produced some motivational loss." [15]

Management has determinedly resisted the recognition of the intensity of group forces among employees—although most managers readily recognize the power of group influence in the executive hierarchy. One reason for this resistance has been the vagueness of much of the supporting research. Some of this objection has been answered by the publication in 1958 of Prof. Leonard R. Sayles's book *Behavior of Industrial Work Groups: Prediction and Control*.[16] In it, Sayles reports on a mammoth field study of 300 work groups in thirty plants in a variety of industries. His conclusions, based upon study of work records, interviews, and clinical observations, bring conclusive evidence to bear on the subject:

> The work group itself is the primary forum for registering discontent as well as the organizational mechanism for releasing productivity. It is not the isolated workman, as so many are prone to believe. . . . These groups are themselves the product of management decisions. . . . The technology and the organization of the plant are the architecture of the work group, constructing with the materials of human interactions a variety of types of groups.

Obviously, Sayles is at odds with the organizational experts who feel that objectives, responsibilities, functions, and authorities can be charted by the men who sit in the front office.

Sayles is convincingly able to identify work groups which he describes variously as "apathetic"—least likely to strike, but not rated as cooperative by management; "erratic"—which display no relationship between seriousness of grievance and intensity of protest; "strategic"—which always seem to be at the center of really important grievances; and "conservative"—most stable in that they do not use concerted action without warning.

Identification of these groups can be made according to occupation and working conditions and to other observable characteristics. Sayles's study supports the belief that the larger the group, the more likely it is to deliver concerted action. Degree of activity is also shown to be directly related to (1) relative position on the promotion ladder, (2) relative size and importance of the group, (3) similarity of jobs within the group, (4) degree to which work is indispensable, and (5) precision with which management can measure work load and pace. This kind of information is the kind management needs, and can use, in predicting employee behavior. It does not, however, answer many problems about how management can influence or control this behavior.

What Managers Can Do about Human Relations

As expressed earlier, the problem is mainly one of attitude, perspective, and skill. Managers must recognize their responsibility for managing human affairs at work. They must always weigh this concern against the urgencies of technical and administrative matters. And finally, management must find effective ways for handling people at work.

Needed: A New Attitude. In the matter of attitude and skill evaluation, Douglas McGregor, professor of industrial management at Massachusetts Institute of Technology, has much to offer management in his thoughtful work, *The Human Side of Enterprise.* Most of today's management thinking was forged to meet the needs of a feudal society, reasons McGregor. The world has changed, and new thinking is needed for top efficiency today. That's the core of his philosophy of pitting Theory X versus Theory Y.

Theory X, the traditional framework for management thinking, is based on a set of assumptions about human nature and human behavior. The assumptions are these:

1. The average human being has an inherent dislike for work and will avoid it if he can.

2. Because of this human characteristic of dislike of work, most people must be coerced, controlled, directed, threatened with punishment to get them to put forth adequate effort toward the achievement of organizational objectives.

3. The average human being prefers to be directed, wishes to avoid responsibility, has relatively little ambition, wants security above all.[17]

Do these assumptions make up a straw man for purposes of scientific demolition? Unfortunately, no. While they are rarely stated so directly, the principles of organization that comprise the bulk of management literature could only have been derived from assumptions such as those of Theory X.

Theory Y finds its roots in recently accumulated knowledge about human behavior. It is based on the following set of assumptions:

1. The expenditure of physical and mental effort in work is as natural as play or rest.

2. External control and the threat of punishment are not the only means for bringing about effort towards organizational objectives. Man will exercise self-control in the service of objectives to which he is committed.

3. Commitment to objectives is dependent on the rewards associated with their achievement. The most important rewards are those that satisfy needs for self-respect and personal improvement.

4. The average human being learns, under proper conditions, not only to accept but to seek responsibility.

5. The capacity to exercise a relatively high degree of imagination, ingenuity, and creativity in the solution of organizational problems is widely, not narrowly, distributed in the population.

6. Under the conditions of modern industrial life, the intellectual potentialities of the average human being are only partially utilized.

Under the assumptions of Theory Y, the work of the manager is to integrate the needs of employees with the needs of the enterprise. Direct control is only rarely appropriate. Here again are McGregor's words:

The industrial manager is dealing with adults who are only partially dependent. They can—and will—exercise remarkable ingenuity in defeating the purpose of external controls which they resent. However, they can—and do—learn to exercise self-direction and self-control under appropriate conditions. His task is to help them discover objectives consistent both with organizational requirements and with their own personal goals. And to do so in ways that will encourage genuine commitment to these objectives. Beyond this, his task is to help them achieve these objectives: to act as teacher, consultant, colleague, and only rarely as authoritative boss.

The assumptions of Theory X would not have persisted—and would not have succeeded in bringing us to this state of industrial development—if there were not some truth in them. But today's knowledge of behavior and motivation goes beyond those time-honored assumptions.

McGregor says this about motivation:

> Man is a wanting animal—as soon as one of his needs is satisfied, another appears in its place. This process is unending. It continues from birth to death. Man continuously puts forth effort—works, if you please—to satisfy his needs.
>
> Human needs are organized in a series of levels. At the lowest level, but of greatest importance when they are thwarted, are the physical needs. (Needs for food, drink, shelter—the things money can buy.)
>
> A satisfied need is not a motivator of behavior! This is a fact of profound significance. It is a fact which is unrecognized in Theory X and is, therefore, ignored in the conventional approach to the management of people.
>
> When the physical needs are reasonably satisfied, needs at the next higher level begin to dominate man's behavior—to motivate him. These are the safety needs: for protection against danger, threat, deprivation. Some people mistakenly refer to these as needs for security. However, unless man is in a dependent relationship where he fears arbitrary deprivation, he does *not* demand security.
>
> When man's physical needs are satisfied and he is no longer fearful about his physical welfare, his social needs become important motivators of his behavior. These needs are for belonging, for association, for acceptance by one's fellows, for giving and receiving friendship and love.
>
> Above the social needs—in that they do not become motivators until lower needs are reasonably satisfied—are the needs of greatest significance to management and to man himself. They are:
>
> 1. Those that relate to one's self-esteem. Needs for self-respect and self-confidence, for autonomy, appreciation, competence, and knowledge.
>
> 2. Those that relate to one's reputation: needs for status, for recognition, for achievement, for deserved respect.[18]

Because of our laws, our economic prosperity, and the power of workers to influence public and business affairs, America today is not always a satisfactory place to practice Theory X. It seeks to motivate by appealing to lower-level needs—which, in American workers, are often already satisfied before the manager has a chance to ask for a little extra effort.

A Deep Sense of Involvement. In more highly academic words, Raymond B. Cattell made a similar observation ten years previously:

> It is no longer possible to speak simply of good leaders and poor leaders, but instead we are required to view the problem in terms of whether a leader is good or bad with respect to a specific "syntality" dimension. For example, a certain leader may in general increase the dimension of group general ability, reduce its dimension of morale, and increase its dimension of dictatorialness of atmosphere. Secondly, it indicates that every man is to some extent a leader insofar as every man has some effect upon the syntality of the group. Thus leadership can no longer be considered as an all or nothing phenomenon, but even when it is formally organized in terms of leaders and followers, there is for each an index showing the extent to which he is leading.[19]

In other words, even the least man in your shop may aid your plan or block it. The leader, to some degree and with some of his subordinates, may find himself following. To the group, and to the organization as a whole, this may be beneficial so long as the group is motivated to proceed effectively toward its goal.

On behalf of participation, John R. P. French, Jr., another "group dynamics" researcher, observes that:

> Group harmony appears to be disrupted when members see themselves competing for mutually exclusive goals. Greater group productivity will result when the members or sub-units are cooperative rather than competitive in their interrelationships.
>
> The greater the degree of involvement, the greater the salience, clarity, and degree of differentiation of the person's perception for the goal, his liking for it, and his identification with it.[20]

Management's problem, then, is how to encourage this involvement without (1) sacrificing management prerogatives or (2) using up too much of its time.

Foundations for Better Human Relations. There is much that can be done by each serious manager who wishes to improve his relationships with people. While the availability of scientific facts may be slight, the fault lies more with the individual than with the research effort. Anyone who takes the time, or makes the effort, can learn a lot about human behavior—his own as well as that of others. It will give him a feeling of humility, of course. But this humility need not destroy his confidence.

Leadership depends upon many things. Demonstrated technical ability to plan and coordinate plans wins many followers. Drive, courage, and persistence build a good foundation for leadership, too. People will respond to the manager who expresses confidence in them. People will lean toward the manager whose behavior is consistent. The manager who searches hard for the people-oriented facts when making decisions, who as a result creates the impression of trying to be fair, gets approval, if not accolades, from his subordinates. These are actions any manager can take without being a psychologist, sociologist, anthropologist, or parlor psychiatrist. These qualities should be considered, however, only as foundations for human relations skills and should not be confused with the skills themselves.

Patterns for Effective Control. Psychologist Rensis Likert (of whom we spoke before) and Stanley E. Seashore (a man of considerable reputation) have long studied an important facet of management by exception—cost control. They came to two rather revolutionary conclusions regarding patterns of success:[21]

PATTERN NO. I—While fiat changes in procedures plus pressure from on high for reduced cost often produce immediate end-results, there is almost always delayed but prolonged decay in a number of sensitive criteria. Not only do attitudes, motivation, communications, attendance, and labor relations deteriorate, but end-results (productivity, waste performance, earnings), product and customer loyalties also suffer. These delayed effects are long-lasting and very difficult to reverse.

PATTERN NO. II—Conversely, when management *gradually* makes changes and increases its demands while at the same time improving its understanding of and skill in securing cooperation, all the factors mentioned in I *gradually* improve. An improvement in attitudes follows first, attended by gains in attendance and labor relations. These, in turn are followed by improvement in end results (not as marked as in I, but more permanent), quality of product or service, and customer loyalties.

Likert and Seashore qualify these conclusions, such as by saying that in companies where work standards have long existed and continual rating of performance against established goals has taken place, Pattern I is less likely to take place. But they do bring forward a weight of evidence and reason that is hard to deny.

Planned Communications. In addition to the failure to motivate members of an organization to cooperate with a management by exception system, there is often the failure to explain the system adequately or to forestall fears about it by providing clear-cut information. The process of conveying organizational information bears the difficult label "communications." Close examination of the processes will show that in many ways it is inseparable from the motivational process—in that in many instances people can only be motivated by communicating ideas and attitudes to them.

Keith Davis has cited a reliable study of communication that shows that, contrary to management's intent, most communication does not flow down the chain of command. In actuality, the study showed, much of the communications engaged in by members of management are likely to be with people not in their own organization. Such communication tends to be at random and irrelevant to the organization's goals. In other words, it is wasted. In the face of such unplanned, heterogeneous patterns, a major problem persists of trying to encourage greater cross-communication within the total management organization.[22]

Since cross-communication is so important to management functions, Davis suggests these tested, routine methods:

• Management lunchrooms, coffee hours, and clubs
• Various types of boards, committees, conferences, and meetings
• Special communications, such as house organs, exclusively for executives or advance releases from forthcoming company house organs

All these practices seek to keep management people better informed about goals, policies, personalities, and current events. Thus informed, they can make sound decisions in terms of the firm's goals and all other relevant factors. If intermanagement communication is to succeed, the facts need to be available and to be surrounded by an information-sharing climate.

Management's communications weakness often lies in its wishful thought that it is easy to get ideas across to other people. In practice, few things are more difficult. The late Dr. Irving J. Lee (of AT & T) prescribed a relatively simple checklist[23] to make sure that

in a communication situation, you would stack the cards of understanding in your favor. In prescribing policy and procedures, Dr.
Lee listed five communications essentials:

• *Motivate.* The best way to get the attention of a second party
is to show him why he should listen to your idea and to show him
how he'll benefit by paying attention to you.

• *Inform.* Planning the content of your message is especially important as is the need to allow adequate time to tell your story.
Instructions should be explicit and presume to answer the questions
of who, what, when, and how much.

• *Stimulate Questions.* Many a person nods his head in agreement
when in reality he has long since lost your train of thought. He can
only be put back on the track if he's given a chance to ask questions
about his assignment.

• *Check Up.* Some sort of built-in control should be installed in
your communications. For example, a person can be required to
check back at a certain time or date or when the job has reached
a prefixed stage of completion. Questioning on the part of the communicator also helps bring into the open vaguenesses or misconcep-
tions before it's too late.

• *Invite Participation.* For two reasons this is desirable. First, it
helps you to avoid the possibility of overlooking an option or flaw
in your system that is obvious to the person who must carry it out.
Second, people who haven't had a chance to present their ideas for
consideration are later characterized by inefficiency, poor morale,
and disinterest.

Communication also suffers frequently from poor timing: for instance, announcing a curtailment in capital spending just as the
executive suite is being refurnished, or alerting your staff about
changes which are not imminent. And much of the wastefulness
in communications is from "overpublication"—dependence upon
memos, pamphlets, etc., rather than upon intimate, personal contacts.

Willard V. Merrihue,[24] formerly manager of community and business communications for the General Electric Company, observes
that a "communication plan is often the missing link" in introducing
change. "Proper planning and timing will not prevent serious reper-
cussions," says Merrihue, "if the communication plan is slighted or
mishandled." He advises that "every advance in operating procedures or any major change in established routines should be looked
upon as a three-stage job. First, there is the technical development,

or physical planning. Second, is the planning for the personnel involved in the change. Third, is the early and continuously modified communication planning to explain to all the need for the change and to obtain their active cooperation in making it work."

There's been so much discourse, however, on the need for greater communications that in sheer reaction, many feel that the problem has been exaggerated. In part, this attitude can be attributed to the feeling by some that when they are communicating, they are not working. Of course this is not so—if the communication is planned and purposeful.

A Favorable Climate

As we have seen, certain kinds of management techniques foster cooperation and encourage the assumption of responsibility and the development of self-discipline. Certain kinds of company policies do the same. And so do certain kinds of attitudes. What is needed in any company that sets out to make management by exception work is to develop these policies, techniques, and attitudes. One of the most intelligent listings of these conditions was made by two industrial psychologists, Lester F. Zerfoss of American Enka Corporation and Roderick F. O'Connor. In abbreviated form, here is what they recommend:

1. *A man's concept of himself tends to mirror his superiors' formal or informal judgments.* For this reason you must remember that whatever competence a man demonstrates in his daily work never represents the limits (in quality, quantity, or scope) of his productivity. In a growth climate this individual can, and will, do much more.

2. *See each job as an important job.* There's a tendency in organizations to talk about "key" jobs, to worship star performers, reward leaders, and forget the followers. When the supervisor of an industrial work group thinks an individual on his team does a job of no great importance, the morale of the entire team is threatened.

3. *Expect a lot from people.* In general, a man wants to do—and is able to do—more than he's now doing. One of the happiest moments between a man and his boss comes when the man, stretching to meet the demands placed upon him, produces beyond expectations.

4. *View mistakes as necessary to growth.* If you convert the mistakes of your subordinate to learning opportunities for him, you've gone a long way toward giving mistakes positive value. A man should know what caused him to make the mistake, what he needs to do next time

to prevent the mistake, and why it's important for him to improve. Only then will his growth reach a new high.

5. *Make accomplishment the basis for security.* The supervisory climate in which a man works must be a secure climate. But this security can't be the conventional kind of security, based on seniority and group protection. It must be a security in which the fairness of treatment is based on four factors that the individual can earn for himself, regardless of the time he spends in the organization.

• *Opportunity* to do as much as he is able to do.

• *Assurance* that his accomplishments will be honestly and accurately understood and recognized.

• *Expectancy* that he will be rewarded for accomplishment as he deserves.

• *Faith* that the company will maintain for him a bank of goodwill so that loyalty, service beyond the call of duty, and all the other extra values he gave will not be forgotten when his productivity is past its peak.

6. *Help subordinates get oriented.* Your subordinates want to know in advance about changes that affect them. To know where they stand. To know the "why" behind their work activity. And they need to know how their work fits into the work of other people and contributes to the objectives of the organization as a whole.

7. *Set the stage for mutual trust.* Perhaps the greatest single element in the rightness of climate to support growth is the faith that a man arrives at through personal experience. His working relationships must tell him, "I'm working with people of integrity. The decisions they make will be based on principles and sound thinking, rather than on expedient or political bases. Administrative action will be guided by what is right rather than by who is right."

8. *Recognize that development breeds development.* A growth climate can exist only where most of the people most of the time are experiencing progress, accomplishment, and attainment of goals. An intelligent man tends to do more of the *things* that work and give him satisfaction and fewer of the things that fail and deprive him of satisfaction. You can always count on the desire to win.

9. *Make work experience meaningful.* A growth climate is highly charged with the "why" behind the activity that the individual engages in. He must know the theory behind the practice, must be able to identify the principles he's applying.

Arbitrary decisions, unreasonable demands, and haphazard behavior frustrate and degrade people. The supervisor who can explain the reasons behind his thinking is far more likely to do right than the one who merely says, "The boss wants it done this way." Don't limit this principle to jobs that are physical. It holds as true for abstract mental activity.

10. *Work for a climate of mutual concern.* A growth climate is a climate of sharing. There must be a willingness to give and take, a regard for the good of the group, willingness to shift roles from leadership to followership and vice versa.

11. *Aim at freedom.* The growth climate is a climate of freedom— freedom to think, to talk, to talk back. Freedom to disagree, criticize, suggest change. Freedom to make choices, and—most important— freedom to live up to the spirit of the rules rather than to be limited to the letter of the rules.

Restraint should grow from consideration of other people rather than from rigid following of a rule. A growth climate depends upon the highest level of insight, courtesy, and consideration for others, as well as upon self-respect.

12. *Recognize the values in change.* There's no time in a man's life when he is more likely to learn quickly and effectively than when he adjusts to a new job. Solving the problems created by change forces people to grow. In a growth climate, change in all its many forms must be perceived as an opportunity for improvement.

Where the people in an organization see change as opportunity, criticism becomes constructive, procedures don't masquerade as policies, and current standards don't become obstacles in the way of progress. The alert administrator, by taking advantage of the changes that affect him and his people, gets growth motivations that are genuine and effective.

13. *Understand a man's right to be himself.* In a growth climate the differences and the likenesses of people are recognized. Where people are alike they want to be treated uniformly. Because people are basically alike in their need to be considered for promotions, they demand that their qualifications be reviewed so no one is overlooked. Where people are different, they want to be treated differently. Because each one recognizes that he is different in his ability to cope with the problems of the new job, he expects the decision on promotion to be in terms of excellence. To the extent that his individuality has been considered, he can accept the decision even when it is unfavorable to him.[25]

References

1. "No Longer Just a Grind at Norton," *Fortune,* August, 1963, p. 123.
2. "The Unfinished Job at W. R. Grace," *Fortune,* August, 1963, p. 113.
3. "Gillette Faces the Stainless Steel Dragon," *Fortune,* July, 1963, p. 159.

4. Ernest Dale, "Functions of the Manager of Tomorrow," *Training Directors Journal*, American Society of Training Directors, Madison, Wis., September, 1963.
5. "McNamara's Problem," *Life*, Sept. 20, 1963, p. 4.
6. Ralph J. Cordiner, "The Nature of the Work of the Chief Executive," paper presented to CIOS, New York, September, 1963.
7. "The Gentle Bulldozer of Peoria," *Fortune*, July, 1963, p. 166.
8. Fritz J. Roethlisberger, "Twenty Years of Management Development," *Training Directors Journal*, American Society of Training Directors, Madison, Wis., September, 1963.
9. Dale, *op. cit.*
10. Hugh Estes, "Some Considerations in Designing an Organizational Structure," in Mason Haire (ed.), *Organization Theory in Industrial Practice*, John Wiley & Sons, Inc., New York, 1962, p. 22.
11. Glenn Gilman, "An Inquiry into the Nature and Use of Authority," in *ibid.*, p. 107.
12. Keith Davis, *Human Relations in Business*, McGraw-Hill Book Company, New York, 1957, pp. 12–14.
13. Robert Saltonstall, *Human Relations in Administration*, McGraw-Hill Book Company, New York, 1959, p. 57.
14. Harold Guetzkow (ed.), *Groups, Leadership and Men*, Carnegie Press, Carnegie Institute of Technology, Pittsburgh, Pa., 1951, pp. 76–84.
15. *Ibid.*, pp. 82–83.
16. Leonard Sayles, *Behavior of Industrial Work Groups*, John Wiley & Sons, Inc., New York, 1958, p. 3.
17. Douglas McGregor, *The Human Side of Enterprise*, McGraw-Hill Book Company, New York, 1960, pp. 33–35.
18. *Ibid.*, pp. 36–38, 45–49, 152–153.
19. Harold Guetzkow, *op. cit.*, "Determining Syntality Dimensions as a Basis for Morale and Leadership Measurements," by Raymond B. Cattell, pp. 24–25.
20. Harold Guetzkow, *op. cit.*, "Group Productivity," by John R. French, Jr., p. 51.
21. Rensis Likert and Stanley Seashore, "Making Cost Control Work," *Harvard Business Review*, Cambridge, Mass., November–December, 1963, p. 102.
22. Keith Davis, "New Angles in Getting Your Story Across," *Factory*, September, 1957.
23. Irving J. Lee and Laura L. Lee, *Handling Barriers in Communication*, Harper & Row, Publishers, Incorporated, New York, 1957, pp. 77–92.
24. Willard V. Merrihue, *Managing by Communication*, McGraw-Hill Book Company, New York, 1960, p. 248.
25. Lester F. Zerfoss and Roderick F. O'Connor, "How to Create the Climate to Make Managers Grow," *Factory*, December, 1957, pp. 136–138.

Chapter 16

IMPROVING MANAGERIAL PERFORMANCE

Lee A. Iacocca, vice-president and general manager of the Ford Division of Ford Motor Company, keeps three books on his desk. One is green, the second is black, and the third is brown. He uses all three to guide him in evaluating and developing the key personnel under his direction. The green book is a detailed guide to a system of annual personnel appraisals. The black book contains detailed personal records of each of 107 executives who report to Iacocca. The brown book contains the master plan for the division's long-range management needs. Together, the three books aid Mr. Iacocca in carrying out a critical phase of a management by exception system—measurement of managerial performance.[1]

Managerial Performance

Mr. Iacocca's system of performance appraisal points a direction for all executives to follow. In this text, we have repeatedly emphasized that the concept of management by exception depends upon measurement. And the measurements considered one by one have been of the major economic inputs into an enterprise. These are money, manpower, materials, and machines. In addition we have considered the major organizational functions, such as finance, operations, and marketing. However, there is a unifying ingredient that runs like a thread through each factor and function. It is the man-

289

agement part of the manpower input. It provides the sinew that binds inputs and functions together to form a whole. It is management that is universally accepted as the key element in determining the profit or loss, the success or failure of an enterprise. And it is management which applies the exception principle and to which the exception principle is applied.

The technique of applying the exception principle to management performance is popularly called "appraisal," "management appraisal," or "performance appraisal." Such appraisals take several forms. An appraisal may be "results"-oriented, in which the measurements are of tangible evidence of achievements. Or it may be of the management methods employed, in which it is concerned with management's use of techniques (such as delegation) which are generally conceded to be beneficial to the organization. Finally, the appraisal may be personality-oriented, in which the measurement rests upon judgments of demonstrated attitudes or behavioral characteristics of the manager. Most appraisals include a little of each technique.

Results Appraisals

The highest form of result in business is the attainment of profit objectives. And it is at the highest executive level that profits become the measurement integer of finance, sales, production, and auxiliary operations effectiveness. The acid test of the chief executive's performance is by the profits (or losses) his efforts generate.

Looking backward from profits, the next plateau of results measurement is at the various cost centers of a business. Cost centers are comparable to profit and loss centers, but they differ in scope. Sales and production departments are typical cost centers, and in some organizations so are regional sales offices, product sales departments, and assembly, machining, and packaging departments.

The next level of results is that which is described by achievement of objectives. For example: Did the research department develop a new product by a certain date? Did the personnel department introduce a job evaluation plan this year? Has the industrial engineering department completed its training program for new products?

The Du Pont System. Probably the most single-minded example of results measurement at the highest plateau is provided by the Du Pont company.[2] Its famous chart system for appraising managerial performance places "primary emphasis upon return on investment." The Du Pont chart series focuses attention on this vital end result without neglecting the factors that influence return on investment: (1) earnings as a percentage of sales (which is the gross profit margin) and (2) cash turnover. Financial people explain the significance of the often-overlooked latter measure this way: If there has been a change in selling price, an improvement in cash turnover indicates that capital is being worked harder, i.e., the business is getting increased sales out of the same plant and working capital.

To provide these key measurements, Du Pont furnishes its board, chief executive, and department managers with the following measurements at the end of each month:

• Annual data for ten years: per cent return on investment, per cent turnover, and earnings as a per cent of sales. These are plotted on logarithm paper, on which the average for the ten-year period serves as a base line for comparison.

• Monthly data projected to an annual figure (current month multiplied by 12) compared to quarterly data projected to an annual figure (current quarter multiplied by 4): per cent return on investment, per cent turnover, and earnings as a per cent of sales. These are also plotted on logarithm paper and compared with the forecast result, which is adjusted each quarter.

These key charts are supplemented by other charts prepared on the ten-year base and on the annual base as above:

• Sales in dollars and earnings in dollars compared with averages and forecasts for the year (adjusted quarterly)

• Expenses as per cent of sales, including separate charts for factory costs, selling expenses, freight and delivery, and administrative charges

Further charts detail desired trends such as:

• Inventories (in dollars and number of months supply on hand) compared with projected standards for raw materials, semifinished products, and finished products

• Inventories (total) plotted according to actual investment and standard investment

• Accounts receivable plotted according to actual investment and days outstanding, compared with standard investment and standard days outstanding

• Cash position

Finally, Du Pont posts a ten-year progressive analysis of:
• Total investment in dollars compared against forecasts (adjusted quarterly), this being broken down into three charts
• Permanent investment
• Working capital in dollars compared with forecasts (adjusted quarterly)
• Depreciation reserve in dollars and per cent of permanent investment

Du Pont's executive committee uses the charts each month to review the performance of a particular profit center *and of its manager*. The charts are characterized by several items:

1. There is a complete absence of narrative so that the observations and comparison are as objective as can be.

2. Favorable deviations from standard are colored in blue, unfavorable are colored in red.

3. Charts show what has happened in terms of return on investment and help put the finger on the broad underlying factors which caused the results to be what they are. This enables the committee to raise questions with the general manager regarding possible trouble spots—and these questions, in turn, may lead to further analysis and presentation.

4. Rigid rules govern the assembly of data for presentation. To the maximum extent possible, the data for all periods are on a uniform basis and afford common measurement of performance for all investment lines.

Du Pont inaugurated this chart system nearly fifty years ago. And it is conclusive that the basic concept, which emphasized return on investment, has never changed.

Cost-centered Appraisals. Cost-centered appraisals are more universally applied than profit-centered ones. These cost-centered appraisals follow closely the performance criteria listed at length in the chapters on operations, marketing, finance, etc. The important difference is that in appraisals, the criteria and goals are used to motivate and to counsel managers.

Objective-centered Appraisals. Objective-centered appraisals turn on the prior establishment of various achievement goals. A plant engineer responsible for building a new plant, for instance, may have been given target dates for completion of engineering design, construction of building, and installation of equipment. His performance would be judged by how nearly his projects were completed by the due dates. Examples of cost-centered and objective-centered appraisals are shown in Figs. 4-1 and 4-2 in Chapter 4.

Dale D. McConkey, vice-president of United Fruit Company, cautions that one of the most critical aspects of appraisal by objectives lies in the responsibility of the manager's superior. Obvious as it may seem, McConkey observes that many managers fail to set the objectives clearly in advance of the performance review. To avoid this possibility, he advises that the superior answer these questions in advance of the appraisal: [3]

1. Does the objective represent a sufficient task for the manager during the measuring period?

2. Is the objective practical and attainable?

3. Is the objective clearly stated in terms of (*a*) the task, (*b*) the measuring period, (*c*) the method of measurement?

4. Is the objective compatible with the company's plans and overall objectives for the period?

Methods Appraisals

Because results are often long- rather than short-range and spring from the efforts of not just one manager but many (i.e., teamwork), and because they often occur in direct relationship to the means applied, the most commonly used form of performance appraisal focuses on the management methods employed.

It may be hard to separate skills from method and work habits. They tend to go hand in hand, and in turn, work habits may be hard to isolate from personality factors. However, an absolutely clear distinction is not truly important.

In judging performance in terms of techniques used, rather than of profits generated, costs reduced, or objectives met, one might ask these questions: [4]

Does the manager use company policy as a base for his decision?

When he deviates from policy, are his reasons sound?

Will he take calculated risks when it is to the advantage of his operation? Or is he overcautious to the point of missing opportunities?

Does he distinguish important problems from less important ones?

Does he spend his energies where the payoff is greatest?

Is he thorough in his analysis and reports?

Is his work accurate and reliable?

Does he handle several diverse problems during the course of the day?

Is his performance consistent despite changing conditions?

Can he handle large volumes of work without impairment of his performance?

Has he trained a replacement for himself and a sufficient number of subordinates?

Has he provided his work force with policies, plans, procedures, measurements, and controls?

Has he clearly defined responsibilities and authority for his managerial group?

Does he constantly communicate to his staff important matters pertinent to their work and goals?

Were any critical incidents traceable to misunderstanding on the part of someone he had directed?

Have there been instances of communications outside the department made by word of mouth, without confirmation in writing?

Is he concerned about the tone of his remarks as well as their content? Points to consider in reviewing his pattern of communications concern abruptness, curtness, bumptiousness, discourtesy, and the like.

Is he a good listener? Or does he interrupt often?

Is he careful to have standard instructional methods and procedures in writing kept up to date?

Are his memoranda concise, complete, grammatical?

What is his "frictional record" in his dealings with people under him? Are there repeated flare-ups? If so, is there a pattern of such explosions?

Is he receptive to suggestions from those he directs?

Does he apply the recognized human-relations considerations about such things as criticism, recognition of work well done, and fairness in allocating work loads?

Does he "oversupervise"?

How does he "pour on the pressure"? Does his manner induce calmness or tension?

Is his group performance spotty? Are some units or individuals under his supervision turning out better results than others?

How is his group's teamwork? Does it rise to an emergency?

Personality Appraisals

It is probably unwise to use the term "personality" in connection with appraisal since so many qualified people have counseled us about the difficulty in making personality judgments. Perhaps a better term would be "behavior" appraisal.

Carl Heyel, who has written broadly on this subject, says:

It has been estimated there are some 18,000 different terms that can be used to describe a person. It's easy to let one outstanding trait overshadow all others. Look over these definitions of some general terms that are often used rather loosely:

A *trait* is a distinguishing quality of a person—a distinctive, definable characteristic. It may be one predominant aptitude, or a combination of a number of aptitudes or behavior characteristics.

A *behavior characteristic* is a pattern that an individual sets by habitual repetition.

Personality is the sum of the traits and behavior characteristics that a person presents to the world and that determine the reactions of others to him. There's no clear dividing line between such terms as personality and temperament. Temperament is the characteristic of an individual as revealed in certain feelings, moods, and desires. We usually describe a person's temperament as cheerful or irritable. In common usage, when we say a person is temperamental we mean he swings unpredictably and violently from one set of feelings, moods, and desires to another. If we say he has a cheerful disposition we mean that this characteristic is fairly stable and predictable.[5]

In judging personality, you can consider many important and desirable qualities: enthusiasm, congeniality, ability to work with many different personality types, dedication to business and to the job, self-reliance, aggressiveness, initiative, decisiveness, maturity, self-confidence, ability to make concessions or to bring about beneficial compromises.

James H. Taylor, former personnel vice-president for Procter and Gamble, emphasizes that no list is complete, no list is just right for your particular company. He adds two other particularly good suggestions for appraising performance:[6]

• Rate only those factors where an individual exhibits real strength or weaknesses. In other words, look for exceptions.

• Rate only what the individual does and not what he is capable of doing or what you wish he might do.

Don't attach nominal numbers to separate ratings and then average them. Averages conceal zeroes in areas where outstanding performance may be necessary. Furthermore, it is the *pattern* of desired managerial behavior that will best serve as a standard with which to compare an individual's own pattern of behavior.

The Appraisal Interview

The main purpose of a performance appraisal is to find out where an individual manager has failed to live up to his responsibilities— or where his outstandingly good performance indicates the need for broader or deeper responsibilities. The appraisal interview, then, is roughly akin to the report phase of management by exception. And this report may be made to two people: the executive to whom the appraiser reports and the manager who has been appraised.

The report to the rater's superior is made for the purposes of (1) keeping him informed of personnel development in his organization and (2) getting his advice where the direction of counseling, discipline, promotion, or reassignment is not clear. The superior utilizes the appraisal in evaluating managerial personnel generally and in matching operational problems or opportunities with the responsible managers.

The report to the appraised manager is made to him mainly for the purpose of providing him with an objective analysis of both his style and his successes and failures. If a subordinate is achieving his goals in a timely and efficient fashion, he may conclude that he need only continue in the same fashion for the coming months. If his performance falls short of the specific goals set for him, he may need to examine these goals again to convince himself that they are fair and attainable. And he will, of course, need to examine his style of managing to determine what it is that he is doing wrong or that can be improved.

The appraisal, for the appraised manager, initiates a decision-making and action phase of management by exception. It is also calls for decisions and possible action by the appraiser. Regardless of the action decided upon by the appraiser, he should always try to relate it to a positive objective—helping the individual to achieve the standards of performance that best suit him and the organization.

Advice varies on how best to conduct an appraisal interview. Contrary to recent criticism, there is merit in applying the so-called "sandwich" technique. This technique instructs the appraiser to begin the interview with an evaluation of a favorable aspect of the manager's performance, to then move into the critical area, and to conclude with another favorable evaluation. Danger lies in the appraised manager's hearing only the compliments, or in his failing to take the criticism seriously. Nevertheless, it's an easy technique to use, and if the interview is well planned this danger can be avoided. Good planning means a careful study of the job itself to provide the interviewer with an intimate, accurate knowledge of what the job demands in full. Time spent at the measurement phase should assure this knowledge. Good planning also implies an objective study of the man himself. This means that the superior must do his homework before the interview, carefully reviewing the manager's record not just the day or week before—but over a period of months.

Probably when conducting an interview your best approach is to do that which comes naturally. Robert Hoppock, professor of guidance and personnel at New York University, has suggested some basic principles which you can incorporate in your approach:

1. *Discuss the job first, the man later.* This way you assure yourself that both you and he agree on the exact nature of his work. If you are not sure, Hoppock urges that you ask questions like: What are *all* the things you do on your job? Which do you think are the most important? Which take the most time? The most skill?

2. *Let him talk before you do.* A man accepts his own criticism more readily than he will yours. Often he will bring out his own weaknesses more sharply than you might be inclined to. Good leading questions to stimulate his conversation are: What do you think are your greatest strengths? Where do you feel less competitive? Is your impression that you are growing more competent on the job? In what activities? Where do you think we could offer you some help?

3. *Listen attentively.* If nothing else, this assures him that you think enough of what he says to pay attention. Interrupt only to summarize his remarks in your own words. This gives him a chance to correct any misconception you may be drawing.

4. *If the subordinate rates himself more favorably than you do, find out why.* Ask him for specific instances. Be sure you understand his reasoning, even if yours is different. Then, if you still disagree, state your position and reasons. You need not secure complete agreement. Just establishing where your viewpoints differ is worthwhile.

5. *Consider the whole picture.* Beware of making judgments on the basis of only a few observations. Try to contrast a man's mistakes with the number of opportunities he has for making them, the freedom of action he has or has not, the difficulty of the job itself.

6. *Avoid your prejudices.* Especially those that have little to do with the job. Typical of these are: You're a clean-desk man, his is cluttered; his mannerisms annoy you but few others; you both have the same hobbies, or attended the same schools; you're punctual, he's usually a little late but makes up for it by working late.

7. *Criticize performance, not the man.* By emphasizing performance, you can expect some changes. Chances are very slim that you can make the man change in extremes of attitudes, interests, etc.

8. *Admit your own shortcomings.* If you are partially at fault for his poor performance, acknowledge it. In the interview, *he's* appraising your honesty and fairness.

9. *Be candid with the truly deficient manager.* Let the individual know exactly where he stands. Don't threaten, but make clear his present and future status. Tell him what you think he can do to improve. If he shows a desire to improve, offer to help him.

10. *Back up your good managers.* Let them know you are going on record concerning their ability and performance. Invite the exceptional man to tell you how he wants to develop himself.

11. *Develop strengths.* It is far better to get the most out of a man where he has real potential than to harp continually about correcting weaknesses. As Hoppock says, "successful companies are not run by little paragons who have corrected all their faults, but by well-balanced teams of able men, each of whom has his weaknesses." Your job is not to produce supermen. Your job is to help managers more closely fit the pattern of job needs for each of the functions for which you are responsible. Rarely will you find the man whose performance can be encouraged to be exceptional in all things. Rarely will you find managers in whom some glaring weaknesses will not show up.[7]

Managerial Incentives

Nearly half of all manufacturing and retail companies surveyed by the National Industrial Conference Board in 1961 (in a study of 1,157 firms)[8] had an executive bonus plan for their top three executives. These bonuses averaged nearly one-third of an executive's annual base salary. In almost all cases, bonuses were related to profits generated by the company. This kind of incentive represents the highest form of tangible motivation for executive performance.

And while the man in the street may have a vision of company executives taking care of themselves financially well ahead of employees, the figures don't bear this out. In a study of forty-one major companies conducted by Edward C. Bursk and reported in the *Harvard Business Review*[9] he found that the percentage increase in gross compensation for management personnel for the years 1939 to 1950 was far less than for others in the same organizations. The study showed top management's gains at 35 per cent, middle management 45 per cent, supervisory management 83 per cent, and white-collar and hourly paid workers 106 per cent. When taxes and living costs were considered, the net gains for management turned out to be serious losses instead: top management −59 per cent, middle management −40 per cent, supervisory management −13 per cent, and white-collar and hourly paid workers +3 per cent. Since a schedule of rewards is obviously essential to our economic system, it would appear that many management by exception schemes (all dependent upon attaining individual, group, and organizational objectives) are weakened by a failure to provide adequate financial incentives for management personnel.

Nonfinancial motivation, tangible and otherwise, plays an important part, of course. Executives, more so than others in the organization, are spurred to their objectives by a sense of responsibility, the challenge to get the job done well, a pride in achievement, a chance to participate in formulating policies and plans, easy and ample access to higher management, and attractive working conditions.

Be all that as it may, Richard C. Smyth feels that maximum performance from executive personnel will only be forthcoming if three financial conditions exist:[10]

1. A sound and equitable base salary structure
2. Short-term financial incentives (such as bonus plans based upon performance)
3. Long-term financial incentives (such as stock plans and deferred compensation plans)

Smyth demonstrates that short-term incentives focus managerial attention primarily on current operations and the current fiscal year. Long-term incentives focus management attention on the long-range picture—typically one to ten years ahead. For top-level executives, both kinds of incentives are needed to make management by exception functional. For middle-level management or for supervisors, a sound salary base plus some sort of bonus plan is desirable.

Conformity and the Exception Principle

One of Texas' many millionaires is not an oil man. He is quiet, bookish, low-pressured. And he has amassed a personal fortune of over $70 million by investing in the seemingly bland field of life insurance. His name is Troy Post. Mr. Post is noted for his ability to spot a company that, in his own words, is "ready to take off." [11] This canny insight for exceptional opportunities was first demonstrated during World War II when he directed his first small insurance company to insure GIs without disallowing benefits for death in combat. If Mr. Post had been an officer of any of the large established insurance companies, chances are he could not have gotten such a scheme past the rigid confines of corporate policy. His creative marketing talents probably would have been stifled by organization-man thinking.

It is unfortunately true that the greatest hazard in practicing management by exception lies in the possibility of establishing standards that demand too much conformity. Yet the very principle of management by exception is almost wholly dependent upon conformance to standards. What's the solution to the dilemma?

At least one management authority, Dr. Joseph M. Juran,[12] sees no real problem here. He conceives of the management process as a continual cycle of "breakthrough" and "control." Like a living organism, a company, corporation, organization, or enterprise strikes out to attain goals, then settles back to consolidate its gains. After a period of consolidation and control, profits inevitably start to recede. The organization, if it is to keep alive and healthy, must break through its current set of standards to new levels of performance. The exception principle, consciously practiced, will aid and abet each phase of this cycle as Dr. Juran describes it. During the control cycle, emphasis is upon meeting standards—conformity, if you will. But at the projection step of management by exception, management can detect receding profit, market, or operational trends and plan again creatively for a breakthrough.

The difficulty in many organizations is that staffing has focused on providing control-type personnel rather than those also needed for creating breakthroughs. A company needs both kinds, of course. But to permit the control mentality to take over completely at the projection stage invites disaster. Robert Anderson, vice-president and director of product planning of Chrysler Corporation, is a forceful spokesman for this viewpoint. He tells of the need for a steady idea flow in business: "No company in any industry can consider itself safe from the challenge of determined competitors. No company, no matter how big and old and well established it may be, however deeply entrenched and financially bulwarked, can consider itself beyond the reach of aggressive, nimble, smaller companies that are alive to the opportunities all around them in a changing environment." And then Anderson concludes, "It is the planners, the men paid to listen to new ideas, who will keep the company on the alert and ready."

Organization Arthritis. *Management Consultant,* a publication of the Association of Consulting Management Engineers, observes that too often management loads the dice against itself when it comes to recognizing and reacting to change. For example, ACME cites these eight shortcomings:

Rationalization of Decision Making. Marketing research, cost analysis, forecasting, statistical decision techniques have become increasingly necessary—and valuable—in modern business. However, they tend to discourage the venturesome spirit unless management holds them in check by emphasizing other values that are important, too. For the new tools tend to focus men's attention on the avoidance of mistakes rather than on the taking of risks. An engineering-type viewpoint tends to dominate instead of an entrepreneurial one; decision makers try to see how close they can get to being 100% sure before moving ahead, overlooking that in a dynamic economy you are lucky in management if your tests and controls can make you even 75% sure.

Knowledge and Tradition. In many companies a large body of experience and tradition is building up. This knowledge can be extremely useful and has in fact, accounted for many an edge that a veteran organization holds over competitors. At the same time, much of this experience is continually being dated in a changing industry and is a liability if not discarded. Therefore, strong leadership is required to show which of the traditions are still valid or valid with modification, and which are not. Turning away from an old and cherished policy can be a painful and agonizing job, as many businessmen know all too well, and it usually must be done from the top down.

Accounting Conventions. Modern accounting focuses a strong light on the profit-and-loss showing and has contributed notably to good management practice. It must also be said, however, that established accounting practices favor conservatism rather than risk taking. For instance, if the question is whether to build a factory that will produce 300,000 items, or one that will produce 500,000, accounting conventions tempt the decision maker to err on the low side. If he decides on the smaller plant, accounting will not show the profits he could have made with more production and more imaginative selling; whereas any excess capacity in the larger plant, if built, will show up clearly in the figures. Consequently, vigorous management is needed to support a "non-accounting" viewpoint and keep accountancy in perspective.

Authoritarian Emphasis. A great many practices in business management (as in the military) favor doing things as instructed and in a uniform manner rather than in an inventive way. This tendency, reinforced by certain traditions of scientific management, often carries over into areas where it is not wanted. In a sense, therefore, management must counter forces for conformity that it has set in motion itself. It is also significant that I.B.M. has made studies indicating that the development of management talent is retarded in departments which are highly organized and overformalized.

Automation and Cost Trends. As we invest more money in automated plants and expensive distribution structures, pressures mount to freeze product design and marketing programs in the interests of further mechanization. Innovative ideas must survive a lengthening process of checking, double checking, revising, postponement, etc. Unless management is continually holding this process in check, mechanization may become its own worst enemy.

Operations Myopia. Ambitious executives naturally like to make a good showing on current operations. This is as it should be. But a kind of Gresham's Law can work here, with the motives for concentrating on operations driving out the motives for critical reflection, which are needed for innovation. If management does not worry about this danger, who will?

Cultural Drags. Chris Argyris of Yale and other behavioral scientists are concerned that certain values in contemporary culture (abetted often by management itself as well as by unions, bigness and specialization of jobs) are infecting executive-employee relations. The tendency is for the employee to agree, in effect, to report to work on time, stay busy, and follow instructions in return for fair pay and being left alone by his boss. Such non-involvement makes it difficult for an organization to do more than follow old routines.

Need for a Flywheel. If innovation and change were to proceed recklessly and unrestrainedly (as they might if only "idea men" dominated), an organization would weaken at the seams and fly apart. Tradition, custom and routine all have value for their cohesive effect. Maintaining incentives for innovation and pressing for new thinking while at the same time keeping the pace of change reasonable, calls for the most discriminating kind of leadership.[13]

Individual Inertia. While it is true that management is often guilty of structuring its organization too much in favor of conformity, there are serious and qualified observers who believe that this condition has been exaggerated. Professor Leonard R. Sayles of Columbia University's Graduate School of Business, for instance, believes otherwise. In his book *Individuality and Big Business*,[14] Sayles debunks the idea that Americans are tragic victims of organization life and that corporations are filled with look-alike robots. He also brands as an illusion the idea that every American is a person overflowing with initiative, eager to have his own way and to take the risks necessary to achieve it. The truth lies somewhere between, Sayles says. And his most conclusive point: "If a lack of freedom is felt in the modern business organization, it usually is not the fault of the organization itself, but of the individual to whom freedom is a burden."

Many other businessmen and qualified observers share this opinion. Frederick A. Stahl, president of Standard & Poor's, said in 1963, "Businessmen all work and operate in unison. They all belong to the same clubs, so business sentiment is pretty much developed through their exchange of ideas." Businessmen, says Stahl, "tend to practice a mass psychology." [15]

William A. Marsteller, head of the advertising agency of Marsteller, Inc., also puts the blame on the individual rather than the business organization. "In the pursuit of security," he observes, "many people forget that the way to succeed in business is by ability and hard work. Somewhere along the line, he finds there is another way— through what the English call toadying and we call politics. Toadying, while historically looked down upon, is widely practiced in business today. But it is almost invariably a certain sign of incompetence, lack of self-confidence, and maladjustment."

Elmer Tangerman, editor of *Product Engineering* magazine, calls attention to the "mental moment of inertia." It is laziness, he insists, rather than real pressures for conformity that begets this follow-the-leadership in industry. But Tangerman observes, "Too often management has the greatest moment of inertia of all." [16]

Guides for Action. Where, then, will you find your center line for action? Here are three ways of putting perspective on this important problem:

1. *A business organization—any organization—needs to secure conformity from its members.* This applies to behavior as well as to results. In order to achieve any degree of harmony in its working relationships, the organization, consciously or unconsciously, formally or informally, sets a standard of acceptable behavior—and this next is very important—that best suits the pursuit of its goals. To become a member, and to stay a member of this organization, an individual must conform or get out. Henry Ford II, speaking to this point, says:

> This kind of pressure, of course, exists to some degree in all organizations. In some it exists to a ridiculous degree. However, in most American companies a man's family life, his social ties, his political beliefs and his religious convictions are his own business. Most companies are interested in performance, not conformance. In a business firm, as in other kinds of organizations—including the family, school, church, and government—there are certain rules that must be observed by everyone. This is not conformity. This is common sense. Efficiency dictates such rules, and without them no organization could stay organized, much less fulfill its functions.[17]

2. *Creativity and initiative are also absolutely essential to organization survival.* Individuals capable of providing these qualities must be selected and carefully placed in any successful enterprise. Their contributions must be encouraged by others who perform the rigorous, and often unpleasant, control functions. Presence of both kinds of individuals gives the organization balance so that it can move ahead, hold its present position, or retreat if necessary.

Writing in the American Management Association's *Management Review*, Prof. Joseph D. Cooper suggests two concrete ways to encourage creativity without damaging organizational discipline:

> A. Place young, active, creative people throughout all activities of the enterprise. If they are to be concentrated anywhere, it should be in activities that call for numerical, abstract reasoning—as in engineering, mathematical statistics, operations research, economic analysis, and complex logistical innovation.
>
> B. The more mature creative people should be concentrated in positions that place a heavy premium on the exercise of judgment embracing economic, social, and ethical values. When we wish creativity

in areas of activity where the unknowns lie mainly in human inter-play, we tend to look for men of maturity who have had sufficiently long, progressive, and varied experiences in the arenas of human affairs. These men need to be recruited from within the organization and from outside.[18]

3. *It is the oddball in the organization who presents the most difficult problem for his peers and his superiors.* Often such individuals confuse erratic behavior with creative contribution. It is up to the more conservative executives to determine how much of the latter is needed to tolerate an excess of the former. Management will always be faced with the problem of deciding how much non-standard behavior it can put up with, or how much conformance it can demand, without either stifling initiative or bringing about anarchy and confusion.

References

1. Lee A. Iacocca, "How Ford Wiped Out $9 Million Losses Each Month," *International Management,* January, 1964.
2. "How DuPont Organizes and Appraises Its Performance," Financial Management Series, no. 94, American Management Association, New York, 1950.
3. Dale D. McConkey, "Measuring Your Managers by Results," *Personnel Journal,* vol. 41, no. 11, p. 540, Swarthmore, Pa., December, 1962.
4. James H. Taylor, *Personnel Administration: Evaluation and Executive Control,* McGraw-Hill Book Company, New York, 1959, pp. 87–90.
5. Carl Heyel, "Five Steps to a Plan That Will Really Measure Your Managers," *Factory,* February, 1959.
6. Taylor, *op. cit.,* p. 86.
7. Robert Hoppock, "Effective Communication on the Job," American Management Association, Inc., New York, 1963, pp. 242–245.
8. "Top Executive Compensation," Studies in Personnel Practices, no. 186, National Industrial Conference Board, New York, 1962.
9. *Ibid.*
10. Richard C. Smyth, *Financial Incentives for Management,* McGraw-Hill Book Company, New York, 1960, pp. 9–10.
11. *Time,* Nov. 30, 1962, p. 86.
12. Joseph M. Juran, *Managerial Breakthrough,* McGraw-Hill Book Company, New York, 1964.
13. "Management of Innovation—Key to the Future," *Management Consultant,* no. 1, 1962 series, Association of Management Consulting Engineers, New York.
14. "How Free Is Organization Man?" *Business Week,* Oct. 5, 1963, p. 100.
15. *Time,* Dec. 21, 1962, p. 67.

16. E. J. Tangerman, "Horizons," *Product Engineering,* Jan. 7, 1963.
17. Henry Ford II, "Choosing a Career in Business," *The Saturday Evening Post,* Oct. 20, 1962, p. 36.
18. Joseph D. Cooper, "Organization: Is This Change Necessary?" *Management Review,* December, 1962, American Management Association, New York.

BIBLIOGRAPHY

Allen, Louis A.: *Management and Organization*, McGraw-Hill Book Company, New York, 1958.

Anderson, Richard C.: *Management Practices*, McGraw-Hill Book Company, New York, 1960.

Barish, Norman N.: *Economic Analysis for Engineering and Management Decision Making*, McGraw-Hill Book Company, New York, 1962.

Batten, J. D.: *Tough-minded Management*, American Management Association, New York, 1963.

Bellow, Roger M.: *Psychology of Personnel in Business and Industry*, 2d ed., Prentice-Hall, Inc., Englewood Cliffs, N.J., 1954.

Berelson, Bernard, and Gary A. Steiner: *Human Behavior*, Harcourt, Brace & World, Inc., New York, 1964.

Bethel, Lawrence L., Franklin S. Atwater, George H. E. Smith, and Harvey A. Stackman, Jr.: *Industrial Organization and Management*, 4th ed., McGraw-Hill Book Company, New York, 1962.

Bittel, Lester R., *What Every Supervisor Should Know*, McGraw-Hill Book Company, New York, 1959.

Black, James Menzies: *How to Grow in Management*, Prentice-Hall, Inc., Englewood Cliffs, N.J., 1957.

Branch, Melville C.: *The Corporate Planning Process*, American Management Association, New York, 1962.

Brown, Robert G.: *Statistical Forecasting for Inventory Control*, McGraw-Hill Book Company, New York, 1959.

Bursk, Edward C., and Dan H. Fenn, Jr.: *Planning the Future Strategy of Your Business*, McGraw-Hill Book Company, New York, 1956.

Carroll, Phil: *Profit Control*, McGraw-Hill Book Company, New York, 1962.

Chane, George W.: *Motion and Time Study*, Harper & Row, Publishers, Incorporated, New York, 1942.

Chapple, Eliot D., and Leonard R. Sayles: *The Measure of Management*, The Macmillan Company, New York, 1961.

Dale, Ernest: *The Great Organizers*, McGraw-Hill Book Company, New York, 1960.

Dale, Ernest, and Lyndall F. Urwick: *Staff in Organization*, McGraw-Hill Book Company, New York, 1960.

Daughton, Paul M., Jr.: *Current Issues and Emerging Concepts in Management*, Houghton Mifflin Company, Boston, 1962.

Davis, Keith: *Human Relations in Business*, McGraw-Hill Book Company, New York, 1957.

Drucker, Peter F.: *The Practice of Management*, Harper & Row, Publishers, Incorporated, New York, 1954.

Duncan, Acheson J.: *Quality Control and Industrial Statistics*, rev. ed., Richard D. Irwin, Inc., Homewood, Ill., 1959.

Dunlop, John T. (ed.): *Automation and Technological Change*, Prentice-Hall, Inc., Englewood Cliffs, N.J., 1962.

Effective Communication on the Job, rev. ed., American Management Association, New York, 1963.

Flippo, Edwin B.: *Principles of Personnel Management*, McGraw-Hill Book Company, New York, 1961.

Foulke, Roy A.: *Practical Financial Statement Analysis*, 5th ed., McGraw-Hill Book Company, New York, 1961.

Gellerman, Saul W.: *Motivation and Productivity*, American Management Association, New York, 1963.

————: *People, Problems, and Profits: The Uses of Psychology in Management*, McGraw-Hill Book Company, New York, 1960.

Gordon, Myron J.: *The Investment, Financing, and Evaluation of the Corporation*, Richard D. Irwin, Inc., Homewood, Ill., 1962.

Gray, J. Seton: *Common Sense in Business: A Digest of Management Procedures*, McGraw-Hill Book Company, New York, 1956.

Guetzkow, Harold (ed.): *Groups, Leadership, and Men*, Carnegie Press, Carnegie Institute of Technology, Pittsburgh, Pa., 1951.

Haire, Mason: *Organization Theory in Industrial Practice*, John Wiley & Sons, Inc., New York, 1962.

Heiser, Herman C.: *Budgeting, Principles and Practice*, The Ronald Press Company, New York, 1959.

Hepner, Harvey W.: *Perceptive Management and Supervision*, Prentice-Hall, Inc., Englewood Cliffs, N.J., 1961.

Herzberg, Frederick, Bernard Mausner, and Barbara Snyderman: *The Motivation to Work*, John Wiley & Sons, Inc., New York, 1959.

Heyel, Carl: *Management for Modern Supervisors*, American Management Association, New York, 1962.

Laird, Donald A., and Eleanor C. Laird: *The New Psychology of Leadership*, McGraw-Hill Book Company, New York, 1956.

Landsberger, Henry A.: *Hawthorne Revisited*, Cornell University, Ithaca, N.Y., 1958.

Leonard, William P.: *The Management Audit: An Appraisal of Management Methods and Performance*, Prentice-Hall, Inc., Englewood Cliffs, N.J., 1962.

Livingston, Robert T., and William W. Waite (eds.): *The Manager's Job*, Columbia University Press, New York, 1960.

Mayer, Raymond R.: *Production Management,* McGraw-Hill Book Company, New York, 1962.

Maynard, H. B. (ed.): *Industrial Engineering Handbook,* 2d ed., McGraw-Hill Book Company, New York, 1963.

————: *Top Management Handbook,* McGraw-Hill Book Company, New York, 1960.

McGregor, Douglas: *The Human Side of Enterprise,* McGraw-Hill Book Company, New York, 1960.

Merrihue, W. V.: *Managing by Communication,* McGraw-Hill Book Company, New York, 1960.

Merrill, Harwood F.: *Classics in Management,* American Management Association, New York, 1960.

Nemmers, Erwin Esser: *Managerial Economics,* John Wiley & Sons, Inc., New York, 1962.

Newman, William H.: *Administrative Action,* 2d ed., Prentice-Hall, Inc., Englewood Cliffs, N.J., 1963.

Payne, Bruce: *Planning for Corporate Growth,* McGraw-Hill Book Company, New York, 1963.

Randall, Clarence B.: *The Folklore of Management,* Little, Brown and Company, Boston, 1961.

Reichmann, William J.: *Use and Abuse of Statistics,* Oxford University Press, New York, 1962.

Rose, T. G., and Donald E. Farr: *Higher Management Control,* McGraw-Hill Book Company, New York, 1957.

Saltonstall, Robert: *Human Relations in Administration,* McGraw-Hill Book Company, New York, 1959.

Sayles, Leonard R.: *Behavior of Industrial Work Groups,* John Wiley & Sons, Inc., New York, 1958.

Schleh, Edward C.: *Management by Results,* McGraw-Hill Book Company, New York, 1961.

Smyth, Richard C.: *Financial Incentives for Management,* McGraw-Hill Book Company, New York, 1960.

Taylor, Jack W.: *How to Select and Develop Leaders,* McGraw-Hill Book Company, New York, 1962.

Taylor, James H.: *Personnel Administration: Evaluation and Executive Control,* McGraw-Hill Book Company, New York, 1959.

Tucker, Spencer A.: *Successful Managerial Control by Ration-analysis,* McGraw-Hill Book Company, New York, 1961.

Uris, Auren: *Developing Your Executive Skills,* McGraw-Hill Book Company, New York, 1955.

————: *The Efficient Executive,* McGraw-Hill Book Company, New York, 1957.

Yoder, Dale, H. G. Heneman, Jr., John Turnbull, and C. Harold Stone: *Handbook of Personnel Management and Labor Relations,* McGraw-Hill Book Company, New York, 1958.

INDEX

A & P, 55
Abbott Laboratories, 248–249
A-B-C Analysis, 25, 93–98, 245
ABC Television Network, 56
AC Spark Plug, 195–196
Academy of Management Sciences, 112
Accident frequency, 234–235
Accountants, 20
Accounting, weaknesses in, 202–203
ACF Industries, 152
Achievement tests, 223
Action, alternative, 102–105
  balance of, 154–155
  committees for, 156–157
  and conformity, 304–305
  control, 173–179
  coordination of, 161–163
  counter attack, 152–153
  decision making for, 147–150
  demand chart, 133–136
  drastic, 151–152
  levels of, 205
  options, 149–150
  personal leadership for, 157–161
  on research problems, 205–208
  timing of, 155–156
  (See also Decision making)
Adams, William R., 11
AFL-CIO, 111
Alberto-Culver Company, 155
Alford, Leon Pratt, 7
Allen, Charles L., 262
Allis-Chalmers, 89

American Association of Industrial Management, 50
  (See also National Metal Trades Association)
American Brake Shoe Company, 85
American Cyanamid Company, 207
American Enka Corporation, 285
American Machine and Foundry Company, 55, 61
American Management Association, 50, 228, 234–235, 304
American Metals Market, 22
American Metals Society, 50
American Motors, 82, 153
American Production and Inventory Control Society, 49, 50
American Society of Lubrication Engineers, 50
American Society for Testing and Materials, 50
American Telephone and Telegraph Co., 283
Anderson, Charles E., 129
Anderson, Robert, 301
Anthropology, 269
Appraisals, cost-centered, 292
  interviews for, 296–298
  methods type, 293–294
  objective-centered, 292–293
  personality-oriented, 295
  results type, 290–292
  sandwich technique, 297
  (See also Objectives; Performance)
AQL (acceptable quality level), 195

311

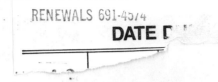